Entrepreneurs
Mastery of the Art of Business

AJ Walton

"Successful people do all the things unsuccessful people don't want to do."

—John Paul DeJoria

GLOBAL TRIBE
Publications

Copyright © 2017 Anthony J. Walton

First published 2017

All rights reserved. No part of this publication may be reproduced or transmitted in any form or by any means, electronic or mechanical, including photocopying and recording on any information storage and retrieval system, without the permission in writing from the publisher.

ISBN-13: 978-1718684942

© Cover Design
Published by Global Tribe Publications
Wellington, New Zealand

SBA Small Business America

A huge thanks to SBA Small Business Administration America for their support, and much of the material on the legal and accounting aspects of starting and managing a successful small business.

The Enterprise Environment

The challenging problem we now face in the US is that there are now 400,000 new businesses being born annually nationwide, while 470,000 per year are dying.

According to the U.S. Small Business Administration, 70 percent of new businesses survive at least two years, but that drops to 50 percent by the five-year mark and 33 percent at the 10-year point, with just 25 percent lasting 15 years or more. Existing enterprise education has to be questioned and reinvented in order to engage the new normal.

The sheer number of small businesses in the USA has made a big impact. Collectively, small businesses have generated over 65% of new jobs since 1995. And according to the Small Business Administration America, they account for 52.6% of all retail sales, 46.8% of all wholesale sales and 24.8% of all manufacturing sales. Moreover, small businesses are our representation to the world, as 97% of all US exporters of goods are small businesses.

Small business has a huge impact on community life and must be empowered. Skills need to be uploaded quickly to meet the demands of the new industries being birthed.

A generation of innovative educators must emerge to serve the new customers that don't want to mortgage their lives with huge debt every time they wish to up-skill. The new reality is that the average millennial will have 17 different jobs in their lifetime.

They say it takes a village to raise a child, in the same way it takes a community of experienced business leaders, educators, mentors and coaches to raise a successful entrepreneur.

For this reason, the Global Tribe team is committed to building a community of creators, thinkers, innovators, lovers, and givers; empowering existing and emerging entrepreneurs to positively influence every area of life—culture, commerce, and community.

Introduction

The Global Tribe story

Global Tribe has come full circle, starting out with the Global Tribe Extreme Cafe, committed to the dream of training thousands of young people in business and practical life-skills, to the launch of Global Tribe Entrepreneurs. We started out with a cafe, with business spaces and mentoring for young entrepreneurs, helping them to start their dream enterprise, which they did with great vigor.

We then based ourselves out of the US becoming involved with the huge fight to make poverty history, building houses in Mexico, learning centers in India, medical aid in Haiti, hospital care in Africa and the list goes on.

The outcome of many years of involvement in working with these countries was the realization that we could never *donate the poor out-of-poverty*, then if we did not assist in building an *economic engine* at the heart of these communities, we may be simply creating a dependency on ourselves and be doing more harm than good. Assisting entrepreneurs in starting new models of businesses is the key to job creation and central in moving communities out of poverty. The best thing that we can do for global poverty is to help start small businesses with a people-loving core at the center.

New model of job creation

Professor Klaus Schwab in his address at the Annual World Economic Summit 2012 in Davos—Kloster, Switzerland, on, 'The great transformation,' introduced four new models that needed to be created in order to push beyond the current global crisis. The fourth new model he suggested must be addressed was, 'The need for a new model of job creation.'

There is now, *Time Magazine* unveiled, in the western world, 75 million young people between the ages of 18-25 who are unemployed. In the US 54% of this age group are unemployed. A high percentage of these have degrees, but no opportunities, their potential left to rot. This is the new poverty and a global crisis.

Jim Clifton, chairman and CEO of Gallup, writes in his new book, *The Coming Job Wars*, "If you where to ask me, from all of the world polling Gallup has done for the last 75 years, what would fix the world—what would suddenly create world wide peace, global wellbeing, and the next extraordinary advancements in human development, I would say the creation of 1.8 billion jobs. The problem we have, is that we have 7 billion people now living on the planet, with 3 billion needing a job. However there are only 1.2 billion full-time formal jobs available.

Professor Klaus Schwab goes on to say, "We also know that hundreds of millions of people will enter the job market in the next decade...The key to mitigating a catastrophic situation is to provide young people with the capability to create their own jobs: to move from the pure concept of unemployment to the concept of micro-entrepreneurship. This will require fundamental changes in educational systems, nurturing a societal spirit of entrepreneurial risk-taking...and making innovation and the support of innovation a key imperative in public and private life."

Global Tribe education

The role of the Global Tribe Educators and Mentors is more about mentoring and coaching than lectures alone. It is a learning community interacting with world-class material and real-world scenarios. Global Tribe is about developing great thinkers; adopting the style of learning used by Aristotle; the style and environment for development is more of a living room than a glass room, an engine-room empowering the *Navy Seals* of business and innovation.

Our goal is to teach the art of business and the art of living, developing multiple intelligence centers—mental, social, physical and spiritual. The original Latin roots of the word for education is *educare* -"to rear or bring up" and *Educere* —"to draw out from within; to lead out of." *Educo* has the same meaning as the two words combined. Education is a leadership role that is dedicated to drawing out the best in people. We also believe leaders create leaders, entrepreneurs create entrepreneurs, the reason Global Tribe's primary role is about connecting people, creating a natural environment for growth.

Global Tribe entrepreneurs

This course, *The Seven Pillars of the Enterprise Ecosystem*, is for entrepreneurs wishing to understand the business universe. The earth's ecosystems are a finely tuned balance of chemicals, systems and particles, many of which are still beyond the grasp of science. In the same way, business is a finely tuned ecosystem, a balancing act of all the component-parts of what makes the enterprise engine tick. This course will introduce you to the component-parts of the business ecosystem. The symbiotic nature of the earth's ecosystem, its design and its relationship to the universe is truly inspirational and a perfect picture of the nature of business. Business is not only organizational, but also relational, a highly complex web or community of relationships. Culture, commerce and community are all connected into what is now a global business ecosystem.

Give a man a fish

You have heard the saying, "Give a man a fish and you feed him for a day, teach him how to fish and you feed him for a lifetime." A great saying, but doesn't go far enough. Education should include working with and being mentored by real fishermen. Then when the apprentice is ready, they then need help with funding in order to purchase a fishing rod and a bike in order to transport the fish to market.

So, give a young person a fish and you feed him for a day, teach him how to fish, mentor him and help fund his fishing enterprise, and you will feed him, his family, and his community for a lifetime.

Business is not divorced from the real world, it is the *economic engine* that is foundational to a great society and the key to making poverty history. These Seven Pillars lay at the heart of the *Global Tribe Entrepreneurs* strategy. If an entrepreneur wants to succeed they must first gain a clear understanding of what the business ecosystem looks like. The universe of this enterprise engine is complex, but an overview, or the basics can be easily understood by learning the *Seven Pillars*, the component-parts of every successful business.

Contents

Entrepreneurs — Art of Business

The Seven Pillars of the enterprise ecosystem

This course is for entrepreneurs wishing to understand the business universe. Every enterprise is an ecosystem of relationships, experience, information and issues that relate to any given subject, decision or problem. Business is a mental, social and spiritual ecosystem. Business is a finely tuned activity; a balancing act of all the component-parts of what makes an enterprise tick.

Part One

Character and the art of thinking

Albert Einstein said, "Most people say that it is the intellect which makes a great scientist. They are wrong, it is character."

Pillar One: The Entrepreneur

It is one thing to know all there is to know about business (marketing, accounting etc.); you may even have the best product or service on earth, but without some basic disciplines, you are doomed to fail. The art of being an entrepreneur is more about strong character and discipline than skill alone; characteristics such as; being a hard worker, creativity, patience, perseverance, and self-control.

Chapter 1	What is an Entrepreneur?	17
Chapter 2	How do Entrepreneurs Think?	23
Chapter 3	A Strong Intelligent Mix	29
Chapter 4	Black and White Thinking	33
Chapter 5	How to Think in Color	37
Chapter 6	Green Thinking - Design Thinking	39
Chapter 7	Red and Blue Thinking	47
Chapter 8	Intuitive Thinkers	51
Chapter 9	Wisdom Thinkers	53
Chapter 10	Rational Thinkers	57
Chapter 11	Honest Thinkers	63

Chapter 12	The Thinking Triangle	69
Chapter 13	The Black Box	75
Chapter 14	Design Thinking	83
Chapter 15	Levels of Thinking	89
Chapter 16	Consciousness	95
Chapter 17	The Core	97
Chapter 18	Big Picture Wisdom	101
Chapter 19	The Ultimate Mindset	105

Part Two

Wisdom and Discipline

Skills must be learned and sharpened constantly for any enterprise to succeed.

Knowledge is now easier than ever to access, however knowledge is not skill. Skills are mastered by training, experience and discipline. You can have all the skills in the world, but without wisdom knowledge is of little value.

Pillar Two: The Customer

A customer is the most important visitor on our premises. He is not dependent on us. We are dependent on him. He is not an interruption in our work. He is the purpose of it. He is not an outsider in our business. He is part of it. We are not doing him a favor by serving him. He is doing us a favor by giving us an opportunity to do so. —*Mahatma Gandhi*

Chapter 20	The Customer is King	113
Chapter 21	What is a Market?	117
Chapter 22	What is Social Media Marketing?	127
Chapter 23	What makes a Great Ad?	137
Chapter 24	What is a Brand?	141

Pillar Three: The Team

Good leadership and great managers bring all of the pieces of the enterprise engine together in order to build the enterprise clock. They draw out the best in people and build them into a healthy, functioning community.

Chapter 25	Team Up	149
Chapter 26	Entrepreneurial Workers	153

Chapter 27	Team Leaders and Managers	163
Chapter 28	The Coaching Edge	167
Chapter 29	Team up with Empowering Companies	173

Pillar Four: The Lawyer

My involvement in property is not simply about the challenge of constructing buildings on time and on budget, but to understand the multitude of laws that relate to tax, subdivisions, resource and building consents, contractual issues, and the list goes on and on.

Laws that govern companies, property, insurance, insolvency, bankruptcy, maritime (the law of the sea), and intellectual property — copyrights, trademarks, and patents.

Chapter 30	Contracts, Tax and other Good Stuff!	179
Chapter 31	The Law	191
Chapter 32	Employment and Labor Law	197
Chapter 33	Hiring a Contractor or Employee	203

Pillar Five: The Accountant

On entering or thinking about the enterprise universe we need to ask ourselves the big philosophical question, is the *bottom line* of business to make money? Are our innovations all about making a large profit? Innovation, when it comes to a new or existing enterprise it is all about making the *customer* wealthy, adding value in some department of their lives. Prosperity, broadly defined touches on a number of areas in a person's life — social prosperity, intellectual health, cultural richness, spiritual wisdom, and material wealth.

Chapter 34	What is the Bottom-line?	215
Chapter 35	How do I do the Accounting?	217
Chapter 36	Developing a Cash flow Analysis	223
Chapter 37	What about Tax?	229
Chapter 38	The Bank	223

Pillar Six: The Manager

Today, a lot is written about leadership and entrepreneurship, and the subject of management is often neglected. The old model of management, Covey points out, is based on the military model, and is not working for a new generation of young employees. Great entrepreneurs are not always great managers, and often especially weak at administration. Management is the ability to coordinate people in order to achieve the goals and objectives of the owner, utilizing available resources efficiently and effectively. Great managers build the enterprise clock.

| Chapter 39 | Building the Clock | 239 |

Pillar Seven: The Innovator

Innovation is best defined by Ian Hunter in his book, *Imagine,* as the process of generating wealth from new ideas - taking what resides in your imagination and converting it into reality, into profit.

Most enterprise startup's come out of an existing job or another business. In fact in my country of New Zealand around half of all entrepreneurs will start their business in the same industry as their present job.

Chapter 40   The Innovator 255

Chapter 41   The Why 259

Chapter 42   The BIG Plan 265

Chapter 43   Developing a Business Plan 271

Chapter 44   Imagineering 279

I have kept these *Seven Pillars* reasonably broad, philosophical and practical so that this overview can be used in most countries as a way to gain a birds-eye view of the *Enterprise Ecosystem*. Some things are universal and increasingly so, but many of the laws and regulations are very different from country to country, and community to community.

However, the foundation principles or the basics of starting and building an extraordinary enterprise are universal. This manual is tailored to the American legal and accounting business system. Most of the accounting and legal technical information, is from SBA Small Business Administration (America). SBA.gov Most countries have their own government website with more detail covering their company law, tax law and business regulations.

How to use this material

This is the textbook used in GT PRO[BOX] educators and mentors events, training courses and connectors that are designed to grow and support entrepreneurs on the ground, doing the hard yards. This is also the source of much of the material in, *Art of Thinking, Mindsets,* and *Vision Book*.

Each of the Seven Pillars of the Enterprise Ecosystem gives the business architecture its strength and beauty. When you first study any subject, you gain an overview and knowledge of the subject, soaking yourself in the subject matter to develop a deeper understanding of how all of the component parts fit together. Finally, you must put it into practice in order to gain experience, and grow in wisdom.

The best way to digest this information is done the same way that you would eat an elephant—slowly, one bite at a time! Digesting this information in dialogue with a friend or friends, in a group setting, will help accelerate, motivate and apply your learning.

Part One
Character and the Art of Thinking

"Most people say that it is the intellect which makes a great scientist. They are wrong, it is character."

— Albert Einstein

Pillar One
The Entrepreneur

"Being an Entrepreneur is Primarily about Adding Value to People's Lives"

— A J Walton

What is an entrepreneur?
How do they think, and develop?
How do I come up with the big ideas?
What is Strategic Thinking?

Chapter One
What is an Entrepreneur?

The way an Entrepreneur thinks is their core competency, their primary asset, and sets them apart as creators. They fearlessly create something of value out of very little or nothing, making the connection between the raw resources and assets at their disposal, and then move things around until they work.

The term **entrepreneur** is a loanword from French, and is commonly used to describe an individual who organizes and operates a business or businesses, taking on financial risk to do so.

The term was first defined by the Irish-French economist Richard Cantillon as the person who pays a certain price for a product in order to resell it at a higher price. The term first appeared in the French Dictionary "Dictionnaire Universel de Commerce" of Jacques des Bruslons published in 1723.

Over time, scholars have defined the term in different ways. Here are some prominent definitions:

- 1803: Jean-Baptiste Say: An entrepreneur is an economic agent who unites all means of production - land of one, the labor of another and the capital of yet another and thus produces a product. By selling the product in the market he pays rent of land, wages to labor, interest on capital and what remains is his profit. He shifts economic resources out of an area of lower and into an area of higher productivity and greater yield.

- 1934: Schumpeter: Entrepreneurs are innovators who use a process of shattering the status quo of the existing products and services, to set up new products, new services.

- 1964: Peter Drucker: An entrepreneur searches for change, responds to it and exploits opportunities. Innovation is a specific tool of an entrepreneur hence an effective entrepreneur converts a source into a resource.

- 1971: Kilby: Emphasizes the role of an imitator entrepreneur who does not innovate but imitates technologies innovated by others, are very important in developing economies.

- 1975: Albert Shapero: Entrepreneurs take initiative, accept risk of failure and have an internal locus of control.

- 1975: Howard Stevenson: Entrepreneurship is "the pursuit of opportunity without regard to resources currently controlled."

- 1983: G. Pinchot: Intrapreneur is an entrepreneur within an already established organization.

- 1985: W.B. Gartner: Entrepreneur is a person who started a new business where there was none before.

The five types of entrepreneurs:
1. Social Entrepreneurs
2. Educational Entrepreneurs
3. Business Entrepreneurs
4. Governmental Entrepreneurs
5. Meta Entrepreneurs

My story

I never saw myself as an entrepreneur, but when enough people tell you then that's how you operate, you begin to believe it. The naming of people however is not as important as the role of and the need for pioneers, innovators or servant leadership.

I started out as more of a *social entrepreneur*, initially developing a course called *New Start Motivation* for young people trying to get a job.

This inspired a number of motivational type programs: Examination Motivation at a local University, a radio program called High Voltage Thinking, and a manual with CD's named the Success N Life Club. This led to speaking engagements at a wide range of functions on a broad range of topics, from Thinking by Design, to Practical Business Skills, and the Art of Leadership.

My journey has involved a multitude of endeavors: Global Tribe aid work, reinventing community organizations and Churches, the Leadership of a Political Party - Future New Zealand, Romanian Child Aid, Body and Soul gyms, and the Global Tribe Cafe for young people.

Global Tribe Cafe was where this idea of Global Tribe Entrepreneurs had its genesis, as already mentioned, with spaces for young people as a safe place to have-a-go at their first business. We gave them a space, mentors and a great environment in which to develop their ideas. This cafe eventually became funded by local government and the name changed to Zeal, which has now spread to many other cities throughout New Zealand under the leadership of a group of young *social entrepreneurs* far more understanding of youth issues than I did.

Politics

My involvement in politics helped me to understand the wider issues of living in community and developing an integrated vision for a healthy society.

As a young political leader in our country I was invited to Washington DC, along with many other leaders from around the world, to a prayer breakfast with President Bill Clinton. This was an annual event started by the US President, Eisenhower, to build relationships globally.

It was there that I heard the story of Mother Teresa's visit to a previous Breakfast to speak on a platform with President Clinton, Hillary Clinton, and a line-up of the world's most powerful speakers and leaders. Apparently when this short, physically frail woman spoke, it had an impact and authority that no other speaker present possessed. She had an impact and authority greater than presidents because of her servant heart, and passionate love for the poorest of the poor. As she spoke, she influenced people's priorities, and carried such a potent level of love, that it deeply affected all of those that heard her for the rest of their lives.

To Romania with Love

Spearheading a major paradigm shift in my thinking was our initiative to help children suffering in orphanages throughout Romania. The result of twenty-five years of dictatorship under Ceausescu saw these children living under hellish conditions.

Late one Saturday evening, I reflected on what I had seen of the Romanian children on the BBC World News that day. Pictures of naked children covered in sores, huddling together like animals in cages splashing in their own excrement. I had only really caught a glimpse of these children while in deep conversation with family and friends while visiting my parents' house, however the images returned to my mind with huge feelings of both compassion and helplessness. I kept saying to myself "It's impossible. What can I really do that will make any difference?"

No sooner had I thought those thoughts, than the most powerful of emotions entered my soul. Feelings and thoughts that had a penetrating punch. I began to feel as if I was one of those children, amongst them, somehow inside their heads; they were saying to themselves "I wish someone would come and take away my pain. Why won't they come? Could someone please come and help?"

This was not a passing fit of passive pity, it was a defining moment, a revelation of what the Creator sees and feels every day. Emotions so cutting that the pain would not leave, echoing through my soul, forcing out the tears and moving me to aggressive action; shifting me out of the feelings of helplessness to becoming their advocate, and an attempt to do my small part in relieving the pain of these children.

'To Romania with Love' was a mission that eventually resulted in a shipment of food, medical supplies, clothing, and teddy bears being sent. This was not without experiencing the extreme frustration of trying to convince people to take action and give a piece of their lives in the form of money or other provisions, taking some responsibility for what was going on in our global village.

I then led a team of twelve doctors, nannies, and volunteers on a trip to Romania to a large castle housing over 300 children, to give what love, affection, or meaning we could.

We flew to Amsterdam to pick up the supplies that the Dutch had donated, and then drove for three days to find ourselves at the gates of the castle I had seen on the BBC World News. Because communication was impossible, we had no way of making contact with the orphanage and had no idea if they would let us in. It was madness looking back. We were hundreds of thousands of miles from home with no guarantee of entry.

On arrival I asked to speak to the doctor in charge, and was led through the chilling hallways of what can only be described as a death camp. The doctor was a gracious man doing his best, powerless and humiliated by years of watching helpless children die of every kind of disease, including Aids. With a few painkillers as his only medicine, and little more than weak tea and soup for their daily diet, the doctor could do little but watch the children die or go mad. When he finally allowed us to enter, we found children rocking back and forth, softly hitting their heads against the walls to pass the time of day. Other kids were drinking their own urine from pots placed on the floor used as a kind-of-toilet. The effect was devastating and it made me feel sick to the stomach.

These children had no father or mother, and for years before we arrived they were caged and left naked in their cells, which looked more like pigpens. To add to their nightmare, the stronger, more aggressive kids would roam around, biting or smashing the other kids against the wall, punching and scratching them at will.

I will never forget one day, taking a group of kids outside the walls of the castle for the first time in their lives to a group of dentists. They had just arrived from England to attend to the raw nerve endings protruding from these children's rotten teeth. It was a sunny day; the sky was blue and the grass long and green. However these kids were huddled together in the middle of a field, obviously frightened by their new surroundings, not knowing where they might be going next. Their home was a picture of hell itself.

That day we talked, through our interpreter, to some older children who were complaining about a predator in their midst. A man who appeared to be in his late twenties, of rugged appearance, who spoke to us with an arrogant tone in his voice, and who was molesting these children every night. I must admit during that night we plotted ways by which to kill him, which I guess wasn't that charitable, considering we weren't going to give him a proper trial.

Although the orphanages throughout Romania had been equivalent to death camps, things were radically changing because of the international aid and huge compassion of truly outstanding people from around the world. Every one of our team spent weeks, even months, in mourning after our visit, with times of deep sobbing and eyes filling with tears at the faintest memory of these children. This experience radically changed the direction of our lives.

Global

For over ten years, I joined friends to ride motorcycles across the deserts of Baja Mexico, a lot of fun, but also the catalyst for our involvement in building homes for families trapped in poverty.

Since then Global Tribe has moved beyond New Zealand into many of the poverty hot spots of the world, focused on assisting those humiliated by poverty. This was until the realization that, the only way to make-poverty-history was to focus on the development of what I call, *economic engines*. Healthy *small businesses* established at the heart of these poor communities.

All of this was only made possible by a life long friend, Wesley Campbell, a truly great business entrepreneur, starting out in the United States with an unknown Rock Band from Australia and a few hundred dollars in their pockets. It was on the back of their global success that News Boys and many other bands promoted Global Tribe teams and raised money to help build houses for the poor of Mexico, Haiti and Africa. It was Wesley that encouraged me to use the equity in my home to purchase my first commercial building. The building we eventually partnered on in order to house ZEAL, the cafe for young people mentioned earlier.

White Cloud Innovations

Many years later I started a building company named *White Cloud Innovations* to build cool small spaces, environments that inspired people, where they could create, rest, and relax. This has always been my passion, architecture that not only looked cool, but also felt cool to live in, built for a cool price!

The ultimate goal of this company was to create a support base, freeing myself to help young entrepreneurs and those trapped in poverty.

The Entrepreneur—Build the person and you build the business

Like it or not, most great companies or community organizations were started by an entrepreneur, and in many cases more than one. This is the person or persons who plant the seed idea, establish the root, and grow the initial fruit. It is one thing to know all there is to know about business (marketing, accounting etc); you may even have the best product or service on earth, but without some basic disciplines, you are doomed to fail. The art of being an entrepreneur is more about strong character and discipline than skill alone. Characteristics such as being a hard worker, creative, patient, will have perseverance, and self-control.

This pillar, The Entrepreneur, is the most fundamental issue to the creation of any enterprise, because it's about the quality of character and the disciplines of the person or persons who lay the foundation and culture of the new enterprise. So time taken to establish the person at the root of the enterprise, makes this the most important section of the book. We need to focus on caring for the goose that lays the golden eggs, and not the golden eggs that they lay. Otherwise, as the story goes, you will destroy the goose. Who we are is the foundation of what we do and how we will operate.

The creation of a great enterprise, no matter what, is more about character and wisdom than talent, about learning an art form more than acquiring know-how, about discipline more than the creation of systems.

Hard work and pain

On reading Ashlee Vance's biography of Elon Mask one of the great modern day entrepreneurs, the man behind *PayPal, Tesla Motors, SpaceX, and Solar City;* you quickly see that his success is not about skill alone, but huge amounts of courage, persistence and pain. In the chapter on Pain, Suffering and Survival, Vance quotes one of the *Tesla* and *SpaceX* investors and Musks friends; he saw a man who arrived in the United States with nothing, who had a lost childhood...who had the ability to work harder and endure more stress than anyone I have ever met. What he went through in 2008 would have broken anyone else ... but he kept working and stayed focused.

You may be the most educated, knowledgeable person in the world but without a strong work ethic and the disciplines of success, you would simply be what is known as an educated fool. To be a successful entrepreneur you will experience extreme pain. Character is the steel-like internal strength to be able to withstand large amounts of pain. Great athletes must break through multiple pain barriers in order to reach another level.

This is reality, and it sucks, but the right kinds of discipline can turn into the pleasure of winning and habits of success. However, once stretched, you will never go back to your original shape or size, you become a bigger person.

Working hard gives you a special kind of victory; self-control. King Solomon in his book called Proverbs says, "A man without self-control is like a city broken into and left without walls". In early times a city or village without walls was left unprotected and in danger of being overpowered and robbed, again and again, until they could rebuild the walls, which was a slow process.

Disciplines of character, like building muscle, or walls, it takes years and lots of hard work. Without certain disciplines in business we are at risk of losing everything. We can have a number of these disciplines mastered, but if we have neglected one area, it can bring everything crashing down. It all starts with our personal character and discipline, which then naturally extends into our business life. Hard work also gives us an empowering confidence, and respect for ourselves. Self-respect comes from self-control and self-control is about self-leadership. Leadership over negative emotions, attitudes, voices and the multitude of interruptions that take us off course.

Chapter Two
How do Entrepreneurs Think?

"You can never cross the ocean until you have the courage to lose sight of the shore."

— Christopher Columbus

An entrepreneur must master the art of thinking; however to achieve this we must understand that it is not a purely academic exercise, but the product the right-kind-of-environments, experiences, and the company of experienced mentors or great coaches.

So how do entrepreneurs think, and how do they develop their thinking? Most business ideas fail due to wrong or incomplete thinking. Human beings, like plants, grow or fail to grow, depending on their environment. For a business to succeed the entrepreneur must grow and develop in his or her thinking by planting themselves in the *right environment*.

Remember, you are the tree on which the fruit grows; healthy tree, healthy fruit! I have never forgotten what Warren Buffet, one of the world's leading investors once said, *that he didn't invest in great companies, but in great CEO's*. This is because he understood that the key to great and profitable business, was and is entirely in the way an entrepreneur thinks.

The following are 10 thinking traits of entrepreneurs; they are:

1. **Strategic Thinkers**
2. **Critical Thinkers**
3. **Creative Thinkers**
4. **Intuitive Thinkers**
5. **Wisdom Thinkers**
6. **Rational Thinkers**
7. **Honest Thinkers**

8. Balanced Thinkers
9. Innovative Thinkers
10. Design Thinkers

An entrepreneur must master the *art of thinking*; however to achieve this we must understand that it is not a purely academic exercise, but the product the right-kind-of-environments, experiences, and in the company of *experienced mentors or great teachers*. Access to these kinds of people is often hard because they are too busy; so this is where the Global Tribe Lounge can be helpful, a place to connect with these people.

Strategic Thinkers

Strategic thinking is:
- Integrating the future into your decision
- Creating processes today by thinking, laterally, vertically and intuitively — (The Thinking Triangle).
- Planning the future in light of present realities, resources, capabilities, contexts, customers, and obstacles.
- Moving people or resources into the most advantageous position prior to the actual event or engagement.
- Thinking ahead!!!

Strategic thinking is an art form and a mindset as much as it is a skill, and is based on large amounts of information, innovation and intuition. This must be gathered, ordered, interpreted, and then applied. Strategic thinking is another framework for ordering our thinking. It is where we take our dream, vision and mission and turn them into a plan of action. This is the art of innovation. Planning the future in light of present realities, resources, capabilities, contexts, customers, and obstacles.

A strategic thinker is an entrepreneurial thinker, they process the same attributes. The true meaning of the word entrepreneur is broader than its use in a business context. As already pointed out, it was coined by the French economist JB Say, around the year 1800; "The entrepreneur," Say wrote, "shifts economic resources out of an area of lower and into an area of higher productivity and greater yield." In other words, an entrepreneur creates a plan in order to use resources in new ways, maximizing productivity and effectiveness.

In business, community organizations, or in our personal lives, strategic thinking has to do with taking what you have and making the most of it. It is taking our personal capital and using it more productively in order to generate a greater yield.

Strategic thinking is often associated with going to war. The formal definition of the word *strategy* has strong military connotations. A common dictionary definition shows that *strategy* is the science of planning and directing large-scale military operations, specifically of maneuvering forces into the most advantageous position prior to actual engagement with the enemy. It seems most dictionary definitions use a military reference. However, strategic thinking is not restricted to military action or even to business. Strategic thinking is used in sports, government, community organizations, and increasingly in planning our family and personal lives.

In his book *Alexander the Great's Art of Strategy*, Partha Bose reveals the secret of Alexander's ability to think strategically. Love him or hate him, Alexander the Great (356-323BC) was arguably the greatest military strategist in history. "At the age of 20, he ascended to the throne of his father's kingdom. By the age of 23, he had defeated Persia, his nation's greatest enemy. And by the time of his death, aged 33, his armies had conquered virtually the entire known world. Form the shores of the Mediterranean to the foothills of India, including the lands of modern-day Iraq and Afghanistan."

Alexander's father Philip wanted his son to have a higher education than what was being provided. He wanted his son to be equipped with a mental framework that would guide him as a military leader and an empire builder. It was at this time that Aristotle was discovered and taken from relative obscurity to train Alexander and a selected group of young leaders. He was to train them to think. Aristotle had just missed out on the top job at Plato's Leadership Academy in Athens, where he had studied and taught for over twenty years.

The art of strategic thinking

Aristotle taught using Socrates method of engaging his students through the use of dialogues. Bose points out, "It was common, for example, to see Aristotle come around the corner, leading a group of students deep in an intellectual dialogue". Chinese philosopher Lao-tzu once wrote: "If you tell me, I will listen. If you show me I will see. But if you let me experience, I will learn." These future leaders of Macedonia were taught how to solve complex problems, practical decision-making, to think strategically, to accurately gather facts, and to recognize patterns within different types of problems. Aristotle taught these young leaders the art of strategic thinking which involved a number of crucial elements:

Alexander's father planted him and his associates in a positive environment for growth.

An amazing environment was built for him in the hilly resort of Mieza, just outside the Macedonian capital of Pella. "The school had on one side, a stunning view of the Thermaic Gulf... on the other, the wilderness. Bose describes this school: "Mieza on most days was a picture of sunny serenity, with cobbled pathways and shaded walkways where enclaves of students discussed Persian poetry or Greek plays. Botanical and zoological gardens had been built surrounding the school to cater to Aristotle's interests in the biological sciences. He spent all of his free time categorizing plants and animals. He would then apply his discoveries within nature to understanding the world of intellect. Another important part of the environment for learning is about whom we mix with. This is why it is a vital part of the Global Tribe strategy to help entrepreneurs go beyond simply being taught to fish, to being connected with the right mentors, coaches or support networks.

Strategic thinkers clearly define the dream, the vision, the big goals or key objectives

For Sir Edmund Hillary it was to climb the highest mountain in the world. For Neil Armstrong it was to walk on the moon. For Alexander it was to conquer the world, something that in modern thinking is unthinkable, and even detestable. In chess the aim is to out think your opponent by being a number of steps ahead, maneuvering them into checkmate.

In business the goal is to create something of value in order to make money. In many communities around the globe the big goal is to survive another day. The dream of still others is to help them survive. Peter Drucker the great business philosopher says, "Efficiency is doing the thing right, but effectiveness is doing the right thing." A strategic thinker focuses on doing the right thing, in the right place, at the right time.

Aristotle taught his students how to frame a question in order to gather facts and discover underlying patterns or trends.

One of Alexander's key skills as a strategic thinker was his ability to seek facts and observe patterns within the information he received in battle. Bose reveals that he would "seek facts about a certain region from a diverse set of sources—from the meteorologist, agriculturalist, botanist, zoologist, civil engineer, hydrologist, historian…and then synthesize the facts so as to arrive at a point of view."

The central skill of leadership is the ability to gain an accurate picture of where you are now, and where you need to go. "Strategic thinking is the bridge that links where you are, to where you want to be." Max De Preen in his book *Leadership is an Art*, says, "The first responsibility of a leader is to define reality." Strategic thinking means facing the hard facts in order to define reality and thus gain a clear picture. In the development of any strategic plan we must ask numerous questions. Questions such as: What resources do I have? What skills do I possess? What systems can I create? Where can I find the information or facts that I need? When do I wish to complete this project? What are the obstacles?

One of the templates I often use in the strategic planning process, is what's called SWOT analysis. This represents standard questions starting with each letter of the word SWOT (Strengths, Weaknesses, Opportunities, and Treats). In every project I initiate, I use this process and others to help define reality.

Aristotle helped his students identify problems correctly and to search for underlying issues.

He taught "that the world they would interact with, as rulers, governors and generals, was a complex world of people, feelings, perspectives, assumptions and biases. He had them build scenarios and work collaboratively with one another in shaping the future of their country."

He created real life situations to test their problem solving skills and help them to think on their feet. Scenario building was a vital part of Aristotle's transformative learning experience. The young students spent hours practicing what they had learned in numerous problem-solving engagements that Aristotle had designed. They had to think through the implications of their actions three or four steps ahead and pin point their consequences. It is said there is no substitute for experience. True, but remember, all of those who are now experienced started out at precisely the same place of inexperience.

In order to develop and sharpen Alexander's responses, Bose reveals that Aristotle, the facts guy, "would throw a continuous stream of facts and situations at him to see how he framed, adapted and solved a problem based on disparate, often conflicting sets of facts. He was taught to think about connections between facts, about soft points in the logic of an argument, and about what information was still needed."

Aristotle exposed his students to a wide range of disciplines.

Although he specialized in certain fields, he designed an academic program that would keep them from forming a narrow view of the world. Alexander's introduction to multiple disciplines led him to write about 150 books on subjects as diverse as meteorology, metaphysics, physics and politics. Strategic thinkers are passionate about learning. In so doing, they create a larger database from which to draw, when considering a situation, or making decisions concerning the future.

Aristotle created an educational environment of open and honest feedback

The key to gaining honest feedback from people is to create an atmosphere where people are unafraid to be open, to ask questions or put forward their point of view. Alexander and the other students understood that everyone and everything was open to criticism. Aristotle encouraged this because at Plato's Academy in Athens he had felt stifled, not feeling he could speak his mind. People will shut down or disengage if they feel their ideas and opinions are not, at the very least, respected. A part of Alexander's success was the result of cultivating a culture of ruthless honesty, where challenges to authority and ideas were accepted.

Alexander was taught to take all the time that he needed to plan before going to battle

Qualities cultivated by Aristotle, such as analytical reasoning, self-criticism and intellectual honesty, built a culture of risk taking based on a platform of strategic thinking. Partha Bose reveals, "After capturing Elatea they sat tight for almost a year planning, preparing, and testing their next set of moves, but not attacking." Michael Porter a professor at Harvard Business School once wrote, "The essence of strategy is choosing what not to do." Strategic planning is where you pull all of the intelligence, facts, ideas, advice and scenario building, into a plan of action. This is where key objectives, long-term and short-term goals, time frames, lines of communication, personnel and budgets are established. The intention in this chapter was not to outline a system for strategic planning, there are numerous available on the Internet, but to discuss the essential nature of thinking strategically.

Chapter Three
A Strong Intelligence Mix

We are free spirits contained within a magnificent body of flesh and blood. We are aware that we exist in a vast universe of stars, planets and other human beings, we are our own person, confined to our own body and not merged with everybody else on the planet. Consciousness is one of the great wonders of the universe.

An entrepreneur is constantly looking at things differently, turning things upside down to see if there is an opportunity. They mix with inspiring, progressive thinkers who fearlessly discuss new ideas, new ways of doing things and of conquering new worlds. James T. Kirk from the original *Star Trek* series was an entrepreneur, describing the mission of Enterprise: "to explore strange new worlds; to seek out new life and new civilizations; to boldly go where no man has gone before."

Thinking by design

Nature inspires us to think, to *think outside of the box*. If we do not question things in a constructive way, we risk living in the darkness of someone else's negative box. Living inside of the box is not always a negative thing, if we are in the right kind of box. For example, the *laws of aerodynamics* are the only box to live in if you decide to go flying.

Thinking is a great gift, and tells us we are fully conscious human beings. But due to negative environments and wrong perceptions or interpretations of the bad experiences we encounter, we can allow our thinking to become boxed-in. Jack-in-the-box, a popular child's toy, was a present I was given as a young boy; you push a lever and Jack jumps out on the end of a carefully disguised spring. Decades later, triggered by the memory of Jack, the thought came; if Jack-in-the-box lived his whole life inside of his box, he would never have enjoyed the color and the beauty of the world outside, or brought happiness to millions of children. Thinking about thinking will help to lift the lid on boxed-in-thinking.

One evening while bathing my seven year old son Levi, he looked up at me and said, "Dad, do you like being you?" This was one of those deeply profound child-like philosophical questions. "Yes, most of the time," I answered. "Do you like being you?" returning the question; "Yes, yes, I do," he assured me. It made me realize that a sense of wonder about who we are and the world around us is our ultimate wealth, the ultimate mindset.

Born in 1596, Rene Descartes was the French philosopher who created the phase, "Cogito, ergo sum." "I think, therefore I am." This was his conclusion upon questioning his own existence. According to Descartes, his belief in his own existence was the firm foundation upon which he could build further knowledge or philosophy. My son was *thinking,* therefore he *was* an air sucking, food consuming, biological organism. In this statement, Descartes was describing the greatest gift of all—*consciousness*. He sensed his personhood, conscious of his own independent existence.

We are free spirits, contained within a magnificent body of flesh and blood. We are aware that we exist in a vast universe of stars, planets and other human beings; we are our own person, confined to our own body and not *merged* with everybody else on the planet. Imagine entering someone else's body, like entering a room, and becoming instantly aware of their most intimate thoughts and feelings. Consciousness is one of the great wonders of the universe. It is where *self* is seated and life becomes real. Where I become my own person, free to be me, free to create, and even free to destroy if I so choose.

At this stage it would be helpful to think-about-thinking. The key to the success of the entrepreneur is not so much in her or his outer world, as it is the inner universe of thinking. We need to learn the systems for thinking in the following chapters, the art form of thinking in color (yellow, green, red and blue) for instance, must become second nature.

Intelligence theory

Howard Gardner, professor of education at Harvard, asks the question: "How would someone from outer space, landing on earth, view the intelligence of the human species?" In his book, *Frames of Mind,* Gardener outlines his "Theory of Multiple Intelligences" which goes beyond the view that the standard IQ test is an adequate measure of a person's intelligence.

In the movie *A Beautiful Mind*, Russell Crowe plays the part of the absent-minded but brilliant mathematician John Nash, who clearly needed to develop his *social intelligence.* In one scene he approaches an attractive woman in a bar and says: "Listen, I don't have the words to say whatever it is that's necessary to get you into bed, so can we just pretend I said those things and skip to the part where we exchange bodily fluids?" With a slap around the face, he quickly learns that sex without love or friendship is not what she wants.

John Nash was highly developed in the area of logical and mathematical intelligence, but he was socially inept. To be educated in one or two departments of *intelligence* can leave us limited or incomplete as human beings. We can have a highly developed intelligence in one area of our lives and be totally under-developed in another. The IQ test only evaluates an individual's ability in a few areas; mainly linguistic and logical-mathematical with some visual and spatial tasks included.

Gardner, in his groundbreaking book, draws from a wide range of research and outlines seven intelligent centers, that he believes better represent a more complete view of human intelligences. These are:

- **Linguistic intelligence** – the ability to read, write and communicate with words.

- **Logical-Mathematical intelligence** – the ability to reason and calculate, and to think things through in a logical, systematic way.

- **Visual-Spatial intelligence** – the ability to think in pictures, visualize a future result, and to imagine things in the mind's eye.

- **Musical intelligence** – the ability to make or compose music, to sing well or understand and appreciate music, and to keep rhythm.

- **Bodily-Kinesthetic intelligence** – the ability to use your body skillfully to solve problems or present ideas and emotions, displayed in athletic, artistic or building pursuits (dancing, acting, construction).
- **Interpersonal [Social] intelligence** – the ability to work effectively with others, to relate to other people, to display empathy and understanding, and to notice their motivations and goals.
- **Intrapersonal intelligence** – the ability for self-analysis and reflection…to contemplate and assess one's accomplishments, review one's behavior's and innermost feelings… to make plans and set goals."

This view of intelligence impacts the world of education and takes us from a preoccupation with Intelligence Quotient (IQ), to recognition of each person's unique intelligence mix. We need to develop in all areas of intelligence; however, the reality is that we will learn and naturally become stronger in certain intelligence centers, more than others.

In their book on *Accelerated Learning*, Colin Rose and Malcolm Nicholl point out that, "In essence, this new way of regarding intelligence tells us that there are "multiple windows leading into the same room" and that "students can be approached and learn from a number of perspectives." This shows that our ability to see is not one-dimensional; it happens at a number of levels, in a variety of ways.

Levels of intelligence

In Stephen Covey's book, *The 8th Habit*, he gives his view of human intelligence. This is similar to what I have already outlined and inclusive of most of the aspects discussed by Howard Gardner. Each intelligent center, Covey says, "corresponds to the four parts of our human makeup: body, mind, heart and spirit."

Mental intelligence: "Our ability to analyze, reason, think abstractly, use language, visualize and comprehend."

Physical intelligence: This is everything our "body does without any conscious effort. It runs your respiratory, circulatory, nervous and other vital systems. It is constantly scanning its environment, destroying diseased cells and fighting for survival." "Doctors", he says, "acknowledge that the body heals itself and that medicine simply facilitates it's healing."

Emotional intelligence: "one's self-knowledge, self-awareness, social sensitivity, empathy and ability to communicate successfully with others." This concept has been popularized and developed by Daniel Goleman in his books on the subject of Emotional Intelligence; stating that, "emotions play a far greater role in thought, decision making and individual success than is commonly acknowledged…and that performance in all jobs, in every field, emotional competence is deemed to be twice as important as purely cognitive abilities."

Spiritual intelligence: pointing out that this area is becoming mainstream in regards to scientific inquiry. "Spiritual Intelligence," he says, "is the central and most fundamental of all the intelligences because it becomes the source of guidance for the other three… Spiritual intelligence also helps us discern true north, truth principles, that are part of our conscience."

Levels of seeing

Ultimately, *seeing*, even physically, does not happen in the cornea, pupil, iris, lens or retina; it happens within our brain. The biological eye puts us in touch with the physical world. Seeing mentally has to do with our ability to reason, understand, think and analyze. When seeing things intellectually we say things like: "It dawned on me; I see it now"; "I understand" or "It's as clear as day (or mud)!" This ability enables us to see ideas, concepts, philosophies, beliefs, truth and the thoughts expressed by others.

Thinking about the concept of seeing intellectually both Gardner and Covey refer to our left-brain activity; talking about seeing emotionally – they are referring to right-brain activity.

At the mental and emotional level, seeing clearly is thinking clearly! Left-brain thinking has to do with orderly, logical, systematic, sequential, and the analytical processing of information. Whereas seeing emotionally involves right-brain activity and has to do with the creative, intuitive, imaginative, emotional, pictorial, artistic, musical, instinctive forms of thinking.

We need to understand that these four intelligence centers [or seven, as Gardner outlines] are not separate boxes; there is a crossover as they mesh and work together. For example, our self-image can begin as an emotional equation, then move to the level of our human spirit and become a spiritual force of either inferiority or confidence. A powerful emotional experience that goes beyond the desktop level of thinking, taking root deep within our hard drive. Viruses such as inferiority can, if not dealt with, penetrate every area of our thinking with self-doubt and fear, just as confidence-building experiences can positively affect our thinking with optimism and courage.

Plastic surgeon Maxwell Maltz tells the stories of those that have undergone major face reconstruction, then upon viewing their new faces insist that, "nothing has changed." Friends and family may hardly recognize them, and point out the change, only to be told that they can see no difference. He says, "Comparison of 'before and after' photographs does little good, except to arouse hostility." This shows that our physical ability to see can be blinded by our mental, emotional and spiritual state.

When it comes to understanding or seeing spiritual realities, it can be difficult due to their invisible nature. Substances such as love, truth, conscience, faith, imagination, intuition, dreams, hope, peace and wisdom; or negative forces such as fear, rejection, bitterness and anger, are all invisible and yet extremely real in our everyday experience. These negative mindsets, as Nelson Mandala points out in one of his famous quotes, can be the mental equivalent of drinking poison: "Resentment," he says, "is like drinking poison and then hoping it will kill your enemies." To be a wise entrepreneur we need to understand how people tick.

Chapter Four
Black and White Thinking

"Critical thinking perpetuates the old-fashioned view of thinking established by the Greek Gang of Three (Socrates, Plato and Aristotle), based on analysis, judgment and argument." Critical thinking, has a part to play, but as de Bono notes, "our success in science and technology begins, not with critical thinking, but from the possibility system. The possibility system moves ahead of our information to create hypotheses and visions."

— Edward de Bono

Imagine a world where there was no color, only black and white. One where there was black and white fish, black and white plant life, a black and white animal kingdom and black and white interior design. In countries where oppressive leadership exists, it seems that everything from the physical environment to their mental environment becomes black and white or gray.

This is where we depart from discovering the wonder of the eye and discover how to think in color. To think in color has to do with creativity, hypothesis, design, innovation, new ideas, strategy, planning, evaluation, possibilities, problem solving, instinct, humor, emotional intelligence, intuition, wisdom, empowering beliefs and analytical, critical thinking.

In contrast, black and white thinkers overindulge in cynical, critical or judgmental thinking. Edward de Bono points out that, "Critical thinking perpetuates the old-fashioned view of thinking established by the Greek Gang of Three (Socrates, Plato and Aristotle), based on analysis, judgment and argument." The Black and white thinker majors in this narrow way of thinking.

The Greek word for *critical,* is *kritikos,* meaning *to judge.* While judgmental thinking has its place, it is only one wing of the bird. With only one wing, our thinking will never truly get off the ground and may end up going around in circles. Critical thinking, as we will see has a part to play, but as de Bono notes, "our success in science and technology begins not with critical thinking but from the possibility system. The possibility system moves ahead of our information to create hypotheses and vision."

This adversarial system of thinking is the reason we have developed a very judgmental, critical thinking society. Our media, politics, law and science search for *truth* through adversarial dialogue, "I am right and you are wrong" – black and white thinking! "Argument and debate," de Bono points out, "are then seen as the proper way to explore a subject."

At a Methodist convention in the later part of the nineteenth century, a young leader took the floor and shared his vision of the future. He told the ministers present that he believed that people would fly from place to place instead of merely traveling on horseback, a concept too far outside of the box for some in the audience to stomach.

A minister by the name of Bishop Wright stood to his feet and voiced his protest. "Heresy!" he shouted, "Flight is reserved for angels!" He went on to explain that if God had intended people to fly he would have given them wings. When Bishop Wright had finished his brief protest, he took his two sons, Orville and Wilbur, and stormed out. As incredible as it sounds, it was Orville and Wilbur Wright that several years later, on 17 December 1903, took to the skies. They achieved four flights that day, the first was 12 seconds and the fourth lasted 59 and carried them 852 feet. The Wright brothers had built the first airplane, the Flyer III, and by 1908 flew 60 miles in less than two hours.

Black and white thinkers consider it their job to point out the problems within each new idea (or person]) before considering the possibilities. Many black and white thinkers have made condemnation and *higher criticism* an art form. Black and white thinkers are often overdeveloped in vertical, left-brain thinking and carry an unhealthy prejudice, wrong belief systems, destructive cynicisms and bigoted attitudes. This can result in a distorted view of self and poor relationships with other people, as they focus on faults before strengths.

Although this is a black and white view of black and white thinkers, it may help in identifying unbalanced, unhealthy thinking habits. Edward de Bono says, "This adversarial system is fundamental to western thinking traditions." We are culturally drowned in this system of thinking and need to unlearn the negative aspects of it. "If we trained a person to avoid all errors in thinking, would that person be a good thinker?" Proactive, creative, design systems of thinking must be developed in order for our society to develop in a balanced way.

Thinking in color

It has been said that, "the eyes are the windows of the soul." Look into the eyes of a person and you will see what's really going on: happiness, sadness, joy, pain, insecurity or confusion. These windows do not only reflect the soul (mind, will, emotions and spirit) – the inside world on display – they also bring the outside world in, through the most amazing portal on earth.

The transparent cells in the lens of the eye allow millions of image-carrying light photons to enter the cornea. The cornea is the primary focusing structure, the place where particles of light pass through the optical fluid on their way to be analyzed and then processed by the retina. Before the photons touch down on the photoreceptor cells of the retina, they must first pass through the iris, which controls how much light is allowed to enter. The iris has the ability to constrict or dilate, and gives the eye its blue-green-brown colors. It has 266 identifiable characteristics compared to the 35 characteristics of the fingerprint.

The retina is paper-thin and only one inch square, yet it contains 137 million super light-sensitive cells. So sensitive, that the eye can detect one single photon of light in a dark room. On the retina, approximately 95% of these cells are rods that have the ability to analyze black and white images, dim vision, night vision and peripheral vision. The balance of these cells is made up of seven million cones designed to analyze color images. When light first strikes the retina, a photon of light interacts with a molecule and is transformed into electrical signals – a process that takes picoseconds. A picosecond is the approximate time it takes for light to travel the breadth of a single human hair. These electrical images travel down the million optic nerves to your brain at approximately 300 miles per hour.

These highly intelligent cells of the retina take the optical image that enters upside down and turns it right side up, before transmitting the image to the brain. The retina cells achieve up to 10 billion calculations per second. Grant R Jeffrey in his book, *Creation*, points out that, "the retina acts as a type of film, receiving the actual image composed of light photons passing through the iris, cornea and eye fluid." Something he says "is more sophisticated in its design than even the most powerful electron microscope or satellite spy camera. For example, the most advanced film available today can differentiate between a range of one thousand to one. However, recent experiments have confirmed that the retina of the human eye can easily differentiate, and analyze, a range of ten billion to one."

After all of the complex processes the eye goes through in order to deliver vision, seeing ultimately happens within the visual cortex of the brain – in full color. We have been designed to see our world in color – to think in full color!

Chapter Five
How to Think in Color

Yellow thinking has to do with generating creative possibilities: new ideas, hypothesis, invention, humor, solutions and design. Many great ideas have been aborted due to critical and analytical thinking being introduced too early in the process. Yellow thinking is allowing ourselves to dream, to create and to imagine the new possibilities, to brainstorm what could be.

Systems of thinking

To develop our thinking to a place of full color we need systems that help guide our thinking processes. Brainstorming, for example, is a system whereby all involved agree not to criticize one another for the common purpose of generating a list of new ideas or possible solutions. This system helps us to focus on and release our creative imagination without fear of rejection.

King Solomon wrote, "As a man thinks in his heart, so is he." If you think in black and white you will develop a narrow view of the world and risk becoming a judgmental, narrow-minded person. To think in color is not always the easy road, and requires characteristics such as humility, grace, honesty, openness, patience, and the courage to ask the hard questions.

Throughout this book, I will introduce many original systems that myself and others have developed. *Thinking in Color* is a system that I have developed in order to help us change gears between different modes of thinking. Using the base colors of yellow, green, red and blue, I have designed four gears for thinking. These gears help you to develop and work through all aspects of a new idea or problem.

Sculptors possess a range of tools for working their design into stone. Each tool carries out a defined function. They have learned to use each tool to get the desired effect. They are skilled crafts people who know which tools to use at any given point to achieve the big picture. In the same way, each color represents a tool in achieving the desired result. This system does not necessarily have a beginning or an end. You simply continue shifting from one mode of thinking to another until you have explored all your options.

Yellow thinking = creative thinking

Yellow is the color said to stimulate creativity, thus it represents creativity in the thinking process.

Yellow thinking has to do with generating creative possibilities: new ideas, hypothesis, invention, humor, solutions and design. Many great ideas have been aborted due to critical or analytical thinking being introduced too early in the process. Yellow thinking is allowing ourselves to dream, to create and to imagine the new possibilities; to brainstorm what could be!

Cell phones, computers, cars and buildings; in fact every product or service in existence originated from a tiny seed idea in someone's three pound brain. It was then designed, developed, tested, improved on, and then sold to you and I. We can fly around the world, travel to the moon, phone the North Pole, listen to the radio, turn on a light and read a book – all because someone had confidence in his or her bright idea.

To engage in positive, creative, optimistic, lateral thinking is to think in yellow. This kind of thinking is the starting point when it comes to problem solving or developing creative solutions. Often, what people think to be their problem is not the real problem. Identifying the real problem must start with thinking in YELLOW.

In his book, *How to Think Like Einstein,* Scott Thorpe identifies the kind of thinking that positioned Einstein for success. Thorpe shows that Einstein's advantage, when he began work on relativity and the solution that ultimately became $e=mc^2$, was that he had a good problem. Many of Einstein's contemporaries had been working on the same phenomena, but they were trying to solve a very different problem. Their problem went something like this: "How can nature appear to act that way when we know that it can't?" They did not succeed. More experiments, more money, or more effort would not have helped. They failed because they were looking for an answer that did not exist. Einstein succeeded because he was working on a problem that enabled a solution. He asked himself: "What would nature be like if it did act the way we observe it to act?" This problem has a solution. Einstein found it and it changed our world.

When facing a problem, creativity or possibility thinking is the best place to start. It often requires lateral thinking to identify or define the problem, so when it comes to problem solving, we are focusing our energy on the relevant issues. Albert Einstein points out: "The significant problems we face cannot be solved at the same level of thinking we were at when we created them."

Yellow thinking is going where no man has been before. It is thinking outside of the box; it is the generation of new ideas and the rearrangement of old ones. Thinking in yellow sheds new light on our fears and creates a way out, a different mindset.

Solomon's father, King David, taught him not to subject his thinking to cynics, scoffers or mockers. He warned his son to avoid the black and white thinking of the skeptics and critics of his day. The dictionary describes a cynic as a person who has little faith in human sincerity. In my experience, this group of self-appointed judges have done little to help humanity. They are the dream killers, skilled at putting a negative spin on everything. Masters of put down, they critique our lives for what they haven't been, aren't now and probably won't be. Our ideas won't survive these people, so don't, as the proverb says, "throw your pearls before swine."

Thinking in yellow requires that a positive environment be built for the incubation of valuable new ideas. CS Lewis along with JRR Tolkien and their group of writers called, *the Inklings*, created this kind of safe place to discuss their writings and test their new conceptions. To effectively think in yellow, it is important that we connect with the right people, creating a safe place to dream and development our ideas, just like the Inklings.

Chapter Six
Green Thinking - Design Thinking

Thinking in green begins with breaking a concept down into its component parts, researching the facts and gaining the advice of the experts. The idea is then crafted by taking it into the workshop of the imagination, a well-equipped workshop that draws heavily on every other mode of thinking to do its job. We move back and forth, thinking about thinking, form color to color in order to create a masterpiece.

Using the earth's rich plant life as a metaphor, green represents design, structure, strategy, research, and the development of detailed plans. Each plant has its own unique design. Starting out as a seed that falls to the ground, then planted into a fertile environment, it finally grows into the exact structure that was programmed into its DNA.

Green thinking is the design stage of an idea. Design as defined by Dictionary.com means: "to prepare the preliminary sketch or the plans for a work to be executed, to plan the form and structure of…to conceive in the mind; to fashion; the development of a plan or project." Design has to do with planning in a systematic way. It means to create or produce, as in a work of art; to form a plan or scheme; to form an outline or sketch an idea; to invent; to project, and to lay out in the mind.

An idea, like a seed, will grow and develop as we set goals, create detailed plans and develop a strategy for its implementation. Thinking in *green* begins with breaking a concept down into its component parts, researching the facts and gaining the advice of the experts. The idea is then crafted by taking it into the workshop of the imagination. The imagination is a faculty of the human spirit, and is a well-equipped workshop that draws heavily on every other *thinking color* to do its job. We move back and forth from color to color in order to create a masterpiece.

Design – Mind Maps

The structure of a tree reminds us of another great thinking or planning system that can assist in the design thinking process – *Mind Mapping*. Mind Mapping is a thinking system built on the way the brain operates best. Not in logical sequence, but like the branches of a tree or the arteries of a leaf. This system allows the brain to reach out in any direction and capture all associated thoughts. Memory works by an activation process that Mind Mapping helps to trigger. In my experience Mind Maps are a powerful tool for thinking, because they enable us to sketch out an idea quickly, and capture any associated thoughts, giving us a birds-eye overview of the subject. Tony Buzan, in his book *The Mindmap Book,* points out that Mind Maps provide an exceptionally useful intermediate stage between the thinking process and actually committing words to paper.

Mind mapping is no mystical new age idea; it was the practice of many of the great thinkers of history such as Isaac Newton, Leonardo da Vinci, Pablo Picasso, Albert Einstein, Thomas Edison, Michelangelo, Beethoven and Vincent van Gogh. This list goes on to include great thinkers from the fields of politics, the military, architecture, art, poetry, science and literature. Criticized for making messy notes or doodling, these great thinkers used words, images, symbols, numbers, diagrams and pictures to give their ideas color, movement, depth and dimension.

Mind Mapping helps trigger a mountain of memory and experience. These maps draw on our personal database; the library of everything we have ever seen, heard, touched, tasted or felt. Tony Buzan points out that, "Each bit of information entering your brain – every sensation, memory or thought (incorporating every word, number, code, food, fragrance, color, image, beat, note and texture) can be represented as a central sphere from which radiate tens, hundreds, thousands, millions of hooks. Each hook represents an association and each association has its own infinite array of links and connections." Mind Maps ignite a huge storehouse of information. This system works by simply placing your idea at the center of a piece of paper. Then, in the same way that most plants grow out in many directions, you draw lines or create branches flowing in all directions, identifying any associated ideas or major subheadings. As illustrated, you may use pictures, words or symbols in this green thinking process. It may be used to stimulate creativity, organize ideas for a speech, brainstorm or develop detailed plans, or to simply take notes.

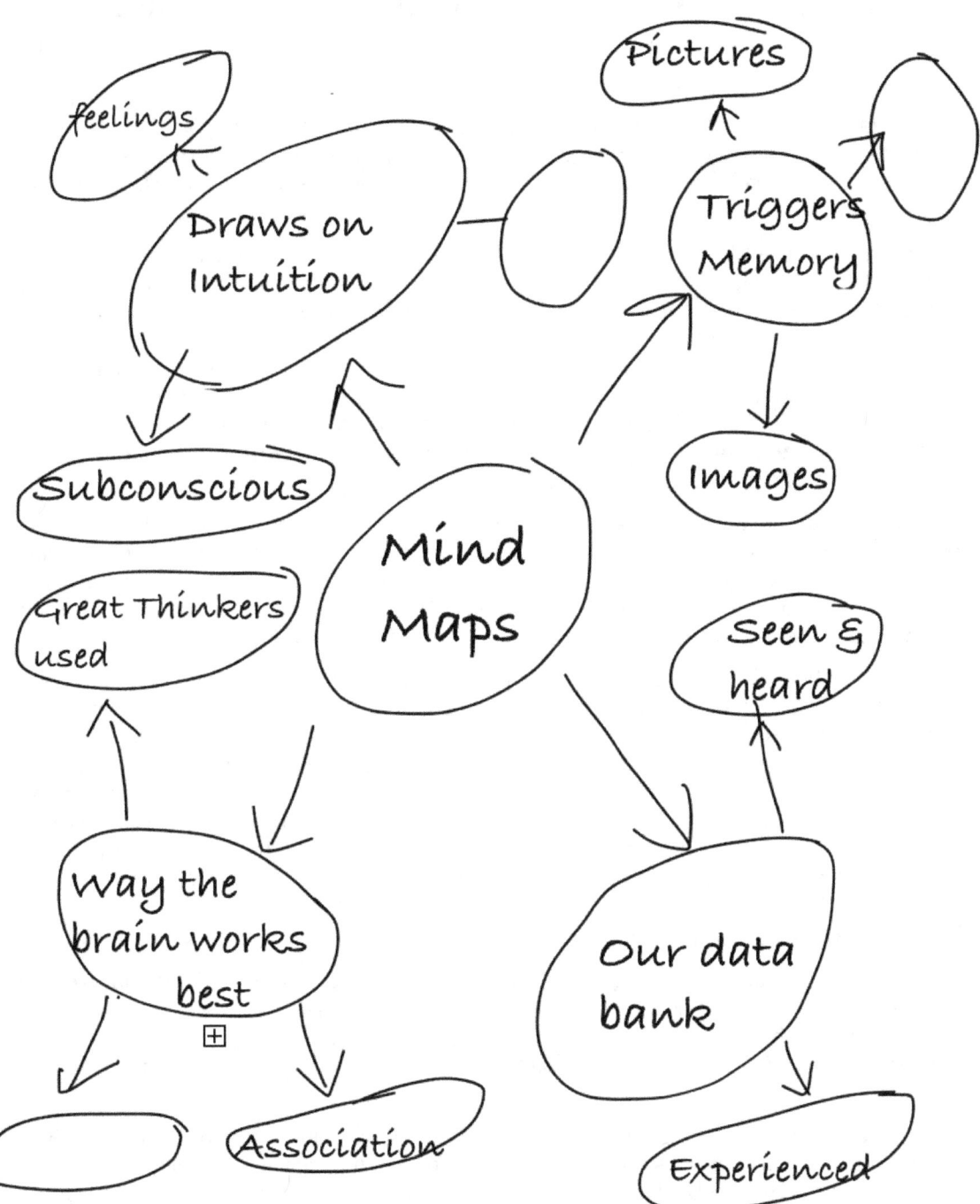

Thinking Green = Goal setting, planning, and daily action

Goals

Before we can fully engage the planning process, we must clarify the *big picture*. Thinking in both *yellow* and *blue* (blue and red thinking is covered in the next chapter) we paint the big picture, hammering out our big goals, as well as defining the key departments of our lives. Numerous words are used to describe the big picture: vision, objectives, the dream; whatever the words used, the concept is basically the same.

Thinking in green and red, we hammer out the structure and the detail: setting medium and short-term goals, planning and taking action. Goals set the direction, planning builds the roadmap. Goals give us a sketch, planning adds the structure and color. Goals are statements of faith about the future; planning creates blueprints so all involved can play their role. Goals are the seeds, planning the growth and development. *Green* thinking will grow an idea from a seed into a living, colorful, fruitful tree. The art of goal setting is an important part of thinking in green, because goals must be set in order to measure our progress–they are a vital part of the planning process. Goals force us to plan ahead and to use our time and resources effectively.

In a book called *Psycho-cybernetics*, Maxwell Maltz reveals that we have all been wired by our Creator with a goal-seeking device called the *servomechanism*. Every living thing has the *Life Instinct,* a built-in guidance system, said to be the most advanced guidance system in existence. It's what wakes us up in the middle of the night, causing our brain to switch on and come alive with ideas, innovations and solutions to problems we may be facing.

Maltz says, "there is within each one of us a *Life Instinct*, which is forever working toward health, happiness, and all that makes for more *life* for the individual". He calls it the *Creative or Success Mechanism*, due to its drive to achieve success and not failure. This built-in automatic guidance system, once the goal is set, doesn't stop processing night and day until it has hit its mark. The science of Cybernetics suggests there is convincing proof that the so-called subconscious *mind* is not a mind at all, but a *mechanism* – a goal-striving *servomechanism* consisting of the brain and nervous system, which is used by and directed by the *mind*.

The key areas of our ecosystem

An important part of goal setting is the identification of the unwritten goals that already exist within our personal ecosystem. These are the major departments of our lives that impact upon each other. If our health is not good, or our relationship with our partner is unhealthy, or our finances are a mess, then our ability to move freely into the future is hindered.

A vital part of clarifying the wider context of our lives, is gaining a snapshot of the Key Areas that make up our lives as they exist now. Green thinking is not only useful in the context of our work and business lives, or one-off projects, but also useful in developing our personal lives. A great starting point in building a life by design, or a personal strategic plan, is to identify the key areas of our lives.

Key areas in my life include: Family and friends, physical health, work life, social life, business life, spiritual life and other areas of interest, such as writing books. Whatever the *KEY AREA* headings may be, we must personalize them so that they give us a quick overview of each major department of our world.

Taking the time to outline these key departments helps us to take inventory of our personal assets and liabilities – a reality check of sorts. Understanding these key areas gives as a big picture, GPS or satellite overview of where we stand now in relation to where we want to be. GPS stands for global positioning system, and is a satellite navigation system consisting of a network of orbiting satellites, originally placed in orbit by the US Department of Defense. A GPS serves us by showing us where we are now in relationship to our map, and where we need to head in order to reach our desired destination.

Planning

Planning is the primary skill of green thinking, and equally applies to organizing our personal lives as it does achieving our goals in business or at work. Planning is the process used to achieve our goals. Planning is the creation of a map, the mental journey into the future in order to calculate the resources needed and the obstacles to be overcome. Great planners anticipate change, look for opportunities, and eliminate the unknown.

Like building a jig-saw-puzzle, planning paints the whole picture, giving us an accurate overview so that we can connect all of the hundreds of little pieces of the puzzle together. These tiny pieces of puzzle are all shaped and colored differently, so if the box didn't have the goal-picture painted on its lid, it would be almost impossible to assemble.

Green thinking sets priorities, creates deadlines, and commits to a timetable for action. In the area of project planning there are numerous planning templates and software packages available online that will give structure and design to your ideas.

There are many planning tools and systems available, from the easy-to-use to the highly complex, depending on your project. They all reveal elements relevant to effective planning, but are not always applicable to every project.

In developing my own personal strategic plan, I have developed my own systems and maps to help keep me on track. I have created *Vision Book* for this reason, something I visit regularly, and something that's always changing. It is a place I can escape to and think, dream, imagine and invent. This is a sanctuary where I can develop my ideas, and update my goals.

My dreams, passions and big ideas should seldom change, but they do mature as I spend time thinking on them. Key areas, on the other hand can change more often, as we change jobs, diets, or exercise plans. In the physical health department for instance, there is constant change and development in order to keep motivated. Goals in the area of health may relate to: books to read, new sports to try, and education concerning diet and health in general. Tasks are then the action points that can be dropped into my daily to-do-list, should I find the time or energy. The mountains we climb become achievable as we break down reaching the summit into bite-size tasks and daily action.

The starting point is to think in *yellow* and *blue*, then move back and forth between *green* and *red*. Thinking in *yellow* and *blue* is essential for clarifying the *big picture design*, whereas thinking in *green* and *red* adds critical thinking, development and detail to our design.

The *Vision Book* is a self-coaching platform that will to you to map your ecosystem, create master plans, projects and tasks for action. It will coach you, and help you to engage others in the process; to THINK, CREATE, INNOVATE, LEAD and LOVE.

Following is an outline of the process taught in the Vision Book—Self Coach Journal.

Vision Book

The 5 Step Process:

Step one: Think
This is where you imagine the possibilities, where you enter the workshop of your imagination and dream big, allowing your passions and wild ideas to roam free. A space you can think like an entrepreneur, fearlessly exploring who you could become, or what you might achieve. A space for looking at things differently, turning things upside down to see if there is an opportunity. A space to mix with inspiring, progressive thinkers who fearlessly discuss new ideas, new ways of doing things and of conquering new worlds. Some of these ideas may not enter the next stages of planning and innovation, but sit in the *Vision Book* for years before activation, but that's okay.

Step two: Create
To create involves imagineering; allowing our ideas to take form and develop structure. This is where, in the workshop of imagination, we design a masterpiece. We write the DNA, generating the building blocks and the blueprints in order to take our ideas into the real world. Like laying an egg then sitting on it until it hatches, this is the pregnancy stage of our idea. Our creative space, a cafe or special room, is where we take the time to think ahead, plan ahead, then move ahead. This planning process is a design thinking, creative process, to help in crafting your ideas into a masterpiece.

Step three: Innovate
Thinking and creativity are about planning, mapping and designing everything in your world. However, innovation is about action, leadership, drive, and execution. Creating is about preparation, but innovation is about implementation. It is not until we have the courage to use our hard earned cash, raise capital, and step outside the door into the fight, that we can be called innovators. These are the people that jump out of the safety of the nest and change the world, make history, and create the new normal. This takes huge energy, a tough mind and relentless determination.

Step four: Lead
Whereas innovation is extremely task focused, leadership is people centered. Taking the lead is seen in the simple acts of courage and care, influencing people for good. Everyone leads in some way – you don't need a title to give leadership. Doing your job with ownership and excellence catches people's attention, and influences a person's thinking. If *thinking* is about dreaming up the possibilities, and *creating is* about planning and developing those ideas, then innovation is about action and execution; *leadership* is, on one hand, a continual *self focus* in order to grow in character, discipline and skill; then in parallel a *people focus* drawing out the best in them, and empowering the team.

Step five: Love
Love is at the foundation of all that is good. Love innovations are the products and services generated from a genuine desire to serve someone else's success and happiness. Love innovations are also the creative acts of kindness and romance that keep our relationships at every level alive and adventurous. All of this requires hard work, but if you learn to enjoy hard work then you will enjoy most of your time here on earth, because most of our time on earth is spent working.

It's all go and we're moving ahead at full speed – the sky's the limit! At this stage we need to move our thinking into a lower gear, *[thinking in red]* for a more analytical, critical thinking approach.

The Vision Book Planning Process:

Think = the Snapshot, Imagineering

Create = the Map, the Plan

1. Key Areas = major departments, dreams or big goals.

2. Goals = for every key area, vision or dream.

3. Master Plans = goals, resource list, costs and quotes, obstacles identified, equipment needed, personal, evaluation times set, etc. The big picture overview.

Innovate = the Road, the Action

4. Project plans = key areas, goals, tasks [why, what, who, how, where, when]

5. Daily Action [to-do-lists] Priorities, communication, and resources.

Create a Master Plan for each Key Area of your life. Project Plans are only needed when you feel that your Master Plan is so large that it needs to be broken down into smaller, bite-size projects. Project Plans are created to achieve or action shorter term or smaller goals.

For example, your goal may be to climb Mount Everest, so you create a Master Plan of all that is involved, something that you calculate will take you and your team three years to achieve, subject to how quickly you can raise the money. Then you break your Master Plan into smaller shorter-term Projects. One project may be to source and price all of the equipment needed, so a decision can be made — where, what, when and how much is needed. Another Project Plan could involve raising the finance needed to climb Mount Everest.

Chapter Seven
Red and Blue Thinking

Thinking in red is about slowing down to smell the roses. Patiently reviewing all that we've researched, judging our ideas in the cold hard light of day. With the disciplines of a world-class scientist we test the idea again and again, viewing the hypothesis from every angle. Like a crime scene investigator, we go where the evidence leads, leaving no stone unturned. Red thinking engages in critical, analytical thinking to uncover hidden dangers and the seeds of failure.

Thinking Blue has to do with the big picture: purpose, values, character, intuition, conscience, our world view, beliefs and spiritual insight. Blue thinking involves flying high, so as to gain a bird's eye overview of a subject or problem. It has to do with the re-evaluation process of thinking itself.

Thinking in Red = critical, analytical thinking

At this stage we continue to bring our grand idea down to earth. We stop and review everything. *Red* thinking has to do with changing gears, into a cautious, more practical mode of thinking. We review the facts, do the figures again, and allow others to offer constructive criticism.

Thinking in Red is about slowing down to smell the roses. Patiently reviewing all that we've researched, judging our ideas in the cold hard light of day. Robert Schuller, the author of numerous books concerning possibility thinking, calls criticism, quality control. In the pursuit of truth, this is where we expose our precious new ideas to those who are brutally honest, but will treat them with respect. With the discipline of a world-class scientist we test the idea again and again, viewing the hypothesis from every angle. Like a crime scene investigator, we go where the evidence leads, leaving no stone unturned. Red thinking engages in critical, analytical thinking to uncover hidden dangers and the seeds of failure.

Thinking Red requires the ruthless application of logic (left-brain thinking) in order to construct an accurate view of reality. What we perceive as true does not always agree with reality. We must search for the contradictions within our thinking. We must allow others to become our mirror, asking questions of those who will give honest feedback.

Geisler and Bocchino, in their book, *Unshakeable Foundations*, point out that, "All thinking (whether about physics or about metaphysics) is alike to the extent that it is governed by this foundational first principle of logic – the law of non-contradiction—Can opposite truth claims both be true?" The word science literally means knowledge. It has its origin in the Latin term scire, to know. Scientific thinking involves the laborious task of compiling all of the facts. All of the pieces of the jigsaw puzzle are needed in order to paint a correct picture of reality. This knowledge picture must be as complete as possible before we can make accurate conclusions. Black and white thinkers are wise in their own eyes – they don't seem to need all of the facts. They mumble, "Don't confuse me with the facts: I've made up my mind."

The honest scientist (and we can all engage in scientific thinking) goes where the evidence is leading. "The first principle of science is a philosophical assumption upon which the discipline of science rests: it is known as the principle of causality." This principle states that every event has an adequate cause [cause and effect]. Geisler and Bocchino point out that, "Homicide detectives use this method to investigate murders, asking questions such as: What was the cause of death? Was it an accident or was it a planned event? Did it happen by chance or was it the result of an intelligent agent?" Forensic scientists think in red with such questions. Then they shift gears and think in yellow: generating a range of alternative scenarios, brainstorming all of the possibilities. They then create movement, and switch to green thinking, bringing everyone involved together to construct a plan of attack. To create a clear picture they set goals and priorities, assign tasks, and build strategies. Like a well-organized Napoleonic army, they build a plan to discover the truth. At any given point, the leader of the investigation may pull everyone together to engage in some further red thinking; such as reviewing the evidence, analyzing the new information, looking for connections that may lead to a clearer picture. True to any good crime story, the lead character usually possesses a trait that sets them apart; a sixth sense that leads them to people and places that no one else had thought of. The skills of analytical thinking are limited in that they can only lead you as far as the physical evidence dictates. However, beyond the knowledge gained through the five senses, there is the spiritual realm of intuition and wisdom. Understanding the voice of wisdom and intuition will give you the edge, and is what thinking in Blue is all about

Blue thinking = philosophical thinking

While on a speaking trip in the Gold Coast of Australia, I was invited by a businessman to join him and his son on a parachute jump, something I had never experienced before. An adrenaline junkie's dream, myself and five others jammed into a tiny aircraft, and climbed to the maximum height of 16,000 feet into the clear blue skies over Byron Bay. This was my first jump, and I wondered how long I could keep my nerves under control, before fear kicked in. Amazingly, I kept mind-over-circumstances intact, which is until the door was opened and I had to jump out into thin air.

Adrenalin flooded my system as I edged my way to the door and jumped out. As I adjusted to falling through the air at 120 miles per hour, I captured the awesome beauty, a bird's-eye-view of the bay and the surrounding countryside. Time seemed to slow down and my mind and all of its cells were on full volume capturing the exhilarating view; the thin strip of golden sand, the ocean waves, the arid landscape, the roads and the little cars and houses below. Viewing things from this perspective I gained a snapshot of everything at a moment in time. I could see where everything is and how it all fits together. This is thinking in blue.

Thinking Blue has to do with the big picture: purpose, values, character, intuition, conscience, our world view, beliefs and spiritual insight. Blue thinking involves flying high, so as to gain a bird's-eye-over-view of a subject or problem. It has to do with the re-evaluation process of thinking itself.

This mode of thinking will involve some in-depth philosophical thinking that may even lead to a complete paradigm shift. It's where you test what you believe. The Little Oxford dictionary defines philosophy as, "the pursuit of wisdom or knowledge, of ultimate reality or general causes and principles." As CS Lewis asserted, "everyone in life has a philosophy– the only question is, whether it is a good one or not."

Geisler and Boccino show that, "The word 'philosophy' comes from two Greek words: phileo meaning love, and sophia, meaning wisdom." It is interesting to note that the word phileo signifies the kind of love that one has for a friend. The true philosopher, as King Solomon points out, loves wisdom as if it were a close friend. He wrote, "Do not forsake wisdom, and she will protect you; love her, and she will watch over you. Wisdom is supreme; therefore get wisdom. Though it cost you all that you have, get understanding. Esteem her, and she will exalt you; embrace her, and she will honor you."

Friends spend time talking over every aspect of a subject, unafraid to explore and secure about placing their wild ideas or new theories on the table. Friends spend a lot of time chatting about seemingly small stuff; they just love hanging together. To be a friend of wisdom means to be at home with our thoughts, to spend time mapping those thoughts – to love the process of thinking itself. To be at home with our thoughts is a strange concept in a world where much of our thinking is done for us. Wisdom is no stranger to those who take the time to think, chewing on a thought like a cow chews its cud.

To be a friend of wisdom also means having friends that are willing to engage the thinking process with you. Solomon teaches throughout Proverbs that friends, family and wise counselors were his greatest source of wisdom. Blue thinking draws on the mind and experience of others, encouraging conversation and philosophical debate in the search for wisdom. The key to wisdom, Solomon taught throughout the Book of Proverbs, was to possess knowledge and understanding, and a multitude of wise counselors close by. He stated that these attributes: knowledge, understanding and wisdom were worth more than gold or silver, because they lead to wealth in every area of life.

Blue thinking gives leadership to our thinking, asking the big picture questions such as:

- What is our vision or dream?
- What is the big picture?
- What are the key departments?
- Why? What? Where? When? Who? How?
- Do we possess all of the facts or knowledge needed?
- Who is best qualified to give me counsel on this subject?
- Do we understand how these facts fit together?
- Why are we doing this?
- Where do my *belief systems* come from?
- Where did those out-of-control emotions come from?
- What philosophy or world view underpins my thinking and why?
- Who can action this task?
- Should we out-source this task, or keep it in-house?
- What mode or thinking color should we engage next?

Spiritual insight

Blue thinking taps into the spiritual dimension at a number of levels. The wisdom of the Creator is discovered in a number of very simple ways, and is not as mystical as we may think. We were designed to hear the Creator's voice, and like a kind of spiritual DNA, we receive the instructions for success in every department of life through a wide range of voices. For example, we hear the 'voice of conscience' when we violate the laws of love and design. These voices of Spiritual DNA include conscience, intuition, instinct, character and wisdom. They will help us think in *blue* and walk the path of design, wisdom and love.

Blue thinking brings spiritual insight to a subject by asking:

- How does this align with our values?
- Is this consistent with our world view or belief systems?
- Is this ethical?
- Are we really passionate about this?
- What is the Creator saying through the voices of conscience and instinct?
- Does this fit our culture?
- Do they have our chemistry?
- Who should we include in the discussion?
- Do they possess good character?
- What is our Creator saying through the *multitude of councilors*?
- What is the *still small voice* of intuition whispering?
- Where did that thought come form?
- What are my motives?
- What books can give me guidance?

The right questions are gold when it comes to thinking blue. In the following few chapters, I expand on the skill and art of thinking in yellow, blue, green and red.

Chapter Eight
Intuitive Thinkers

"Under all that we think, lives all that we believe, like the ultimate veil of our spirits."

— Antonio Machado

Although our subconscious brain draws on a massive storehouse of experience and information, stored as memories, intuition goes beyond the natural process of reasoning.

Imagine a world without words, a life of silence with no vibrations that form any meaningful or not so meaningful conversation. No small talk or big talk. No music, no verbal dialogue, no connection to the world of sound!

The ear, one of our five senses, is a most amazing biological machine, and possesses approximately one million moving parts. It also has one hundred thousand hair cells functioning as motion sensors that give us our sense of balance. The super sensitivity of this incredible organ makes it possible, on a still night, to hear a cricket chirping from one and a half miles away.

This is how it happens. The sound waves or vibrations of the door shutting, or a person's laughter, travel into the inner sanctum of the eardrum touching or hitting its super sensitive membrane. This membrane is like the skin covering a drum and is approximately the thickness of a piece of paper. It is so sensitive that the brain can detect sound wave impressions less than the diameter of a hydrogen molecule. In this highly sophisticated studio there are the tiniest bones in the body. They are commonly known as the hammer, anvil and stirrup. When the eardrum vibrates, it's through these tiny connected bones that the sound waves are transferred to the cochlea and the organ of corti, the next destination on their journey to the brain.

The organ of corti is described by Richard A Swenson in his book, *More Than Meets the Eye*, as "a musical instrument of sorts; if a piano has eighty-eight keys, the organ of corti has over twenty-thousand keys. It can distinguish between two thousand different pitches." Within this organ, the vibrations are processed through thousands of super sensitive hair cells, converting them into electrical impulses to be transmitted to the brain through the auditory nerve.

Richard Swenson points out that, "The ear is a microphone, an acoustical amplifier and a frequency analyzer." Thinking about this most amazing process I stand in awe yet again at the genius of our Creator. Without this ability, communication, conversation and friendship is made difficult. The ability to hear the voice of our Maker transmitting thoughts of love, knowledge, inspiration and correction, is also an amazing gift. Spiritual vibrations end up in the same place as natural vibrations. Instead of making their entrance through our eardrum, spiritual vibrations enter via our spirit and are immediately transmitted to the brain to become a thought or feeling.

Jesus taught that, "Man [or woman] shall not live by bread alone," but by every word or vibration that is transmitted from the Creator. Some call it a *hunch*! Mother Teresa teaches that, "Silence of heart is necessary so you can hear the Creator everywhere—in the closing of a door, in the person who needs you, in the birds that sing, in the flowers and in the animals." "In this place of silence," she taught, "we will find a new outlook on life, a new energy and true unity with the love of Christ." Originally the human spirit was designed to be the sanctuary where our Creator lived and communicated with us, but sadly no longer functions to the degree it once did.

The sixth sense

At a purely physical level we listen to the sounds, sensations and voices of our world through the five senses: sight, taste, touch, smell and hearing. The vast array of information fed through these amazing receptors is fired off to the brain to be analyzed and processed for action. No matter what the input, it lives on in our memory as a huge database of information and experience.

Hearing the voice of our Creator happens by learning to hear the voice of intuition. Known as the sixth sense, intuition is a powerful inner voice warning us in time to avoid impending danger, prompting us to do good when we know we should. It is the voice of instinct, imagination, self-honesty, conscience, truth and wisdom. This is a voice of both good and evil, of Gollum, and Smeagol—an interesting character from the movie, Lord of The Rings. It is the Creator's voice of inspiration, information and confrontation. It is *thinking in blue*.

Intuition is a part of our *spiritual intelligence,* something that goes beyond the level of processing the information being received through our five senses. Intuition is the voice of the human spirit giving us knowledge or wisdom, and seems to come from nowhere: the *premonition* you experience that gives an uncanny knowledge of a future event, the supernatural knowledge that tells you someone is coming to visit, or as in the experience of a friend, that someone has just died.

Premonitions are evidence of what we call *miracles,* because they surpass natural reasoning abilities, and are unobtainable through the five senses. Intuition is a guide for many business people in the decision-making process, often called *a hunch.* The intuition of a woman when assessing a hidden motive or the character of person, is intuitive knowledge—and deadly accurate at times!

Although our subconscious brain draws on a massive storehouse of experience and information stored as memories, intuition goes beyond the natural process of reasoning. It is imparted. It is knowledge from beyond the walls of the five senses. It is the Creator of the universe giving us what King Solomon taught was *the gift of wisdom..* We have an intelligent designer who generously gives us His wisdom, whether we use it or not. This wisdom is received through the faculties of *perception*. Perception includes: intuition, instinct, conscience, sub-conscious thought, and imagination. *Blue* thinking draws on these Creator designed abilities, helping us to navigate our way through life.

Chapter Nine
Wisdom Thinkers

"A person of wisdom seeks out quality advice by questioning the experts and reading the books of great thinkers. Solomon teaches again and again throughout the book of Proverbs that, "There is victory in the multitude of counselors."

— King Solomon

Solomon's thinking process—thinking about thinking

It used to be that land was the most valuable real estate one could possess, however, the *digital revolution* has made, the *great idea* a highly valued commodity equal to striking oil or discovering a gold mine. Today, Intellectual property can be the most expensive real estate on the planet.

Amidst the teachings of Proverbs you will discover that the secret to the Wisdom of Solomon was his ability to tap into *ultimate intelligence*. Woven into the tapestry of Proverbs are three words that were foundational in Solomon's thinking process: *knowledge, understanding and wisdom.* These are the key ingredients in Solomon's pursuit of ultimate wisdom. As these three thinking skills become a habit, we will enjoy the wealth and freedom that wisdom brings. As you search for wisdom using these three guides, at some stage the light will turn on, the windows will clear, the sun will rise, and you will gain the Creator's perspective. A still small voice, a hunch, a dominant thought, something someone says, instinct, or the voice of conscience all communicate an idea or message for those who have learned to listen. Solomon teaches us to "tune our ears to wisdom," something that made him the most creative, innovative leader of his day.

Each of these three words will lead you to a different mode of thinking. Again, view thinking within this process as changing the gears of a car: the first gear being knowledge, the second understanding and the top gear, engaging wisdom.

1. Knowledge = Facts, information and honesty

The first step toward *wisdom* is the discipline of gathering all of the facts. Knowledge in this process has to do with digging up all of the relevant information in order to gain a clear picture! Solomon taught that, the wise accumulate, or store up knowledge. *"Any enterprise,"* he said, *"is built by wise planning and becomes strong through common sense and profits wonderfully by keeping abreast of the facts."* Whether it is processing an idea, dealing with a problem, evaluating a philosophy, or questioning a belief system, to discover wisdom we must fearlessly face the facts.

Like a good judge, this requires putting aside our personal prejudice, opinions and any initial negative emotions in order to view the facts objectively. We must remain open and ruthlessly honest as to where the facts might lead. It is going where the evidence leads, using the skills of a great scientist or crime scene investigator. It is searching out the facts and laying out all of the pieces of a jigsaw puzzle ready for assembly. If pieces of the jigsaw are missing, this will result in an incomplete picture. In decision-making, missing *facts* give an incomplete picture and may mean the difference between success and failure.

Solomon taught that the key to the accurate accumulation of the facts was the art of listening. It has been said that the reason we have two ears and one mouth, is so that we can listen twice as much as we talk. A study of people from a variety of professional backgrounds showed that 70 percent of their waking hours was spent in communication. Of that time, 9 percent was spent writing, 16 percent was absorbed in reading, 30 percent talking, and a huge 45 percent occupied in listening.

Although we spend a lot of time listening to oral communication at a purely informational level, researchers claim that 75 percent of this is ignored, misunderstood or quickly forgotten. Listening is not only the key to gaining knowledge, it is the skill needed to succeed in all four modes of thinking. The art of listening is the art of asking the right questions, the hard questions. It is asking probing questions in order to uncover the truth of a matter. Questions that open up the door to a vast storehouse of valuable knowledge locked away inside of other people. Accessing this information and experience often costs little more than swallowing our pride and showing a bit of humility.

We must also ask the tough questions of ourselves. Questions that dig down, in a constructive way, in order to peel back any layers of possible self-deception. Asking the kind of questions that question the way that we have viewed or have done things in the past. You don't need a Harvard Degree in order to learn or exercise the art of listening; however, it does require characteristics such as patience, sensitivity, insight, honesty, courage, optimism, confidence, discernment and discipline.

2. Understanding = Education, experience, mentors and teachers

Understanding is the process of learning how all of the facts fit together. It is the summing up of the facts or evidence, in order to make our case. We may have gathered all of the component parts of a watch, but have no understanding as to how they fit together. It is one thing to have an accurate knowledge of all of the parts of the human cell and not understand how the system works as a whole. There is no easy road to be a person of great understanding, it means a life-long commitment to education and the gaining of a wide range of experience.

Solomon is blunt about those who are wise in their own eyes saying, "A fool finds no pleasure in understanding but delights in airing his own opinions." He also says, "The purposes of a man's heart are deep waters, but a man of understanding draws them out." Again asking the tough questions is vital during this process of gaining *understanding*. Knowledge has to do with the observation of the facts. Understanding is the interpretation of the facts and how they fit together. Wisdom then, is the application of the facts. In a nutshell, Knowledge asks, 'What?' Understanding asks, 'How? While Wisdom asks, 'Why? Who? Where? and When?'

3. Wisdom = Knowledge, understanding, intuition and wise advisers

Wisdom is the application of knowledge and understanding. Wisdom is the ability to make the right decision, in the right place, at the right time. A person of wisdom seeks out quality advice by questioning the experts and reading the books of great thinkers. Solomon teaches again and again throughout the book of Proverbs that, "There is victory in the multitude of counselors." Applying this principle is the highest form of self-education, because a person, unlike a book, is interactive, and emphasizes, with emotion the critical success factors. Solomon points out that, "Wisdom shouts in the street, she lifts up her voice in the square; at the head of the noisy streets she cries out; and at the entrance of the gates in the city she utters her sayings." Solomon was saying that wisdom is accessible to all of those who have a listening ear and a teachable spirit.

This process and the key to wisdom in general is built on the foundation of accurate listening. How we hear and the filters we use to establish a clear picture is what keeps us from falling into the trap of self-deception or living a lie. The information being processed through our five senses is not always what it seems. Often laced with deception, our five senses can feed us an equally distorted picture of the truth. Listening carefully, honestly and with the help of our Creator we will find and travel the path of design and success.

Chapter Ten
Rational Thinkers

"People almost invariably arrive at their beliefs, not on the basis of proof, but on the basis of what they find attractive"

— Blaise Pascal

We appeal to an invisible, often unlearned set of guiding principles or laws that we perceive govern what is correct or incorrect thinking. It is as if the brain is wired with the software of logic.

Principles of logic

In thinking about questions such as those proposed in this book, it's important to understand some of the laws of logic and a few basic principles of good thinking. The questions and arguments concerning the enterprise ecosystem are often more about personal opinion than correct or objective thinking. Remember the Blaise Pascal quote, "People almost invariably arrive at their *beliefs,* not on the basis of proof, but on the basis of what the find attractive." We see what we want to see. We see what we are used to seeing. We see what our emotions have sensitized us to see. We all like to think that what we believe to be true would, if questioned, stand the test of logic.

Our appeal to logic is a daily event, saying things such as, "that doesn't add up," "our logic is flawed," "that's illogical," "give me ten good reasons to believe you!" We appeal to an invisible, often unlearned set of guiding principles or laws that we perceive govern what is correct or incorrect thinking. It is as if these laws are instinctive, a natural built-in guide to good reasoning. Our brain is wired with the software of logic. We like to believe that our logic, or the process we use to determine *truth,* is clearly one step ahead of others—our identity is often linked with being *right*.

Thinking about thinking is vital in determining *truth*. If we do not understand the laws and principles that govern good thinking, we open ourselves up to the possibility of believing a lie, a half-truth, or generally being deceived more easily. It has been said that *perception is reality;* a statement that is not true, but makes the point that our perceptions appear to be *real* until we gain more information or think things through systematically. Our belief system is then formed from what we *perceive* to be true, not always based on what is actually true.

Of course, logical thinking alone is not always complete without creative thinking. In the area of science our starting point requires creativity in the form of a *hypothesis.* Once we believe a thing to be true we have created an assumption, a perception that is now, to us, a *reality*. If that belief or assumption is in fact wrong or false, then we may suffer any number of consequences. The assumption that the Titanic was unsinkable was one of the major reasons so many died--1500 people lost their lives that day. The assumption that the earth was flat could have been the reason that many were afraid to explore the *far reaches of the sea* before they did, afraid of falling off the edge of the earth.

Logic is not total protection, but another line of defense against a false belief, a faulty world view or a wrong assumption.

John W. Robbins in his article *Why Study Logic*, notes that in our elementary education we study what is correctly regarded as basic to all further education; reading, writing and arithmetic. He says, "One cannot study history, botany or computers without being able to read... could there be something more basic than the three basics? This is something so obvious that most people do not see it, let alone study it? What is there in common between calculating, reading and writing? The answer, of course, is *thought*. One must think in order to read and write." Just as arithmetic explains the rules to follow in order to arrive at a correct answer, similarly, logic assists us in reaching a right conclusion. The laws of logic and skills in thinking are vital to the execution of rational thought and lay a solid foundation for stable thinking; they give us an intellectual lens through which to see the world.

A powerful tool for discovering and determining *truth* is intuition, but this is a loose cannon without logic. *Logic* is an important branch of philosophy and helps us to keep things objective. Aristotle called *logic* the instrument of all science. He taught that all meaningful thinking and communication is dependent upon logic for its weight and force. We often lack the capacity for independent objective thought due to indoctrination, bigotry, pride or prejudice. For instance, prejudice within our thinking will cause us to pre-judge situations. We jump to conclusions before all the facts are clear: "Don't confuse me with the facts, I've made up my mind!"

In order to be a logical thinker we must act as a wise judge, remaining open to all of the facts, reserving our judgment until the appropriate time. The judge and jury form their judgments from the evidence and the arguments put forward by the lawyers and the witnesses. They listen carefully to the prosecution and defense lawyers in an attempt to understand their line of reasoning. The legal teams put forward their logic and state their conclusions. The lawyers make their appeal to logic, constantly questioning the assumptions or the facts laid before them. Logic is the honest evaluation of the available evidence in search of what is true or what is not.

In an age where most of the information on planet earth is at our fingertips, we should be better positioned to think for ourselves. We live adrift, on an ocean of thought, and will go with the loudest most forceful opinion unless we learn to think for ourselves. When we judge something too quickly, we risk shutting the process of logic or sound reasoning down, limiting our ability to see the truth or the reality of a situation. Logic is a step-by-step processing of ideas, information and experience, so that everyone can follow the concept or idea to its conclusion.

Communication tool

Logic is not only a thinking mechanism, but a communication tool; the science of presenting our arguments in a clear and systematic way. It puts forward its proposition in a tightly defined, easy to follow manner. It is used to defend or prove our ideas and lead others to the same conclusion. *Logic* is putting our thoughts in order, based on fact, not fiction. The study of logic trains the mind to distinguish between factual and emotional appeals in processing a subject. It is one of the tools of wisdom. It is the mining of an idea in search of gold. Just as the digestive system breaks food down, logic breaks ideas and concepts down into their component parts. To further understand the principles of logic, an outline of the *laws of logic* as proposed by Aristotle.

We appeal to an invisible, often unlearned set of guiding principles or laws that we perceive govern what is correct or incorrect thinking. It's as if the brain is wired with the software of logic.

Passion versus reason

"All of our reasoning ends in surrender to feeling, such is the power of emotion or passion."

— Blaise Pascal

Passion is a raging river of feelings, ideas, inspiration and experience, while reason is a deep pool of knowledge, logic and wisdom. Passion can operate devoid of reason, but when coupled with reason it is a most powerful mix.

Winning the race against over 200 million potential brothers and sisters to fertilize the female egg, I started my journey toward life on planet earth. It was only three weeks after conception that a sheet of electrically charged cells organized themselves into a tiny immature heart, then started beating. Then within just fourteen weeks it was pumping seven gallons a day throughout my tiny little body. Now it's "pumping 75 gallons an hour, 1800 gallons a day, and 657,000 gallons every a year (enough to fill four Olympic sized swimming pools) in order to keep all of my cells freshly oxygenated."

In his book, *More Than Meets the Eye,* Richard Swenson points out that "every day this ten ounce muscle contracts 100,000 times, never missing a beat." Over a lifetime of faithful service, the heart, a self-lubricating, self-regulating, high capacity organ, beats 2.5 billion times, and pumps 60 million gallons of blood through 60,000 miles of blood vessels; enough blood vessels to stretch two and a half times, around the earth's equator.

This high speed, high pressure transportation system pumps millions of microscopic molecular machines throughout every organ of our bodies, and carries every kind of precious cargo, including: oxygen, water, glucose, proteins, and carbon dioxide to name a few. Like an express train filled with balloons, the red blood cells are a cleverly engineered transportation system that carries this life-giving oxygen throughout the tissues of our bodies. "We breathe approximately 23,000 times per day and 630 million times over an average life span" generating much needed oxygen. Each red blood cell can carry up to a million molecules of oxygen because of the cell's complex iron-rich substance called hemoglobin. This oxygen-filled train then travels the 60,000 miles of the body's blood vessels in search of oxygen-starved cells. Every second we manufacture over two million of these red blood cells, which if laid side by side would go around the earth's equator four times.

It is hard to conclude that such order and precision came *mindlessly* into being? The production of platelets that are involved in the critical process of blood clotting was no mistake. The immune system, with its fifty-billion white blood cells ready to go to war against harmful microbes in a picosecond, is no accident, but seems to be the work of a great thinker.

Heart and head

In Hebrew thought, the heart is the sanctuary of the soul. It is the spiritual dimension of the *mind, will, imagination* and *emotion*. Metaphorically it is the center of love and compassion, seen as the seat of intimacy and affection, the very core of who we are. It is the seat of *self*, the place of human consciousness. The heart is where our *passions* are birthed and take root, then produce fruit both good and bad. Solomon teaches, "Above all else, guard your heart, for it is the wellspring of life." The heart is where our passions originate, the place they can be developed or defiled.

In Solomon's day the *wellspring* was a very important place. This was a place to guard with your life because it was, to the family and community, the very source of life itself. Raiding armies would fill in or poison their enemy's wells in order to wipe them out or bring them hardship. In the same way, our hearts can be corrupted with bitterness, fear, hatred, prejudice, or jealousy; mindsets that will infect our thoughts. These kinds of attitudes will pollute or poison the *mind*. Our inner drive can be crippled and our thinking distorted by a preoccupation with such powerful yet negative emotions. When we lose heart we lose our passion for life, and it affects our thinking capacity. The heart is a wellspring of passion; we must guard this fresh water of pure inspiration, from pollution.

As oxygen is to the body, passion is to our thinking. We suffocate without passion and creative self-expression. We have all been wired with unique gifts or passions that forever need expression. Passion is the inner drive and relentless pursuit of the *someone* or *something* we love. Passion is a spiritual force that seems to come from nowhere, yet gives energy, motivation, and imagination to our thinking. It is thinking in bright *yellow*!

Passion is an invisible force drawing on every megabyte of our mental capacity; it is spiritual adrenalin! A passionate person is the one on fire with an idea, or sacrificially driven to serve the ones they love. Passion is the difference between the good and the great. Passion is a *wellspring* of inspiration.

Passionate people don't spend their days trying *not* to be bad, instead they step into a world of greatness. Why someone gives themselves to a field of study or work for a lifetime is a mystery. I cannot imagine what the world would be like, if some of the great leaders in medical care and research, lost their passion. The passionate desire to help those in pain, is still the great mother of invention.

Social innovation

In the areas of medicine and health, there were few as passionate as Florence Nightingale. She led the way, and helped lay the foundations of modern medicine and health-care. Florence Nightingale (1820-1910) was the founder of modern nursing, who did her work, she believed, under the inspiration of Christ. When she was 17, she felt God calling her into His service. Theodore Fliedner (1800-1864) deeply influenced Nightingale, by organizing deaconesses within the Lutheran Church who were involved in helping with education, ex-convicts, and nursing instruction. Florence Nightingale became famous, traveling to far off battlefields, cleaning soldier's wounds, and comforting those who were dying. She was a legend, known as the *Lady with the Lamp*. Throughout history passion or compassion has truly been the *wellspring* of invention.

The innovations of love continued. When returning to England, Florence Nightingale wrote a book called, *Notes on Hospitals* published in 1859. This had a profound effect throughout the world on hospital care and hygienic design. Then in 1860 the Nightingale School for Training Nurses was opened at St Thomas's Hospital in London.

Balance

Passion is a raging river of feelings, ideas, inspiration and experience, while reason is a deep pool of knowledge, logic and wisdom. Passion can operate devoid of reason, but when coupled with reason it is a most powerful mix. Passion and reason need to be kept in balance. Overly passionate and we blow up; totally rational, and we dry up. Passionate people, at times, can find themselves adrift on an angry ocean of emotion. On the other hand, rational people can suffer from what is called the *paralysis of analysis*. They analyze things to death. Passion and reason are the two wings of a bird, the two sides of a coin–the perfect marriage.

It has been said that the heart has its reasons that reason knows nothing about. Passion can often throw reason out of the window. This is probably why Blaise Pascal said, "*All of our reasoning ends in surrender to feeling*," such is the power of emotion or passion.

This is why we must be disciplined, because too many truly great people have become the victims of their out-of-control passion. On the other hand, reason can drag us into a deep rut, a surreal world of boredom, never engaging the things we are really passionate about.

It interests me that we all like to be considered a rational person, but truly admire those who live life with passion. Reason is a great servant, but a poor master, due to the fact that if reason dominates, we can lose the power of instinct, intuition and conscience.

Unpolluted passion gives thinking the power it needs to climb the highest of life's mountains—however, we do need reason as our guide. In essence, thinking in *yellow* and *blue* flows form the wellspring of passion, whereas thinking in *green* and *red* comes from the world of reason – keeping us safe. Passion without reason is like a boat without a rudder, it will drift in whatever direction the winds are blowing, or the tides are going. Building a successful enterprise requires both of these powerful forces.

Chapter Eleven
Honest Thinkers

"Honesty and transparency make you feel vulnerable. Be honest and transparent anyway."

– Mother Teresa

Honest thinking is the art of seeing beyond our indoctrinated thinking, prejudice or strong personal opinions in order to discover the truth of a matter. In business, there is a world of half-truths, lies and deception. Then inside of us can be varying levels of self-deception holding us back, or distorting our view of things. To build any enterprise we must conquer our need to be right, and gain an honest perspective.

For over a thousand years, millions of Chinese women were subjected to the very painful custom of foot binding. Foot-binding through the centuries spread from the court to the upper class, and in turn, to the majority of the population. Over time small feet became synonymous with beauty, so much so that it was difficult for a woman with large feet to find a husband. The perfect foot was, tiny, small, pointed, crooked, perfumed, soft and symmetrical. A mother would take a long piece of cloth and bind her young girl's feet. All of the toes, except for the big toe, were bent up under the sole of their feet until they eventually snapped. If started too soon the girl could be crippled for life. Many were restricted to their bed because it was too painful to walk. Even when this physical process was complete, they could never walk very far from home for the rest of their lives. Binding usually began when the girl was four and took about five years to complete. This tradition was said to have started during the southern Tang dynasty (407-923) during the reign of Emperor Li Yu, who was one of China's great romantic poets. Being more interested in wine, women, and song than matters of state, he did not stay on the throne for very long. He supposedly had one of his favorite wives bandage her feet to make them pointed in order for her to dance more beautifully. This caused great excitement in the court, and others followed suit. For Chinese men, small feet were extremely sensual. In these times a man would not see a woman's naked feet until after marriage, and then only during sex. Over the centuries, Dr Ko, a Taiwanese surgeon, says over 3 million girls have experienced this cruel fetish.

Cultural indoctrination such as this can turn something abnormal into something socially acceptable. Bound by the bandages of our cultural and personal pride, hating to admit we were wrong, we can hang on to destructive ideas for many years, even generations before questioning them. Without honesty, our ability to think is bound or crippled. Honesty is a vital part of the reasoning process because it keeps us from being self-deceived, and helps us to remain open to new ideas. The definition of self-deception is, *the process of denial or rationalizing away the relevance, significance, or importance of opposing evidence and logical argument.* The result of dishonest thinking is living in denial, a self-induced mental blindness. Honesty protects us from corrupted characteristics that blind our ability to reason with integrity.

At the level of our human spirit there is a kind of honesty box, that we call conscience, giving us an intuitive knowledge of what is right and wrong, and a sense of responsibility to do what is right. This *honesty box,* not only warns us of what is wrong, it is the voice of good and honest character. Characteristics such as: courage, honesty, loyalty, patience, and humility, all sit beneath the surface of our thinking, and like white blood cells, protect us from harmful unwanted invaders. *Honesty* is character, and character is the foundation that under pins balanced healthy thinking. Albert Einstein said, "Most people say that it is the intellect which makes a great scientist. They are wrong, it is character." Good and bad character speaks to us throughout our day, directing our behavior. Laziness has a voice telling us to take the path of least resistance, which is not always the best decision. The voice of honesty tells us to cut the crap and admit that we were wrong. Both good and corrupted character influences us more than we care to admit, or are even aware of. Good character helps us walk with balance and run with agility. Poor character cripples the thinking process. The bandages used to cripple literally millions of these beautiful little Chinese girls represent those characteristics that bind our thinking. The following are some examples of traits that sit beneath the surface, and kill or distort honest thinking:

Indoctrination

Destructive indoctrination cripples our thinking due to the assumption that we have arrived at *the truth*, and no further thinking on the subject is required.

Negative indoctrination carries an attitude of pride and superiority. Although we have become confident of certain conclusions, we must always remain open to our ideas being tested. Indoctrination stops us asking any further questions—we have made our judgment and that settles the matter.

As much as anything, indoctrination in the negative sense, lacks humility and fails to respect those who do not hold to our point of view. It is an attitude of, "Don't question me, I'm right and you're wrong!" This is something that has halted progress throughout history. The word indoctrination has both positive and negative connotations. In its widest sense it can refer to the teaching of the basics within education: the alphabet, the basic methodology of a profession, or the foundational principles of a subject, such as science. In the fields of psychology and sociology, the terms that describe aspects of indoctrination include: socialization, propaganda, manipulation and brain washing. In the education system, as in our personal lives, we need to distinguish between undesirable and acceptable indoctrination. Closing our mind to the point of no return shows no humility and is the reason many fail. Indoctrination clearly kept people from questioning this detestable tradition of foot binding for thousands of years.

Cynicism

In rejecting the manipulative bigoted attitudes of negative indoctrination, we can swing to the opposite mind-set of cynicism, which is an equally destructive and unhealthy way of thinking.

Cynicism is the *bandage* of mistrust and a deep seated fear of being deceived. It is built on the assumption that most people are motivated by self-interest. Cynicism questions everyone and everything in search of ulterior motives. There is something deeply appealing about cynicism because it lets us off the *commitment hook*. The voice of cynicism says, "Watch out, don't be taken in." So when an appeal for aid is made, we can justify doing nothing. In his book, *Seeing Through the Eyes of Cynicism*, Dick Keyes suggests that, "Cynicism promises a more sophisticated way of seeing. It promises to protect you from getting conned, disgraced or disillusioned." He points out that it is "seeing through and unmasking positive appearances to reveal the more basic underlying motivations of greed, power, lust and selfishness. It says that every respectable public agenda has a hidden private agenda behind it that is less noble, flattering or moral."

There are many good reasons to be cynical; the politician who breaks their promise, the father who hurts his children, or the community leader that controls or manipulates people. Unhealthy cynicism places a harsh judgment on every human being—guilty! Cynicism is a necessary protection against deception and is a part of thinking in *red*. However, the problem with a cynical attitude is that it assumes that everyone is guilty until proven innocent. This is the opposite to a healthy concept of justice, where you are innocent until proven guilty. The outcome is a society where trust is never given an opportunity to grow. It is the assumption that everyone is selfish; an indoctrination of sorts. It is true that we have selfish motives to varying degrees; however, to lock down on the dark side of human nature will fail to draw out the best in people. Solomon's father, King David, taught his son that a wise man does not sit in the seat of scoffers. An environment filled with toxic levels of pessimism, sarcasm, suspicion and skepticism, does not foster healthy, balanced thinking.

Honest thinking

Honesty has as much to do with pointing out the greatness we see in people, as it does not lying, or telling *the negative truths* about our poor character or behavior.

Wikipedia defines honesty as, "The human quality of communicating and acting truthfully. Stating the facts as best one truly believes them to be. It includes both honesty to others, to oneself, and ones motives, and inner reality." Other dictionary definitions talk about adherence to the facts, the refusal to lie or deceive, and about choosing not to be corrupted or false.

Honesty pushes aside prejudice, withholds judgment, buries pride and listens to all points of view. Honest people pursue the facts, evaluate the facts, test the facts, and then judge the facts. Honesty gives us an accurate picture of reality. The voices of indoctrination and prejudice cry: "Don't confuse me with the facts, I've made up my mind." Honesty is the pursuit of truth, within and without, and begins with being honest with ourselves. King David in his prayer asked his Creator, "to keep him from lying to myself."

It is interesting to note that most surveys to identify the kind of leaders we prefer show that honesty is at the top of every list. It is strange, but we often want from others a higher standard than we are willing to impose upon ourselves. Honesty in thinking is having the confidence to seek the input, feedback, and constructive criticism of others.

John Naisbitt in his book, *Mindset,* deals with eleven mindsets concerning seeing the future. He says, "My premier mindset is understanding how powerful it is *not to have to be right*." He points out that, "People are culturally conditioned to have to be right. The parents are right, the teacher is right, the boss is right. Who is right overrules what is right." He concludes, "Once you experience the power of not having to be right, you will feel like you are walking across open fields, the perspective wide and your feet free to take any turn." This attitude, not taken to the extreme, is genuine humility.

Honesty must possess the humility that allows our thinking to be challenged. Mother Teresa said, "Honesty and transparency make you feel vulnerable. Be honest and transparent anyway." Honest thinking is also foundational in gaining wisdom. Remember, wisdom is the ability to research the facts (knowledge), interpret those facts (understanding), and then arrive at a conclusion or application (wisdom). Wisdom requires an honest interpretation and a fearless application of the facts. Honesty is thinking in *red*. Honesty is the steel that runs through the back-bone of great thinkers. Honesty bravely admits, "I'm sorry I was wrong, you were right." William Shakespeare wrote, "Honesty is the best policy. If I lose mine honor, I lose myself."

Solomon teaches, "Faithful are the wounds of a friend." *Honest thinking* requires the help of others, who can fearlessly ask the probing questions, giving honest, sometimes brutal feedback. It is written that Jesus was a man full of *grace and truth*. Truth without love or grace in the mix, can appear ruthless and even cruel. This is an important balance because without the *grace calculation* we would be forever discouraged. Wisdom is needed in calculating how much truth a person can take about their weaknesses or wrong doing at any given time. If someone were to tell us the absolute truth, and nothing but the truth about our flaws, our self-esteem may never recover. Truth or honesty reports the cold hard facts, while grace is the shock-absorber communicating with wisdom and understanding, keeping the bigger picture of relationship in mind. Solomon taught that, "There is one who speaks rashly like the thrusts of a sword, but the tongue of the wise brings healing... The heart of the wise teaches his mouth, and adds persuasiveness to his lips." Honest conclusions are one thing, communicating them is another. Remember this quote: "Under all that we think, lives all that we believe, like the ultimate veil of our spirits."— Antonio Machado

Snapshot - Personal Honesty

Are you honest with yourself? Write down the lies you have told yourself in the past.

1.
2.
3.
4.
5.

Were you honest with your parents, guardian or brothers and sisters?

1.
2.
3.
4.
5.

Are you honest with yourself and others (where appropriate) about your strengths and weaknesses?

List 5 strengths:

1.
2.
3.
4.
5.

List 5 weaknesses:

1.
2.
3.
4.
5.

Do you take the time to point out the positive characteristics you see in others?

Chapter Twelve
The Thinking Triangle

"As a man thinks in his heart, so he is."

— King Solomon

Lateral — vertical — intuitive

The headline news in the September 1960, Popular Science magazine, revealed that Italy's 800 year old, world famous Leaning Tower of Pisa, now 17 feet out of line, may collapse. Pisa's globally renowned tower began in 1174, and was completed two centuries later. One of Italy's most well-known tourist attractions, it was closed down in 1990 and given a much needed face lift and new foundations.

There were 50,000 cubic meters of unstable dirt and sand removed from one side of this 56 meter high structure. Concrete was then poured to create a solid foundation. It took 11 years with a construction cost of £17 million. This architectural wonder was now fixed firmly in place and reopened in December 2001.

Originally designed as a bell tower by the architect Bonanno Pisano, it only became famous when it developed a lean, sinking into the soft sandy soil beneath.

Joining the million other tourists that now come to see this work of art annually, I couldn't help thinking that if this bell tower was reconstructed to become straight, it would become ordinary and of no global interest. So it was fixed forever in solid concrete foundations at a 13 foot lean.

Pisa was famous because of its weird tilt. In the same way that people become news worthy or famous because of their peculiar bent. At a more personal level, because of an incomplete education or negative life experiences, our thinking can form an unhealthy lean, like Pisa, even to the point of collapse.

There are ways of thinking that are both constructive and destructive. For instance, a poverty mindset can prevent us from understanding or contributing to wealth creation. This mindset can subconsciously affect all of our financial decisions in a negative way. This lean in our thinking may be the result of the culture we were born into, or a philosophy we have believed and embraced.

A lean in our thinking may have formed concerning our identity for example. Our self-image may have been distorted or defiled because of a comment someone had made while we were growing up. This chapter however is not designed to help you identify bent thinking as much as to understand how innovative or creative thinking is best developed.

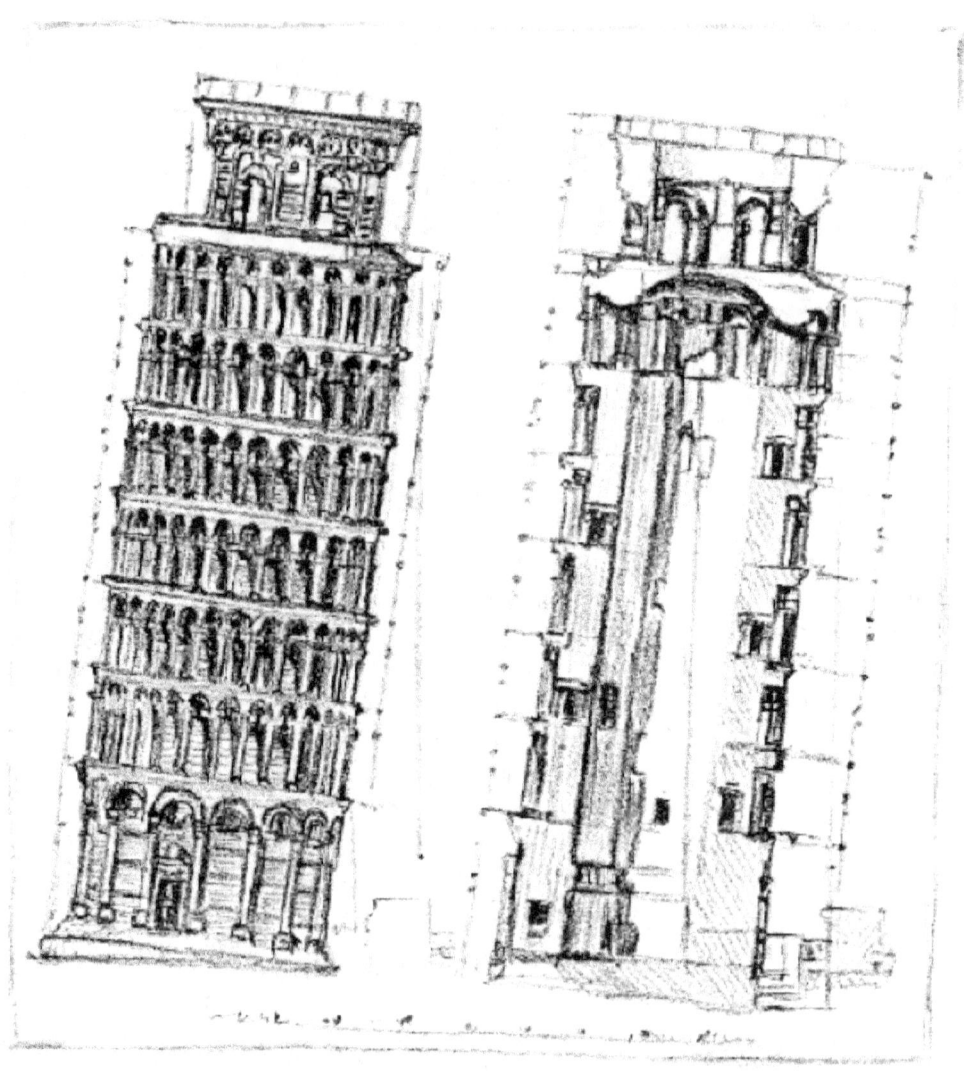

Balanced thinking

In order to stop a *lean* forming within our thinking, we need to understand what balanced thinking looks like. Federal agents taught to identify counterfeit money were not shown counterfeit notes or coins; they had to learn what the original looked like, to the point that they would spot anything that looked different. It is important when it comes to this pivotal area of thinking that we understand what *balanced thinking* looks like in order to help identify imbalance, or a *lean* within our thinking. The concept of *thinking by design* arrived while speaking to an audience on the subject of lateral thinking. Like the mythical concept of storks delivering babies to their parents, this idea seemed to arrive from nowhere, and it stuck. I asked the question; "what is the best starting point when thinking about a new subject, idea or problem?"

Sometimes as a speaker you say things spontaneously and are then forced to back them up. The question was not planned; however, my answer was like one of those babies delivered by a stork. This baby idea has helped me to understand what balanced thinking could look like. I continued, "Thinking is like marlin fishing; once you have caught a big idea or identified a problem, you need to play the fish by first letting the line out, and then at the appropriate moment, you begin winding it in a little. This is done in order to tire the fish and avoid breaking the fishing line. The best way to think on a subject, or process an idea, is to first let out the line of lateral, creative thinking; then wind it in with a bit of vertical, critical thinking, at the same time listening to the voice of intuition."

As I developed this concept, I choose the triangle, the strongest engineering structure in existence, to symbolize a stable, balanced, and healthy thinking process. This model gives us an understanding as to how we can maintain a balanced approach in developing an idea or solving a problem. Many ideas are aborted or simply fall over due to one-eyed, one sided, short-sighted thinking. Without balance we cannot walk properly. Without balance we cannot think in a straight line. This concept will give you a philosophical overview of the three key areas vital to balanced thinking. It's thinking about thinking! Thinking by design is helped by applying and understanding the triangle concept. We design cars, roads, houses, cities and communities, often neglecting to recognize any design in this important area of thinking.

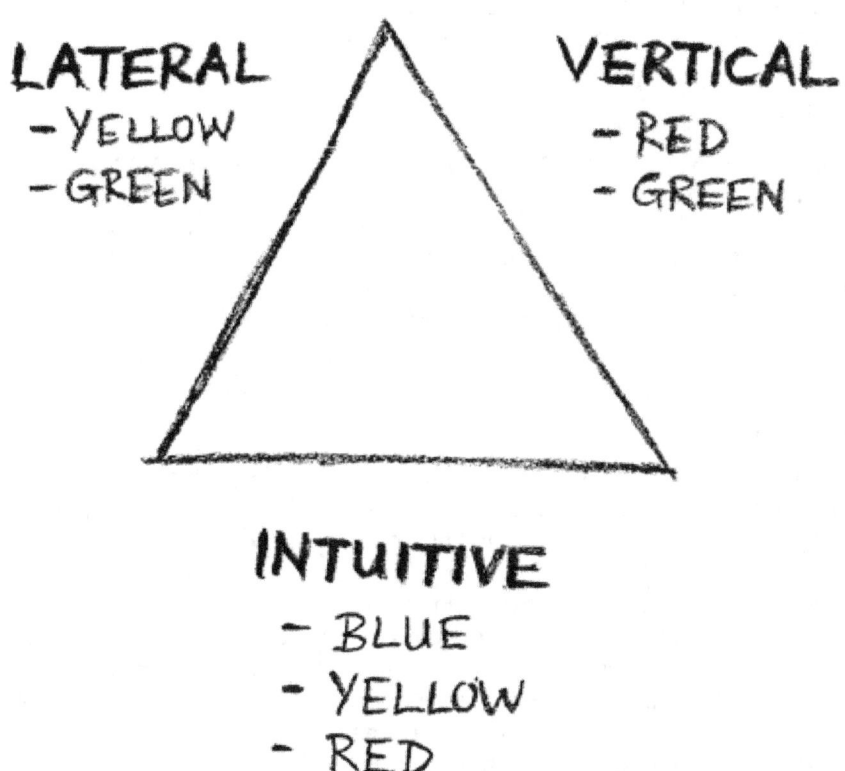

The triangle overview

I have come to see that the best starting place in developing an idea or solution comes under the general heading of the *lateral* approach, which is the subject of numerous books and articles. If we start with a more critical mode of thinking, we can abort new ideas or shut down possible solutions. If we allow others to critique our ideas too early in the process, they can kill the dream and the dreamer. Thinking by design helps us to narrow down much of the thinking processes into three major categories – creative, vertical and intuitive. This is not so much a system of thinking as it is an understanding or overview of how thinking best functions:

1. Lateral thinking

In developing this concept I recalled all of the books I had read over the years that were dedicated to stimulating this area of thinking. Books written by Norman Vincent Peale dealing with the power of positive optimistic thinking, and Edward De Bono's books giving practical insights concerning creative, innovative, and lateral thinking. In general, *lateral* thinking has to do with the power of possibility thinking; of generating new ideas, hypothesis, invention, humor, design and creativity. *Lateral* thinking is having the guts to jump the ruts and create new paths. With the courage, optimism and innovation of the great pioneers, lateral thinkers look for solutions, new concepts and new ideas. *Lateral* thinkers will always create the list of possibilities before forming a list of problems. They place their creative ideas into the workshop of imagination, unafraid of dreaming. Lateral thinkers turn their seed ideas into visions, goals, strategies and detailed plans.

2. Vertical thinking

The weakness of the lateral thinker is that they may never change gears. At some point we must slow down and fearlessly evaluate. Vertical thinking is placing your ideas on the anvil of analytical and critical thinking; researching and reviewing the facts with ruthless honestly. With the disciplines of a crime scene investigator you allow the evidence to speak for itself, and eventually lead you to the truth of a matter. Vertical thinkers build up a picture made up of the facts, leaving no stone left unturned. Then after laboriously noting the facts, using sound logic and watertight arguments, they present their conclusions.

3. Intuitive thinking

These are the philosophical, spiritual, instinctive and emotional aspects of the thinking process. This concept evolved as I observed valued advisors who, including my close friends, challenged my logic with what I initially called *feelings thinking*. In many cases their advice ran contrary to the apparent facts. Their advice was motivated by a hunch, instinct, and spiritual intuition, beyond the realm of the five senses. Beyond the immediate evidence, they trusted their emotional and spiritual intelligence. To begin, I found this expression of *feelings thinking* disconcerting, until I developed a discernment to know the difference. *Intuitive* thinking flows from a combination of faculties often hard to pin down due to their invisible nature. Intuition is a faculty of the human spirit. The *spirit* of a person contains the conscience, instinct, imagination, and the will. It draws on values, beliefs and the subconscious mind; as well as spiritual perception, inspiration, and dreaming.

The thinking triangle

Lateral thinking is something that does not always come naturally to people who are strong in *vertical* thinking, or on the other hand, *intuitive* thinking. For me however, *lateral* thinking comes easily and I have needed to focus on developing the *intuitive*, and more especially, vertical thinking skills. The concept of *the thinking triangle* helps us to understand the key movements needed within our thinking at the most basic level. Without movement, a stream or pond will stagnate. When we have let out enough of the lateral, creative or hypothesis fishing line, we then need to wind it in a little with vertical, critical, analytical thinking. We finally land the fish with some intuitive wisdom, and the advice of those with experience.

Like the gears of a car, understanding the *triangle* concept generates constructive movement in a forward motion. We could view vertical or critical thinking as the reverse gear of a car, but when used constructively, this mode of thinking gives forward motion as well. *Lateral* thinking is the best first gear, ideas that come from out of the blue, from intuitive inspiration, or revelation (a stork delivering a baby). This concept will assist us in choosing the appropriate mode of thinking—which gear to choose next. It helps someone avoid sitting in first gear, sending the rev-counter off the gauge and spinning its wheels. On the other hand, we can start out in third gear and risk stalling the car. The *triangle* pulls all aspects of thinking into three easy to understand categories – *lateral, vertical, intuitive*. It's the big picture view of the basic ingredients of the thinking process.

Art or skill

Learning to play basketball or soccer is generally recognized as a skill, whereas the ability to dance or play an instrument is seen as both an art-form and a skill. Thinking by design is an art-form and a skill. An art-form, in that the way we think is what makes us unique. It is our self-expression. Remember the words of King Solomon, "As a man thinks in his heart, so he is." Our choices and responses are not created for us – we create them. Thinking is a reflection of *self* at the deepest level, it is the seat of our self-consciousness; the awareness that we are set apart from every other human being on the planet. Consciousness is a huge gift!

Thinking by design is also a skill to the degree that we can discipline our minds in ways of thinking that are constructive. We can learn methods or create systems that stimulate or activate our thoughts. Tools to help turn over the fertile soil of the mind, such as thinking in color. Each color represents a different aspect of thinking, giving structures that act as scaffolding while our ideas, beliefs, concepts, or philosophies are under construction. These systems of thinking are skills we use in order to master the art of thinking.

The thinking triangle is another system for understanding the thinking process, especially the need to create movement, or change modes when thinking. So spend the time to test yourself using the Core Art Form Work Book and the questions following each section?

Chapter Thirteen
The Black Box

"A great civilization is not conquered from without until it has destroyed itself from within."

— W. Durran

The *black box* is most commonly known as the flight recorder on an aircraft, designed to analyze what went wrong when there was a failure, before or at the time the airplane was going down. However, in science, computing, and engineering, a *black box* is a device, system, or object that can be viewed in terms of its inputs and outputs, without any knowledge of its internal workings. Almost anything might be referred to as a black box: a transistor, an algorithm, or the human brain. The *black box theory of consciousness* states, that the mind is fully understood once the inputs and outputs are well-defined. We may not fully understand what is going on inside the box, but we can observe what certain inputs create in terms of output. Garbage in, garbage out!

The internal workings of our mind, emotions, and DNA, and how these all affect our decisions or behavior, is for the most part, a black box. The black box within our thinking may be a mystery, but one thing is clear, if we experience negative inputs on a constant basis, those experiences can rewrite our self image and define us in a negative way. The good news is, our outlook, output or behavior may have become negative, but by rewriting the script, we can affect a better outcome. We can create new pathways within our thinking. When we experience hurt, we can allow it to make us better, or bitter. We can allow failure to define us or drive us to greater highs. Pain can stop us or sharpen us. Fear can either paralyze us or energize us.

We understand that we must prepare an athlete or a soldier for the mental strain of competition, opposition, or survival in a war zone, marketplace or otherwise; but when it comes to starting or growing an enterprise, we do little or no preparation in the area of building mental toughness. The battle to win is mostly within the mind, in our thought life, in the face of enormous pressure, fear or even depression. The real fight in the business jungle is about maintaining courage under fire, and not allowing ourselves to be conquered within.

The language of thinking

DNA not only impacts our physical identity, but our social and spiritual identity as well. The personalities or temperaments of the past are written deep within our physical and psychological make up. Embedded within that first drop of DNA is the characteristics of generations gone by. Grandfathers, grandmothers, great aunts, great uncles, and many others from the past have all written us a letter of sorts – our DNA. These letters, if not vetted, can become life-defining *scripts*. Just as deformities occur physically, they can be inherited psychologically and spiritually as well. Just as DNA is the *script* for the construction of every living organism, our lives are also the sum total of the scripts that our family, social, spiritual and physical environments have engraved upon us, that is, unless we exercise the power of choice. The following questions arise: Who am I? Whose philosophy directs me? Where did my world view originate? What *mindsets* possess me? How do I create the future?

Steven Covey in his book, *Seven Habits of Highly Effective People*, summarizes three widely accepted theories of *determinism* that explain human nature or why we do the things we do!

Genetic determinism—*Basically says your grandparents did it to you. That's why you have such a temper.*

Psychic Determinism—*Your parents did it to you. Your upbringing and your childhood experiences essentially laid out your personal tendencies and your character traits."*

Environmental Determinism— *"Your boss is doing it to you, or your spouse, or that bratty teenager, your economic situation, or national polices. Someone or something in your environment is responsible for your situation."*

The truth is that all of these factors influence our thinking. These thoughts, attitudes, ideas and philosophies become a *language*. This language then both reflects and determines our behavior. The language of our thinking is formed by a wide range of pressures, from the past and present, and all influence who we are now. Thinking throughout the centuries has manifested itself in approximately 7,000 complex but colorful languages both verbal and non-verbal. The definition of a *natural language* is a language that is spoken, written, or signed (visually or with a gesture) for the general purpose of communication and connection. We have computer languages, a mathematical language, a musical language, scientific language, body language, and now a highly developed texting language.

We now live in a period where songwriters, movie makers, and TV producers are all shaping culture at a manic pace. It is as if the whole world is watching a screen somewhere, all day, every day; images, vibrations, words and sound bites competing for a space in our brain. They all contribute to our world view and the language of our thinking. This tsunami of images and new ideas is sweeping the globe with ideas both good and bad. This wave of media is a powerful force for good; highlighting the needs of those trapped in poverty for instance. It is also a destructive force undermining *ideas* that keep us safe. People will drown if they don't climb to higher ground, to the place of *thinking for themselves,* and not allowing peer pressure and the whirl pool of popular culture to swallow them up. When I entered the political arena in New Zealand, politicians were allowing themselves to be pressured into doing away with the word and concept of *family,* even in the face of its biological reality. I learned through this experience that when a concept appears to reach *critical mass,* people simply give in and accept all kinds of cultural indoctrination.

We wrap our ideas, concepts, philosophies and insecurities in a language. We even create *languages* to reflect a wide range of attitudinal and emotional states. Optimism has a language of faith and confidence. Pessimism – a language of cynicism and mistrust. Love has a language of truth, and grace. Bitterness is a language of criticism and hatred.

DNA, in its widest sense, is defined as the code or language that is constructing or even deconstructing our lives. Our self-image for instance is a kind of DNA giving us powerful images of who we've judged or perceived ourselves to be. This cluster of images and information deeply affects how we act and what we believe we can achieve in life—the me I see, is the me I'll be! The imagination is the most creative and destructive *workshop* in existence. What we imagine to be true about ourselves becomes our personal DNA and identity. This code or language then reinforces the judgments we have made about ourselves and our world.

Thought life

The concept of *self-talk* reveals the power of a thought. Our thoughts impact our world with both positive and negative emotions. *Self-talk* is the *language of thinking* that operates at a subconscious and conscious level. *Self-talk* is the private conversations we have with ourselves throughout the day. In every-day conversation we talk at a rate of approximately 150 to 200 words per minute. Research suggests that we talk privately to ourselves, in our thoughts, at a rate of approximately 1300 words per minute. These conversations are at the heart of the *language of thinking.* They not only reveal where we are now, they can also become a self-fulfilling prophesy. Fear is a good example of one of those emotions that can become an inner conversation loaded with self-destructive language. As a language of fear is developed we can increasingly come under its influence.

The underlying theme of Mel Gibson's movie, *Apocalypto,* reveals the need to conquer the language of fear. The movie begins with a quote from W. Durrant: "A great civilization is not conquered from without until it has destroyed itself from within." This is the story of the violent end of the once-great Mayan civilization. Jaguar Paw, the son of a great Mayan warrior, is carried to a world ruled by fear and oppression, but not before his father teaches him to exercise self-control over the words he speaks.

There is a scene near the beginning of the movie where Jaguar Paw is out hunting with his father and a number of other warriors from his village. They have just killed a wild boar when a tribe appears, like ghosts, from amidst the undergrowth of the jungle. They have the battle wounds of war and defeat etched in their faces. Then with what seemed to be a tribal custom, they exchange gifts, and moved on. His father, while on the way back to the village, tells his son not to speak of what he has seen in the forest that day. His father asks, "Those people in the forest, what did you see on them?" His son replies, "I don't understand?" His father says, "Fear! Deep rotting fear. They were infected by it. Did you see? "Fear is a sickness. It will crawl into the soul of anyone who engages it. It has tainted your peace already". He went on, "I did not raise you, to see you live with fear. Strike it from your heart. Do not bring it into our village."

Fear creates a language that produces deadly self-destructive self-talk in an individual, community or organization. Studies show that more than 70 percent of the average person's self-talk is negative. When we place ourselves in the *fear-gear*, our mind, imagination, and emotions can be turned against us. I have noticed that many great artists seem to experience and express life at another level. However, their imagination, which is their strength, becomes their enemy when it becomes infected with fear. If we allow it, the language of fear then begins to express itself. As someone once said, "Fear is the darkroom where we develop our negatives." As Solomon put it, "Life and death are in the power of the tongue." This language of fear can be learned from a young age. It can become embedded in the languages of an entire culture. In the movie called *Latcho Drom*,

Tony Gatlif tells the story of the Gypsy culture. The remarkable glimpse he gives us of this nomadic culture reveals their songs of sadness, and a belief that they were the cursed of the earth. Their language was saturated with fear, self doubt and inferiority.

One little girl, while sitting on the train with her family, starts to sing as the others join in: "The whole world hates us, we're chased, we're cursed, condemned to wandering throughout life… The sword of anxiety cuts into our skin… The whole world stands against us… At the foot of a blooded Jesus, God have mercy." Another lady, under a gray sky, sitting on the top of a hill that overlooks the city, sings: "I'm a black bird who has taken flight. Why does your wicked mouth spit on me? Why does your wicked mouth spit on me? What harm is it to you, that my skin is dark… and my hair gypsy black? From Hitler to Frankl we have been the victims of their wars. Some evenings, like many evenings, I find myself envying the respect that you give your dogs." An older lady, sitting on the snow covered banks of a brook, with a tattoo from Auschwitz on her arm, sings of the pain and horror of the camps: "In huge sheds they imprisoned us… we can't find bread anywhere. Life is so far off… and death is so close… The black bird wants to tear out my heart."

It is a good thing to remember the past, but not to relive it in such a way that it imprisons us in the present. The language and the spirit of the songs throughout this movie seemed to resurrect the past and bring hurt, fear, bitterness or rejection to life, again and again. Our language has the power to take the seeds of the past and plant them in the present, and in the hearts of a new generation. Our language can replay what has been, or create new outcomes. Our language creates an atmosphere, and healthy people, like plants, grow in a healthy environment.

Dr David Stoop in his book *Self Talk,* points out that, "Our thoughts create our emotions". The Greek philosopher, Epictetus, said, "Men are disturbed not by things, but by the views they take of them." He understood that in every situation, our responses are based on how we choose to interpret an event, and our subsequent choices then create our emotions. Our perception of an event, not the reality of the event becomes the language of our thinking. For example, the beautiful girl who thinks she is ugly. The ugly guy who thinks he is a stud. The skinny person who thinks they are fat.

Even the *self-talk* of a society can be influenced by the development of a new language, such as the introduction of *politically correct* speak. This is a politically motivated language that has challenged the thinking of modern societies for better and for worse. In some cases it has removed destructive language, helping identify words that have stereotyped people. In many cases removing these labels has liberated people from the cages of racism, sexism, and prejudice. However, it has gone too far and become destructive, promoting ill-conceived values and laws, invading people's lives beyond what is acceptable. In policing the behavior of society, politicians have invaded the family and criminalized parents. Self-talk is also revealed on a more personal level in those small but exclusive parties we throw for ourselves from time to time. Pity-party self-talk drags us into a swamp of doom and gloom: "No one likes me; no one cares; it's not fair; I deserve more; I don't care anymore; I'm better off dead." The words we speak not only affect others, but direct our own thinking and behavior, subconsciously much more than we realize. Solomon teaches that our words can ensnare us, like a wild animal caught in a trap. Changing the way we speak, can change the way we see ourselves, and consequently change the way we respond to opportunities that present themselves. If you change the way you speak and act, your feelings will follow. The words we speak about ourselves, live on in our subconscious mind well beyond the point that they were written or spoken. They get replayed over and over, again and again. However we can create new pathways of behavior by learning a new language. A language of confidence instead of inferiority, a language of possibility thinking in place of pessimism, and a language of fearless love in place of bitterness and anger.

The question is, how do we rewrite our DNA when it is faulty? Unlearning our native language is nearly impossible, so how do we unlearn the language of fear or criticism, and introduce a new script? It is interesting that 497 languages of those cataloged have been flagged as *nearly extinct* due to lack of usage. We cannot unlearn the old language; however, it is possible for a negative, self-destructive language to lose its power and become *nearly extinct* through a lack of use. If you don't feed the fire, it will die out!

The first step in altering our self-talk and rewriting our DNA is to simply allow the old language to become extinct, and in parallel to replace it with a new one, a language of confidence and optimism. Life and death is in the power of the tongue.

Identifying the roots of our negative self-talk is the second step towards changing the fruit. Our language reveals the kind of software we are operating; our personal confessions unveil the DNA planted deep within our subconscious mind. Identifying the old fruit and any associated roots must happen before you can render them *extinct*. Our language and belief system must be carefully checked. This is an exercise that must be executed with both courage and respect. Changing our language has the power to influence our thinking, and in turn our emotions. Thinking affects language, and language affects our thinking. Our language and our thinking shape our emotions. If our emotions are negative, they distort our language and thinking in an endless cycle that imprisons us. If somebody hurts us, for example, a language of pain can develop into a root of bitterness. Our emotions, in turn, can become infected with anger, hatred, and revenge.

The third strategic step in altering our self-talk, and in turn our thinking, is to change our environment. Atmospheric conditions are the difference between a desert and a rainforest, a living plant and a dying one, a thriving fruitful vine, or a sick one. The deliberate decision to place ourselves into a new environment can short-circuit our old destructive self-talk, and trigger new possibilities.

The people we associate with create an environment, and have a far greater influence on our thinking than we realize. One of my favorite stories is the influence Winston Churchill's nanny, Mrs. Elizabeth Anne Everest, had on his early life and thinking. In his book, *Never Give In*, Stephen Mansfield points out that, his parents, Randolph and Jennie Churchill, "gave themselves completely to their social ambitions". True Victorian parents, they maintained an astonishing distance from their children, receiving them only on prearranged times and under the watchful eye of servants, but the Churchills were remote even by these standards. Of his mother, Winston later wrote, "I loved her, but at a distance." His father thought Winston was retarded, rarely talked to him, and regularly vented his mounting rage on the child. If it was not for the love and encouragement of Mrs. Everest, his great leadership and political achievements may never have been what they were. She taught him to memorize the Scriptures, and knelt with him daily as he said his prayers. Mansfield notes, "It is hard to overestimate Mrs. Elizabeth Anne Everest's influence on Winston." Violet Asquith wrote, that in Churchill's "solitary childhood and unhappy school days Mrs. Everest was his comforter, his strength and stay, his one source of unfailing human understanding. She was the fireside at which he dried his tears and warmed his heart. She was the night light by his bed. She was security." He, in turn, adored her and regarded her every word as on a par with the law of God. Seventy years later, when Winston passed away, her picture was at his side.

We need to be constantly aware that our environment is affecting us on a daily basis. Our interaction with others literally shapes our lives. We shape theirs, they shape ours. Some people we allow to be there, some we inherit, and others force their way in. To be surrounded by the right people is gold. It is wisdom to assess the impact that those in our world are having on us. Nothing in the world will positively affect our self-talk, or thinking, like the love and encouragement of a friend, family member, or associate. The opposite of course is equally true; our associations with the wrong people can limit us, or even destroy our lives.

The fourth DNA altering suggestion has to do with finding the right coach. Athletes that become great cannot do it alone, and need a mentor or a coach. Life coaching, for example, has become a vital part of developing leaders. In order to go to another level we need to find a person that we can trust, and give them permission to speak into our lives. Achievement in athletics has as much to do with coaching as it does physical training and development. Mrs. Elizabeth Anne Everest was Winston's coach, one of the most powerful leaders in his life. An influence that reached far beyond the bounds of her seemingly small and insignificant job. She coached a giant slayer, a man that led and inspired England in its darkest hour.

The fifth step involves creating a Master Plan. This requires setting goals and developing plans, leaving lots of room to move and to adapt. A good coach or planning process, such as Global Tribe PROBOX, is the key. Companies create and develop elaborate plans to succeed in business or in a new field of endeavor but in our personal lives we can leave things to chance, to be shaped by the random forces of nature, unseen, unquestioned forces. There are a number of templates out there that give creative ways to achieve this, but time must be set aside, we must see the importance of the this strategic process, and just do it!

Black Box *inputs* Snapshot

What have been the most consistent negative or positive *inputs spoken or unspoken,* that you remember being communicated to you while growing up—what ideas or concepts were repeated over and over, again and again? What suggestions or attitudes *[inputs]* did you perceive or feel?

Positive   Negative

2. What life altering experiences *[input]* have you encountered during your life to date.

Positive   Negative

Chapter Fourteen
Design Thinking

"Design is not just what it looks and feels like, design is how it works."

— Steve Jobs

If we explore the inner workings of nature, we witness award-winning design! Painter, sculptor, engineer, mathematician, philosopher, inventor, architect, and anatomist: Leonardo da Vinci, spent long hours observing nature as it gave his art and design depth and dimension. Michael White, in his book *Leonardo, the First Scientist*, says "Leonardo never lost sight of the primary purpose of the artist; to represent the *soul*, to depict the inner essence of a thing, whatever that may be." Leonardo said, "Knowledge of the structure of the body is only a preparation for the knowledge of the form."

Leonardo spent long hours studying the face. The artist needs to understand how the muscles of the face and the rest of the body generate expression, he taught. White reveals that "Leonardo's scientific investigations clearly added to his abilities as an artist. To him, art plus science equals transcendence."

He studied the work of the ultimate designer and this stimulated his thinking to reach beyond the walls of the *box*; the limited thinking of his era. The deeper understanding of anatomy, plant life, animals, water flow and nature in general, enriched his thinking and inspired endless creativity.

We live in a global community surrounded by design; fashion, the arts, communication, media, architecture, entertainment and engineering. For every area of life to be improved on, or go to a higher level, it requires design. With the explosion of information, design will be the most important skill of the future.

However, to better understand the subject of design, it can help to contrast it with its opposite—the enemy of creativity. So, before developing the concept of design, it's important to understand the way the brain is wired and the traditional modes of thinking that can block the development of design thinking.

Judgmental thinking

At the risk of overkill, this problem of judgmental thinking and a preoccupation with critical thinking needs to be addressed again, not only due to it's affect on design thinking, but most other aspects of thinking as well. One dictionary definition defines it as *fault-finding*. The original purpose of critical thinking was to uncover the truth by attacking and removing all that is false. The problem with this adversarial system of thinking is that we can destroy valuable ideas and relationships in the process: dividing a family, business, community or nation.

Judgment is concerned with right and wrong, black and white and often blocks seeing in color. Judgment thinking is however a vital part of our thinking because in many situations speed of judgment is vital. For example, an object flying toward you at high speed requires an instant judgment. Judgment thinking creates boxes, and once we have processed or identified something and placed it in its *box,* there is no need to think any further about it. We have created a standard response, a stereotype, a definition, a prejudice.

De Bono, in his book *New Thinking for a New Millennium,* points out that, "Judgment is an effort to place everything in its right box." Some of the negative walls that create these boxes are made up of destructive attitudes such as: pride, fear, stereotypes, prejudice, inferiority, insecurity and peer pressure, to name a few. Thinking inside the box, is thinking within what is already accepted as *the norm*, within what is judged as good or proper. Thinking inside the box is judgment thinking.

It must be said that *judgment* is also a valuable system of thinking. Certain laws, values, truths or principles are best kept in their boxes. Many of the laws of physics do not need to be revisited annually; they have been tested again and again and found to be consistent. The judgment that one plus one equals two is solid and does not need continual re-evaluation.

The laws of a country are judgments arrived at by politicians and policy makers, and these do need to be revisited. One such law, that made Britain's top 10 most ridiculous laws, stated that, 'It was illegal to die in the Houses of Parliament. Self-evident social principles such as *forgiveness* and *doing unto others as you would have them do to you*, are good judgments. The procedures of a franchise system, such as Starbucks, are judgments relating to how every aspect of the business must be run. The design of the business is set in concrete and the managers simply follow the instructions in the operations manual.

Judgment is helpful in building standardized, consistent operations, but weak at creating more effective, competitive ways of serving the customer.

De Bono states, "The difference between judgment and design is that judgment deals with what we have experienced, whereas design allows us to create new experiences and new perceptions."

Traditional thinking of the past based on analysis, judgment and logic is not enough in building a better future, instead more innovative and creative design systems of thinking must be added. Critical thinking can show us why something will not work and give us a sense of superiority, but leave no creative energy for designing possible solutions. Edward de Bono says, "Traditional thinking is largely based on judgment… concerned with recognizing standard situations and applying standard solutions."

Judgment thinking is important, but has become a destructive force in societies where it is not balanced with design thinking. It's easier to engage in judgment thinking because it comes naturally to the brain. The brain is designed to fit new information into its existing boxes. A new face is scanned by the memory in search of a match, for example. In conversation, the brain wants to complete the sentence or thought.

De Bono teaches, "The brain is designed to learn through repeated exposure. Gradually patterns are formed, patterns that are then used on future occasions. The choice of the appropriate pattern depends on judgment. The brain, he says, has a very discriminating flip-flop system. The activated nerves flip into A or flop into B state. There is no in-between. In fact, the brain does very much what Aristotle said it did: Makes sharp and firm judgments. There is no natural mechanism in the brain for creative, constructive or design thinking."

Judgment is essentially a backward-looking system of thinking. In judgment thinking we seek to find a standard response for a standard situation. Judgment then gives *closure* to our thinking as quickly as possible. This system of thinking is important, but the problem with it is that it can block or shut down much needed design thinking. It can create deep ruts and abort new ideas vital, not only to our future, but to the future of a business or even a nation.

The designer

Design thinking is a world of color and beauty. Design thinking is a skill that can be learned and continually developed; there is no one way of stimulating it. For many, design does not come naturally due to our cultural programming and the way the brain is wired. The knowledge that we must find ways to stimulate lateral movement in the area of design thinking, is not properly understood, or even widely taught.

A starting point in design thinking is to see ourselves as a designer. The me I see is the me I can be. Our self-image is built on the assumptions we make concerning ourselves; and the truth is everyone can tap into the reservoir of imagination, one of the greatest faculties of the human spirit. We must not view ourselves as being in competition with anyone else. We are one of a kind, not to be compared with others. We should not see ourselves as a part of the *human race,* but as running our own race, creating our own space. Design is fundamentally about self-expression. Everyone can possess and express creativity. Insecurity can spend a lifetime trying to copy somebody else's design, conforming to fashion or the standardized media image of what a person should be. Although, it can equally be said that trying too hard *not* to be like everybody else can also be a sign of insecurity.

Solomon teaches in one of his proverbs, "The sluggard says, "There is a lion in the road, a fierce lion roaming the streets!'" In other words, the mind that allows fear to rule generates images of things that don't exist. Fear builds mountains out of molehills. Fear slams the handbrake on possibilities, hypothesis, and invention, and on anything outside of the box. Our fear projections keep us inside of our comfort zone, stopping us from venturing beyond the walls of the box into a world of imagination.

Design inspiration

Design is heavily reliant upon creativity, and creativity draws from a world of inspiration. The Greek word for *inspiration* means *God-breathed*. Creativity flows from a deep well inside of the human spirit causing thoughts, pictures, ideas, aspirations and revelations to bubble up and move us *laterally* over the walls of our rutted minds. Creativity is not simply a one-dimensional biological process, but spiritual in nature.

Creativity is something that comes from behind the walls of our five senses and ignites songs in the soul, expressions of color, and a frame of mind that appreciates beauty. Whenever we look at the world, we are often blinded or restricted in our thinking because we see the world in terms of our existing mental pathways, or patterns. The term lateral thinking refers to moving sideways, across those patterns, instead of moving along them as in normal vertical thinking.

The brain is our conscious link with the realm of the spiritual. Intuition, premonition, conscience, dreaming and imagination are some of the faculties of the human spirit. All evidence suggests that the mind behaves as a self-organizing neural network. The brain is a wonderful device for allowing incoming information to organize itself into patterns, but it requires the spiritual faculty of imagination to jump the ruts, to see and to develop new realities. Humor and romance are the result of this kind of lateral movement.

Inspiration sparks imagination and creativity. Imagination and creativity then flood the mind with new ideas, the abstract, and a wide range of feelings or moods; the river of design begins to flow. Imagination moves us from the grip of left-brain thinking (logical, mathematical, judgmental, analytical) into a more right-brain function (creative and emotional).

GK Chesterton once said, "God created both the natural world and human beings as any artist creates, forming something separate from himself and then setting it free." The creator has set us free to love, free to hate, free to give, free to be selfish, free to create, free to destroy; choices we face every day. It is true that the gift of *free will* gives us the power to create evil, but this gift also gives us the power to create love. It is out of this position of freedom we *create* – create a mess, create evil, create good, create the future.

The key to design thinking is to find and use strategies that unlock the imagination and stimulate creative thinking.

Snapshot Design Thinking

What are your design thinking spaces, places that inspire you, an atmosphere that generates positive energy?

1.

2.

3.

Who inspires you, and why? Authors, directors, actors, musicians, business people, social entrepreneurs, artists, architects, scientists, engineers, figures from history?

1.

2.

3.

4.

5.

Design is involved in almost everything; products and services creation, solving environmental issues, policies that help communities run smoothly, keeping romance alive, property development, growing a family, building business systems, managing people, inventing a communication system – the list is endless.

If money was no object, what area of design would you engage?

How would you unleash your powers of design?

1.

2.

3.

4.

5.

Chapter Fifteen
Levels of Thinking

"Under all that we think, lives all that we believe, like the ultimate veil of our spirits."

— Antonio Machado

Culture — belief systems — truth or reality

By introducing the following three levels of thinking I am not outlining another system of thinking. These levels of *thinking* already exist and are the foundations of our world view. These are the tensions within our thinking, pressures from within and pressures from without. The first level of thinking has to do with culture, the second, belief systems and the third, truth or reality. It is important to understand the connection between these three concepts in order to have a balanced world view. For example, in ancient times some cultures may have accepted that the earth was flat, but *truth* has told us otherwise. The truth is the truth, regardless of our acceptance of ideas to the contrary. These three levels of thinking will help us to understand the central issues in identifying a faulty world view.

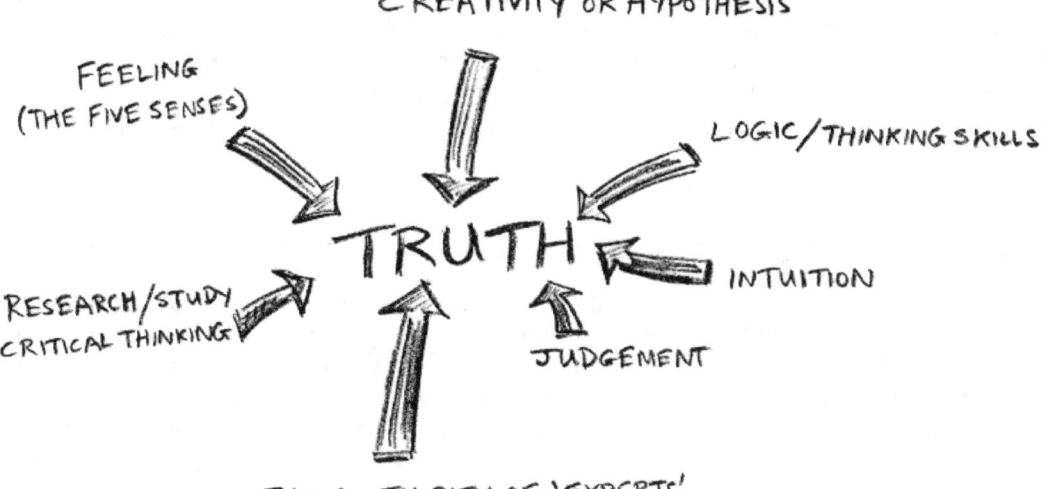

Level one: Culture

This first level of thinking has to do with the *ocean of thought* we are swimming in, the strong ocean currents of *culture*. If we allow it, *culture* will do our thinking for us. Culture has to do with popular opinion, national or community values, and the numerous philosophies society has concerning life and the universe.

In its widest sense, we talk of a nation, tribe, race, community organization, business or sports team, as having a culture. The word culture comes from the Latin word for culture, stemming from *'colere'*, meaning "to cultivate." Culture is found in what society has cultivated. Seed thoughts are planted, eventually growing into the behaviors and customs of a society. Culture is revealed in our language, music, literature, painting, sculpture, theatre and film. It is also revealed in our products and services and in the way we do business in general.

The Wikipedia encyclopedia describes culture as "the way of life for an entire society." As such it includes codes of manners, dress, language, religion and rituals. Whether it is a family sized community or a nation, norms of behavior are set in law, and belief systems are developed. The United Nations Educational, Scientific and Cultural Organization (UNESCO) describes culture as follows: "... culture should be regarded as the set of distinctive spiritual, material, intellectual and emotional features of society or a social group and that it encompasses, in addition to art and literature, lifestyles, ways of living together, value systems, traditions and beliefs."

Daily conversation, media, and inherited values fill our minds with all sorts of cultural voices, pressuring us to go with the flow and ride the waves of popular opinion. This generation is an experience-oriented, visual generation, that listen with their eyes and think with their feelings; gaining much of their philosophy through media, which is then developed around the kitchen table and over cups of hot coffee. Our culture gives us gross generalizations that shape our world view; such as: "If it feels good do it! How can it be so wrong if it feels so right? Be tolerant to everyone! " Our world view can be a mixture of a number of cultural philosophies, often never really thought through.

Our world view needs to be built on a more solid foundation than culture. While there are many great things within every culture, it can also be a seedbed of deadly ideals. Culture is the desktop level of thinking, and many of its ideas and philosophies are left untested and the consequences ignored. It is as if society does not question its fruit (consequences) in an honest way—if the masses believe it, then it must be true. Our world view is formed by these unseen forces of culture, and go largely unquestioned. This level of thinking forms our *judgments about the world*, and these *judgments* form our belief systems, and our belief systems dictate our behavior.

Level two: Belief systems

The designers of the Titanic believed that it was unsinkable. While the first car was being developed some believed that people traveling over 30 miles an hour would suffocate. One publisher wrote a letter rejecting a work of George Orwell: "It is impossible to sell animal stories in the U.S.A." His book, *Animal Farm* went on to become a super success. For thousands of years people believed it was impossible to break the four minute mile. In 1954 Roger Bannister proved that belief to be wrong. Within one year thirty-seven others did the same, and the year after that three hundred runners did what they said could not be done.

Our belief systems are a powerful force. They are at the foundations of all that we think. The question is what percentage of what we believe about ourselves, and our world is wrong or faulty? Where do our belief systems come from? What are our belief systems built on? We often never check our belief systems in order to find out. In discussion with some, you soon get the idea that their world view is never to be questioned.

These belief systems affect our thinking at a number of levels. Firstly, they can block our thinking from exploring new possibilities or arriving at what is in actual fact, reality. And secondly, they form our world view, the *glasses* through which we see the world. Our view of the world is constructed slowly at the core of who we are and shapes our values, character, and behaviors. Our belief systems become a subconscious auto-pilot controlling our reactions and many of our behaviors. Belief systems create maps that guide us through life. They create paths within our thinking that, if left unchecked, can undermine the many positive, creative and innovative aspects of thinking. Because we believe something to be true, it does not automatically follow that it is built on correct principles or aligns with reality.

From childhood we develop belief systems from a combination of personal experiences, including family scripts and cultural influences. The Free Online Dictionary says, a *belief* is *"a feeling of certainty or confidence about something; the mental acceptance of and conviction of the truth, actuality or the validity of something."* These beliefs vary in strength from popular opinion to a deep conviction. They are like strongholds within our thinking that we are prepared to defend, at times, even to the point of death. These strongholds are often based upon what we perceive to be *true*, not necessarily on what is *true*. Belief systems are built on what we *judge* to be *the truth*. They are our perceptions of reality, the conclusions we set in concrete, forming a part of the very foundations of our thinking. We set our belief systems in place by making a *judgment*. We pass sentence on a matter after rational examination or an extreme emotional experience (good or bad) or as a result of cultural conditioning.

We also receive belief systems at conception, from the DNA of our parents. At some point in our lives these need to be questioned to see if they are aligned with the self-evident principles that govern physical, social and spiritual design. When what we believe is in opposition to the natural laws that govern peace of mind and quality of life, we base our lives on illusion and set ourselves up for failure. In a sense, we do not break the laws of the universe (physical or spiritual) we break ourselves against them. Once accepted, our *beliefs* become unquestioned commands to our values and character; they become cultural norms ultimately determining our behavior. At this level of thinking our belief system is only as good as the foundations upon which it is built—reality or illusion.

In the book, *Awaken the Giant Within*, Anthony Robins points out that our beliefs either empower or disempower us. He asks the reader to write a list of empowering beliefs on one page, and a list of the disempowering beliefs on another. I spontaneously listed the first things that came to mind, identifying the ideas that sat just beneath the surface of my conscious thinking; firstly concepts that empowered me, such as: positive is better, creativity is freedom; giving is living; I must do my part for those who are poor, my family needs me, serving a human need is the foundation of marketplace success; confidence is my choice; all attitudes are a matter of choice; the creator is my life source. I then listed the disempowering thoughts planted within my mind: I'll get in really good shape soon; certain people are holding me back; I can't do much to change world poverty, so why try. The list went on, revealing under-tows that daily drain energy and helped to sabotage my thinking. Antonio Machado says, "Under all that we think, lives all that we believe, like the ultimate veil of our spirits".

Level three: Truth or reality

According to James Allen of Harvard Business School, 80% of businesses state that they offer a great customer experience. This is in stark contrast to the 8% of customers who feel the same way. Sometimes reality sucks! Self-perception can be built on self-deception!

The third level of thinking has to do with understanding the concept of *truth*. Dictionaries describe truth as something in accord with reality and therefore accurate, reliable, and in conformity to fact or reality. Truth is the accurate picture of the way the physical, social, mental and spiritual universe is designed to be (including the consequences of stepping over the boundary lines of that design). For example, truth is an accurate picture of the laws of physics; the self-evident, self-validating natural laws that do not change or shift. Truth has to do with integrity, reality, facts, honesty, principles, accuracy, and correctness. It is the fact that has been verified, the hypothesis found to be true. Truth is what a healthy belief system or culture is built upon.

Blaine Lee puts it this way: "the principles you live by create the world you live in, if you change the principles you live by, you will change your world." The lesson of history is that to the degree people and civilizations have operated in harmony with correct truth principles, they have prospered. Principles are not invented by us or society. They are the laws of the universe that pertain to human relationships as much as they do to physics. Principles such as the Ten Commandments can be rationalized away, however the consequences remain the same. When we view them, placing ourselves as the victim, as the one being stolen from or cheated on, we take a different view.

Truth is the inner compass that centers us on *true north*. True north represents those beliefs, values, goals, and principles that produce a healthy life. The reason it is known as *true north* is because there is another force that can take us off course, known as *magnetic north*. If we allow ourselves to be tossed about in the ocean of culture, driven by the opinions of others, we could find that we end up at a destination we never intended. True North is a genuine compass direction that leads to the North Pole. For most people the North Pole is not their ultimate goal; however, it gives them their position, their co-ordinates in relation to where they are on their map, and as to whether or not they are heading in the desired direction.

Magnetic North if followed will take you to some interesting places, but not to the place you had mapped out for yourself. In reality Magnetic North will lead you to Baffin Island; the fifth largest island in the world situated northeast of Canada. It is a beautiful place to visit, but not the desired destination. If the magnetic needle of your compass locks in on Magnetic North, then no matter how good your map is, you will never get to where you want to go. In the same way many have set goals, plans, and dreams (maps) but will never achieve them because they have not aligned their belief system with correct principles. They have not built on a foundation of truth. Starting with the truth about themselves; their character, and their core competencies.

There are principles that build healthy relationships, thinking, businesses, and communities; and when we align ourselves with them we experience a sense of harmony. Principles such as, "Do unto others as you would have them do unto you." Jesus Christ taught that all good law should be built on this concept. When we create laws that are built on, *the things we would expect from others*, we establish a loving society, and a fair legal system.

What we believe comes from what we perceive to be true, and what we perceive to be true for the most part comes from who we believe, and who we believe is a matter of faith. The question is, within our cultural ocean of thought, who do we believe? Who is leading our thinking and in what direction–True North or Magnetic North? A great test for any philosophy, is to ask whether or not the philosophy is livable. Does it work in the real world? What kind of fruit does this philosophy produce? (You can tell a tree by its fruit!) We often try to change the fruit of our behavior, without checking the root. Our belief systems are the root systems of our thinking. Instead of living mindlessly out of cultural scripts handed down to us from generations gone by—think! "Is the culture and belief systems I have inherited built on truth or illusion?" Just think much of what we believe right now may be wrong. Absolutely wrong! It is possible that our present belief systems and cultural pressures may be preventing us from stepping into a new universe of possibility.

A life by design is based on truth and truth is ultimately found in the mind behind nature's design. The intelligence within every living thing reveals the personality and thinking of our designer. If you are wanting to discover a life by design, then what better place to start than forming an understanding of how the Creator thinks. When nature truly comes to life, as was my experience, you find a person who is more approachable than you could ever have imagined.

Overview

Level one: Culture—Once accepted, our *beliefs* become unquestioned commands to our values and character; they become cultural norms ultimately determining our behavior. At this level of thinking our belief system is only as good as the foundations upon which it is built—reality or illusion.

Level two: Belief systems—Our belief systems become a subconscious auto-pilot controlling our reactions and many of our behaviors. Belief systems create maps that guide us through life. They create paths within our thinking that, if left unchecked, can undermine the many positive, creative and innovative aspects of thinking. Because we believe something to be true, it does not automatically follow that it is built on correct principles, or aligns with reality.

Level three: Truth or reality—Truth is what a healthy belief system or culture is built upon. Blaine Lee puts it this way: "the principles you live by create the world you live in, if you change the principles you live by, you will change your world." If we allow ourselves to be tossed about in the ocean of culture, driven by the opinions of others, we could find that we end up at a destination we never intended.

Snapshot reality

What 5 things did you believe to be true, that you have now discovered are not true?

1.

2.

3.

4.

5.

What do you consider to be the 5 greatest influencers on, or within your thinking?

1.

2.

3.

4.

5.

How do you think your culture or belief-systems may have influenced your world view? Your values, principles, attitudes, and behavior.

1.

2.

3.

4.

5.

Chapter Sixteen
Consciousness!

"I think, therefore I am."

— Rene Descartes

Our state of consciousness, has been explained by some, "As no more than the behavior of a vast assembly of nerve cells and their associated molecules. In a materialist worldview, our mind, soul, spirit, and free will are simply an illusion created by electrical charges in the neurons of our brains." John Searle, Professor of Philosophy at Berkeley, said, "In my world view, consciousness is caused by brain processes." British philosopher, Bertrand Russell stated, "Man is the product of causes which had no prevision of the end they where achieving; that his origin, his growth, his hopes and fears, his loves and his beliefs, are but the outcome of accidental collocations of atoms." In other words, my every action is the result of how the evolutionary dice rolls. If this is true, and consciousness is no more than a biological equation, then there is no such thing as soul, spirit or free will. Therefore there is no such entity as *self*. The reality is, there is no *you* in you at all. Your consciousness, your sense of *self,* are illusions bolstered by folklore. If all of our decisions are the product of *our computer-made-of-meat* (the brain), then conscious thought and all decision making is reduced to a mechanical output!

If consciousness is the result of the free-wheeling activities of the human brain under the dictatorship of our environment, then it follows that we have no ability to choose, no ultimate power of choice. American culture critic, Tom Wolfe, put the materialistic mindset succinctly when he said, "Since consciousness and thought are entirely physical products of your brain and nervous system, and since your brain arrived fully imprinted at birth, what makes you think you have free will." If true, then there is no such thing as premeditated murder, only pre-programed murder or random murder, the result of biological conditioning and our environment. Every crime is not the result of choice, but the sum total of the laws of physics and chemistry. No offender held responsible, no one guilty as charged, they simply couldn't help it! If this materialistic world view is applied to justice as we know it and the offender killed someone while driving under the influence of alcohol, we may have to place the drunk driver and their car in prison! In fact neither of them are really responsible, all who influenced them during their entire lifetime, and those who manufactured the car, are partly to blame.

We are more than one-dimensional physical beings. We are a powerful spirit expressed through our body and soul. Neurologist and Nobel Price winner, Sir John Eccles, said, "We are spiritual beings with souls in a spiritual world, as well as material beings with bodies and brains existing in a material world." Human consciousness is a universe all of its own, a complex arrangement of thoughts, emotions, sensations and beliefs. Life within is not always easy, but we are one of a kind, made in the image of our Creator – body, soul, and spirit. Keeping an open mind, we need to continue to probe the big questions of life: Is the world around us all that there is or is there something beyond what our physical eyes can observe? Did mind create matter or did matter create mind? Did God create man, or did man create God? Are we the product of intelligence or random natural forces? The answers to these questions determine the foundation of all thinking. If there is no ultimate outside intelligence then atheism is our world view. Which means all of our thinking will be placed through this filter. Our core beliefs shape or frame our thinking in every area, however – if the foundations of our thinking are wrong, then there can be far-reaching consequences. If you believe this life is all there is, then it is all about the survival of the fittest.

Snapshot consciousness!

What are 5 questions you have concerning your existence?

1.

2.

3.

4.

5.

What are your conclusions concerning the following questions: Where you came from? Why you are here? or Where you are going?

1.

2.

3.

Chapter Seventeen
The Core

"People are unrealistic, illogical and self-centered; Love them anyway."

— Mother Teresa

The center of our Galaxy

If you were to jump on a 747 and fly to the sun, 93 million miles away, it would take you 23 years and a lot of coffee. Only now are we truly beginning to understand and appreciate this powerful thermonuclear reactor we call the sun. This fire in the sky rains down billions of photons, taking eight minutes to reach the surface of our planet, giving us 99 percent of all usable energy on earth. What's amazing, is that every second the sun converts five million tons of mass to energy, soaking our earth with light. This swirling, raging fire storm of exploding gas pumps out enormous amounts energy, of which earth only intercepts one-billionth of its total solar energy, revealing a Creator of extravagant abundance. In one-second the sun gives off more energy than all the people in history have produced during their entire stay on earth.

In July 2004, *The National Geographic* printed some of their latest pictures of the sun, which revealed giant bubbles the size of Texas covering the surface of the sun. They explained: "The superheated gases that form the sun, mainly hydrogen and helium, exist in an electrical state called plasma. Below the surface of the sun, plasma can push and drag magnetic field lines. But when lines are strong enough to arc out, they can easily loop the height of ten earths."

The temperature at the core of the sun is fifteen million degrees centigrade, a lot hotter than the average summer's day at the beach! It is so hot, says physicist Sir James Jeans that a pinhead heated to the temperature at the sun's center "would emit enough heat to kill anyone who ventured within a thousand miles of it." Solar flares, equivalent to millions of nuclear bombs, release such explosive energy that they send gigantic magnetic clouds to earth. Richard Swenson notes that in 1989 one such "solar storm caused a province-wide blackout in Quebec". "The same event", he said,"melted coils in a transformer station in Salem, New Jersey, leading to a fire and a regional power outage." Swenson also cites a more recent solar flare that produced a magnetic cloud moving toward earth at a million miles an hour, thirty-million miles in diameter. What an amazing source of light, life and energy this fire in the sky is! This is a special effect that deserves the ultimate Oscar Award.

What drives our thinking?

The sun is the center of our solar system, the origin of virtually all energy that sustains life; the source of our weather and compared to other stars, is highly stable. Its light output only varies by 0.1 of 1 percent over a full sunspot cycle, which takes about eleven hours, thus preventing wild climate swings on Earth.

Just as the sun is the center of our solar system (with a diverse array of planets, moons and asteroids circling in an orderly fashion), we too have something or someone at the center of our lives who more than anything else, impacts on all that we think and do. Stephen Covey, in his book *Seven Habits of Highly Effective People*, talks of the various *centers* we all possess and their all-encompassing impact on every aspect of our lives. He says that, "Each of us has a center, though we usually don't recognize it as such...[and] whatever is at the center of our life will be the source of our security, guidance, wisdom and power."

If we have an unbalanced, unhealthy obsession, it colors our view of the world and drives our thinking. Our sense of security can become weak or even false (a false sense of security), and our guidance can become based on circumstances and the emotion of the moment. Our wisdom can become distorted by greed, hatred or selfishness and our power derived from putting people down, manipulation or image.

There was a point in history where the scientists of the day thought that the earth was the center of the universe and that the sun and the planets revolved around it. This assumption meant that making sense of how the universe worked was frustrated and confused for many years. Scientists' thinking was driven by a wrong assumption. Until they came to the point of knowing, that what they believed was wrong, they could not proceed. The same is true when we place ourselves at the center of the universe, our thinking is built on a wrong foundation.

Self-centered thinking

Total self-centeredness, most would agree, is unhealthy. Thinking that, "It's all about me," and that "we should look after number one," is destructive thinking. When a child will not share their toys with their brothers and sisters or friends, it is viewed as childish and immature. When an adult does the same thing with their resources, we see it as their right. Self-centered people are rarely admired for their preoccupation with themselves. This is why Jesus taught, that we find our lives as we learn to lose our lives, primarily in loving and showing generosity to others.

We were never designed to place ourselves at the center. Covey suggests that even *good things* placed at the center can throw our thinking out of balance and cause us to become self-destructive. For example, if we become *money-centered* it can distort many of our decisions in an unhealthy, counter-productive way. We can define ourselves by our occupation, and view our personal worth by our net worth. When our sense of security comes from what we possess, we become controlled by or vulnerable to anything that affects our net worth. We can also become obsessed with how well we are doing compared with our contemporaries or those we have chosen to envy. Profit, and not those important to us, can determine our decisions. Covey says making money can become "the lens through which life is seen and understood, [the source of our wisdom, security, guidance, power], creating an imbalanced judgment. Money-centered people often put aside family or other priorities assuming everyone will understand that economic demands come first."

Enemy-centered people nurse and rehearse past hurt. Then their sense of security comes from holding the offender in a kind of mental prison, putting them down mentally and verbally, whenever the opportunity arises. This kind of judgmental attitude cultivated toward the enemy poisons the mind with bitterness and distorts personal character. It then defiles our sub-conscious attitude or our response toward others who we imagine pose a similar threat.

Consciously or subconsciously we can place things or people at the center of our affections. Covey then goes on to talk about becoming a principle-centered person who practices the art of standing "apart from the emotion of the situation… and looking at the balanced whole." The universe does not revolve around us; we are all a part of a bigger picture, a larger community. We were not created to be an independent spirit, in fact a life by design is found in our connections and relationships with others.

Just as life on earth is dependent on the sun, our soul and spirit are dependent upon being connected with others and our Creator. Being centered on our Creator is not a sign of weakness, but completeness. Being dependent upon *The Creator* is a part of our original design. Just as a car was designed to run on fuel, we have been designed to plug into our Creator as the source of life, love and wisdom. Living disconnected from the Creator is like trying to be a tree without roots or soil, a light without electricity, or a fish without water.

Building a positive atmosphere

Although we have no control over the weather produced in our physical environment we can influence our mental, social and spiritual weather. Stephen Covey, in his book *Seven Habits of Highly Effective People,* points out that, "Reactive people are often affected by their physical [and social] environment. If the weather is good, they feel good. If it isn't, it affects their attitude and their performance." Proactive people, he says, have learned to carry their own weather with them wherever they go.

A life by design requires that we shift from being controlled or driven by our social, mental and spiritual weather patterns, to building healthy environments for growth and development. Just as our physical atmosphere contributes to the earth being the habitable zone that it is, we must proactively design ways to build and maintain a positive atmosphere for ourselves and others to enjoy. Our atmosphere is more than the gaseous envelope surrounding the earth, it includes our moods and attitudes, our relationships, and the numerous forces that we find ourselves influenced by daily.

In building a positive atmosphere we cannot focus on one thing, but all aspects of our entire ecosystem. In a practical sense it will include: our home environment, work environment, social environment, and most importantly our mental and spiritual environments. Wisdom thinking must be developed in order to understand all of the elements and how they interact in building a healthy atmosphere. Wisdom thinking is the key to developing the entire ecosystem.

Snapshot personal drivers

What are 5 things that you focus on that you think may be out-of-balance?

1.

2.

3.

4.

5.

What drives you?

1.

2.

3.

4.

5.

Chapter Eighteen
Big Picture Wisdom

"Common sense [wisdom] is genius dressed in its working clothes."

— Ralph Waldo Emerson

Wisdom

Wisdom is the ability to apply all aspects of thinking to a problem or subject. Wisdom acquires knowledge of all of the facts, gains an understanding of how those facts fit together, then uses the faculty of perception to evaluate the evidence.

Edward de Bono says that, "Wisdom has to do with the broader view. Wisdom has to do with the deeper view. Wisdom has to do with the richer view. Wisdom seeks to gain the helicopter view, so that everything can be seen in perspective and in relation to everything else."

In Los Angeles for example, helicopters report to radio stations concerning traffic conditions during peak hours. They take the broad view of what is going on, no motorist stuck in the traffic could possibly get this view. "With wisdom we seek to climb into a helicopter to get a broad overall view."

When we think of the Swiss-made watch, we think of precision engineering. Watches that are so finely tuned, that it only takes one tiny piece to be out of place and the entire system can breakdown. Wisdom is the craftsman that understands the interplay between all of the working parts of these highly sophisticated, highly complex machines.

The human body operates numerous systems, such as the circulatory, digestive, respiratory, nervous, and immune systems. Just as the brain orchestrates the functions and the interplay of the different bodily systems, wisdom gives leadership to our thinking, overseeing the thinking process. When it comes to our health, wisdom understands the interplay between diet, exercise and rest. In business, wisdom must understand people, markets, sales, accounting, and the interplay between all of these systems and relationships.

Wisdom is both a skill and an art-form; the development of research skills, analytical skills, planning skills and thinking skills; then on the other hand, the art of perception, discernment and intuition. Wisdom makes its judgment from all the available evidence, but also from the more subjective, emotional and spiritual forms of intelligence. Wisdom is not a clinical or mechanical approach and may involve the discernment of a person's motives, for example. Wisdom goes beyond the superficial and relies on our instinctive abilities in order to probe a little deeper.

Wisdom is the ability to take something from common sense to common practice; to take a product from research to design, and then to the market. Ralph Waldo Emerson said, "Common sense [wisdom] is genius dressed in its working clothes." Wisdom requires endlessly thinking about thinking, knowing which step is next. Wisdom listens carefully, asks the hard questions, gaining a comprehensive overview.

Life experience

There is no substitute for life experiences – the truth is we often learn more from failure than we do success. Thomas Edison failed over 10,000 times to get his light bulb working– then he succeeded–the rest is history.

Wisdom is the hardest level of thinking to achieve, because it is not acquired in the classroom or as a result of hours of research, it is formed in the school of hard knocks, the university of life. Pain is a great teacher, giving us the lessons of what *not* to do. I am still amazed at the level of pain we often endure before we acquire wisdom.

Remember, we do not break the laws of life, we break ourselves against them. We either discipline ourselves, or life has a way of disciplining us. This is not to say that we cannot gain wisdom from the experience of others, but without our own experience we often do not appreciate its importance or significance. We do not see it when it is in front of us. We don't hear it when it is screaming in our ear.

Proverbs of Solomon

Solomon's wisdom went way beyond his study of nature, people, and information in general; he embraced the inspiration and revelation of his Creator. Something the Hebrew scriptures taught him was foundational to wisdom. Although he acknowledged this, he still sought to widen his database, to increase in knowledge concerning all areas of life. It's as if education in a wide range of subjects gives the Creator a platform through which to communicate wisdom on a broader plane. The following Proverbs are loaded with this concept of widening our frames of reference, thus increasing the likelihood of receiving our Creator's wisdom. Common sense is easy to find, her voice is everywhere for those who have a hunger for wisdom, but turning commonsense into common practice is where discipline must take over.

"Does not wisdom call out? Does not understanding raise her voice? On the heights along the way, where the paths meet, she takes her stand; beside the gates leading into the city, at the entrances, she cries aloud: [this was where the wise counselors where located]...

You who are simple, gain prudence; you who are foolish, gain understanding...Choose my instruction instead of silver, knowledge rather than choice gold, for wisdom is more precious than rubies, and nothing you desire can compare with her. I, wisdom, dwell together with prudence; I possess knowledge and discretion...Counsel and sound judgment are mine; I have understanding and power... I [Wisdom] love those who love me, and those who seek me find me.

"With me are riches and honor, enduring wealth and prosperity. My fruit is better than fine gold; what I yield surpasses choice silver."

In these Proverbs we are taught that wisdom is to be found amidst prudence, discretion, understanding and wise counselors; that wisdom is the reward of those who go on an honest search for it.

The search for our Creator's thinking on a matter is not a passive activity, sitting back and waiting for the bright light. It's found as we get off our backsides and think. Ignorance is not bliss, it's something our Creator finds hard to work with.

Solomon was wise as a result of listening to his Creator, but at the same time expanded his mind to understand all areas of life.

Chapter Nineteen
The Ultimate Mindset

Developing a sense of wonder is discovering the beauty in things. Mother Teresa saw beauty in the poorest of the poor, looking beyond external appearances to the person beneath and showed them unconditional, fearless love.

If a mental state was real-estate, then the ability to enter the moment and see the beauty there would be the most expensive property one could acquire. To possess a sense of wonder, or an appreciation of beauty, is priceless. This mindset is the richest mental state a person can achieve. Relaxed and at peace with ourselves, we can drink in the wonder of it all!

It is said, "Beauty is in the eye of the beholder." This statement implies that beauty is in the mindset of a person. The implication being, that beauty is not necessarily about the external object as much as our internal response to it or interpretation of it. Every mother is beautiful to the son or daughter that has been loved and nurtured by her.

The landscape is filtered by our mind-scape when it comes to seeing beauty. With this mindset we become like an artist with our senses on full volume. We soak in the small things, the smell of a farm early on a sunny but crisp winter morning. Lungs bursting with fresh oxygen, we feel the warmth of the sun kissing our skin, inhaling the smells, noises and images of nature's best. The smell of fresh cow dung, the loud noise of a pig snorting, and the site of tiny hummingbirds riding sunbeams as the sun creeps over the ridges and filters through the trees. It is the childlike mindset that captures the wonder in the smallest of things.

As the noise in our head is turned down and our thoughts thaw out, we begin to see, hear and enjoy the simple things in life. Beauty happens when the noise of the past fades, the sensations now go into slow motion, and when we hit the pause button enjoying the moment.

Finding beauty is like looking for gold, sometimes it requires digging beneath the surface for. When we see the ugly side of a person, we a dig a little deeper in order to discover something of value. When we hear something negative about someone, we search out the truth before passing judgment. When we see the negatives we fly higher to capture the bigger picture of what the person or situation can become. Beauty is the celebration of who a person is, not the preoccupation with what they are not. A sense of wonder is the mindset of greatness, a choice to focus on the uniqueness of those around us, the uniqueness of the human spirit.

You may live in a cardboard box at the edge of a slum and still find beauty. In my work for Global Tribe, a missions and aid organization, I have spent many years visiting slums in some of the poorest areas of the world. Against a backdrop of dust, dirt, a lack of food and little medical care, I find vibrant spirits, laughing, playing, singing, dancing and spending long evenings in rich conversation. Children who have no Lego or the latest Star Wars toys, entertain themselves for hours with sticks, dirty bottles, old car parts and hairless dogs or scruffy little kittens. Fun is in the mindset of the beholder. There is something to be envied about their simplicity of life, and the ability to adapt and thrive where they are.

The ultimate mindset

"The object of education is to teach us to love what is beautiful."

— Plato, The Republic

Drawing out the beauty in people is both a skill and an art form. A sense of wonder is said to be the hallmark of a genius. These people do not look at things in the same way that most people do. They look with a sense of wonder at the design and the detail of an object. They stay a little longer, look a little deeper, and ask the bigger questions. With this mindset you become more alert to the seemingly small aspects of an event or object. This mindset goes beyond creating beauty to enjoying beauty. As important as creativity is, a sense of wonder or beauty is on an even higher plane. It goes one step further than creativity to a state of enjoyment or appreciation. Many have great wealth, and yet confess they cannot enjoy it. It is possible to gain the whole world and lose your soul.

The beauty-mindset both causes and reflects our state of happiness, contentment or pleasure. Being ungrateful, constantly critical and habitually pessimistic is not always a sickness, but the product of choice. Ultimately our mindset is something we must choose. An optimistic attitude, for example, focuses on the good in people and is something we must choose. Many have a faulty belief-system that reassures them that they cannot help the way that they are; their attitudes are there by default and not design. They have not been taught, and thus do not believe, that they have the power to choose an attitude. Our DNA can be altered by our power of choice. We have the steering wheel, we can turn it in whatever direction we choose. A positive mindset does not grow overnight, it is like laying the foundation of a house; we must dig down into solid ground, build the boxing and pour the concrete. It's hard work!

This concept of beauty is a mindset that affects the value we place on people. Instead of putting up with people we must slow down and fully engage. Seeing the best in people is what this mindset is all about. Drawing out the beauty in someone is a great skill and an art form.

Drawing out the beauty

My parents possess this great ability, demonstrated in the way that they dealt with our very special little sister. My mother and father came home one day with a little girl named Tracy, who they announced would be our new sister. She was to be fostered by us for a few months as her mother was a drug addict and very abusive. Tracy turned up with a big suitcase. A scruffy little note was attached to it saying that she was afraid of the dark and needed the light on at night. It wasn't long before we decided as a family that we could not let this beautiful, smiley-faced little girl go.

She was four years old and truly beautiful, although clearly, she wore the scars of deep rejection. Coming from an environment of fear and rejection she immediately became very clingy. She would constantly do things to attract the attention that she was deprived of and so desperately needed. But instead of gaining the acceptance she deserved, she soon set herself up for more rejection. I remember hearing my parents regularly discussing this problem, and then encouraging us to accept her anyway, which we did. In trying a number of things to free little Tracy from the damage done by her mother, they finally had a breakthrough. Until then, they constantly spoke reaffirming words, encouraging words, affirming their love for her, something she couldn't seem to accept. She seemed to increasingly reject words of love and affection. They decided that if she wouldn't accept these kinds of self-esteem building words while she was awake, they would say them to her while she was sleeping. The change was almost instant. Each night they would sit on her bed and speak loving words into her broken spirit and subconscious mind. It wasn't long before the beauty of her personality flowered. I was sixteen at the time, and can still remember her bushy black hair and radiant smiles as she came out of her shell, as she began to believe in who she was. The change was amazing! My mother and father had drawn out the beauty within, beauty that was accentuated by where she had come from.

"Once you see the good in someone, it's hard not to notice the good in everyone."

— Cassia Leo

Tracy ended up staying with us for five years, but because of her insistent grandmother, she was taken away from us when she had just turned ten years of age; one of the great mistakes of the welfare system. She would visit often, and with tears in her eyes, beg to stay. It was sad to see the light in her eyes slowly go out. Like her mother, Tracy became a drug addict at a young age, having her first baby at sixteen. At aged seventeen and three months pregnant, Tracy was stabbed to death by the man she was living with at the time. Although a tragic end, she lives on in our memory and we will never regret the day she walked into our lives and radiated her beauty. Seeing the best in people needs to be cultivated. If my parents had focused on Tracy's faults and insecurities, then the beauty that existed, may never have been discovered.

The beauty-mindset changes our everyday, seemingly ordinary experiences, into something of wonder. We can walk past beauty all day long, preoccupied with the issues of life and miss the mystery that's there.

There are moments of beauty to be discovered everywhere, if we slow down to drink it all in. To think, to create, to innovate, to lead and to love.

In his book The Four Loves, CS Lewis masterfully describes one such moment with his friends, "He is lucky beyond dessert to be in such company. Especially when the whole group is together, each bringing out all that is best, wisest, or funniest in all the others. Those where the golden sessions; when four of us after a hard day's walking have come to our inn; when our slippers are on, our feet spread out toward the blaze and our drinks at our elbows; when the whole world, and something beyond the world, opens itself to our minds as we talk; and no-one has any claim on or any responsibility for another, but all are freemen and equals as if we had first met an hour ago, while at the same time an affection mellowed by the years enfolds us. Life–natural life–has no better gift to give. Who could have deserved it?

Life takes on a mystical dimension when we possess a sense of wonder and the beauty-mindset.

Part Two
Wisdom and Discipline

"No person is free who is not master of himself."

– Epictetus

Pillar Two
The Customer

"A customer is the most important visitor on our premises. He is not dependent on us. We are dependent on him. He is not an interruption in our work. He is the purpose of it. He is not an outsider in our business. He is part of it. We are not doing him a favor by serving him. He is doing us a favor by giving us an opportunity to do so."

— Mahatma Gandhi

Who am I targeting?

How do I let people know what I have to offer?

What is branding all about?

What is network or social-media marketing?

How do I develop an online presence?

Chapter Twenty
The Customer is King and Queen!

Over the years I have heard countless people say that they are sick of working for somebody else, and wish to be self-employed, starting their own business some day and working for themselves. If I get the chance, I remind them that when we start a business, the customer is our boss! We are never self-employed, but in a very real way customer-employed. We exchange one boss that pays us a weekly or monthly wage, for another boss that is more uncertain, and may or may not decide to pay our wages. Henry Ford once said, "It is not the employer who pays the wages. Employers only handle the money. It is the customer who pays the wages." In fact they can fire everybody in the company from the chairman down by simply spending their money somewhere else. Ultimately customers are people like you and I who want a *need met or a dream realized.*

As a customer, when I enter a restaurant, the host may be busy but all I ask to begin with is to be acknowledged. "Hello, I'll be with you in a minute." Then the long list of customer experiences begin. Do they get back to me quickly? Do they seem genuinely interested? Do they ask for my name? Do they remember my name? Do the chefs love me with their food? Are the interactions I have positive? Does the sum-total of my small interactions add up to, "Wow that was great," or "Hmmm that was average?" I never forget when Air New Zealand management must have decided to train their staff to remember and use the customer's name: "Hello Mr Walton, would you like a drink?" Wow…I'm important!

So many companies spend big money on advertising and brand development, but fall over when they send a grumpy waiter out to serve me, or employ a chef that was good at interviews but couldn't cook to save his life. Customer experiences happen every day, at every level, in every business on earth, but our attitude behind all of these interactions is all-important and comes through.

I started out calling Pillar Three, *The Market,* however I then realized that I was focused on the *process,* and not on the *person* at the heart of every businesses: *The Customer*. Businesses that are loyal to their customers allow the customer to drive the enterprise, the services and the product development; in fact every aspect of the business.

Terry Leahy turned Tesco, a struggling supermarket chain in the United Kingdom, into the third largest retailer in the world. When asked by British government senior officials how he did it, he said, "We focused relentlessly on delivering for our customers." In his book, *Management in Ten Words*, he reveals the heart and soul of his awaking and subsequent strategy. "My task was simple: to find out why Tesco was struggling, and to fix it…Although

Tesco was a retailer, we hardly ever took any account of what our customers thought. Yes, we did customer research, we talked about what focus groups told us, we discussed how sales had risen or fallen, but the truth was that the customer was not driving the business, day in, day out. Customer satisfaction was seen in a silo, the responsibility of a department to address, not something that the whole company should focus on."

He was awakened to what he already knew to be true, that successful companies do not just focus on what customers want, but put the customer the center of all they do. That the customer should drive the entire business. Putting the customer at the core of everything we did may sound exceptionally obvious—yet how many organizations truly listen to what their customers, clients or users think of the service or product they provide and then act on what they hear? His passion to serve the customer became the culture and focus of everything they did, he placed the customer in the driver's seat.

When I started my property development and construction company, *White Cloud Innovations*, I was passionate about building smaller homes that were affordable, but that still looked cool. It made me angry to see neighborhoods of new, low-cost homes that where ugly or cheap looking—an environmental disaster! Our success as a company has come from a genuine desire to serve people with great quality, beautiful spaces, but at an affordable price.

The customer experience

According to *Peppers and Rogers* 2005, "The customer experience has emerged as the single most important aspect in achieving success for companies across all industries." Customer experience is the sum of all experiences a customer has with the supplier of goods and/or services, over the duration of their relationship. According to James Allen of Harvard Business School, 80% of businesses state that they offer a great customer experience. This is in stark contrast to the 8% of customers who feel the same way!

A positive customer experience does not happen by accident, but by design. A company or not-for-profit must define and understand all aspects of the customer experience in order to have long-term success. Then they train and empower the team to deliver the proposed experience, and *deliver it genuinely and consistently*. A company must constantly teach, train and develop in order to keep up with the constant demands of providing an exceptional customer experience. A company's ability to deliver a great experience that sets it apart in the eyes of its customers will, research reveals, increase the amount of consumer spending and inspire loyalty to its brand. Building great *customer experiences* is a complex enterprise, involving strategy, integration of technology, orchestrating business models, brand management and CEO commitment.

The increasingly online nature of the modern marketplace does not alter the fundamentals of sound business practice; in the long term, there is no substitute for providing good products and services at a reasonable price, and delivered with love.

"According to James Allen of Harvard Business School, 80% of businesses state that they offer a great customer experience. This is in stark contrast to the 8% of customers who feel the same way."

The spirit of new generation enterprise

The foundation principle of business is *the creation of products and services that meet people's needs.* These 'innovations' (products and services) must 'love people' in a way that causes the customer to want to part with their hard earned cash. Kevin Roberts, once the worldwide Chief Executive of the advertising agency Saatchi and Saatchi, when speaking on building a great *'brand'* introduced the idea of *"the love-mark."* Brand creators used to speak in terms of brand *names* and brand *image*, but these days it goes much deeper. Roberts says, "You can plot any relationship—brand or otherwise—by whether it's based on love or respect. High respect ratings used to win. These days a high love rating wins. If you don't love what you're offering me, go home!" Roberts argues that consumers do not want any more information. "They are suffering from information overload and what they want now is a relationship. They want connections." What Roberts is saying in essence is that successful businesses of the future must build a relationship with their customers, offering products and services which people love—the love-mark.

One of the leading characteristics of successful business people is their passion and belief in their product or service. Successful business is about serving people with innovations that love them. Love innovations are the products and services generated from a genuine desire to serve another person's success or comfort. Love innovations are the creative acts of kindness and romance which keep our relationships at every level alive and adventurous.

The first business I started was a gym named *Body and Soul*. This was something that was inspired by reading the story of the YMCA, the organization that popularized basketball and gymnastics. *Body and Soul* was a not-for-profit organization set up under a Church called *The Rock*, meeting in a large warehouse with over a thousand people attending. This gym would help fully utilize their facility and contribute to the mortgage. I started it because, at the time there was no gym in the area, and I was passionate about having a gym that was a beautiful space, low cost, with friendly staff and where ordinary people would feel relaxed. In our city, at the time, gyms where very sterile, cold and unfriendly; with lots of big mirrors, muscle men, tanning oil and the annual subscription had to be paid up front.

So to make it an inspiring place to be for the average person, we created a cool space, great art, a cafe, child care, and an aerobics room with two huge palm trees either side of the stage. The place looked like a large cafe with a gym in the corner. We then advertised, inviting people to join for $1 a day. It was full to capacity within a year of starting, and stayed that way year-in, year-out.

Chapter Twenty One
What is a Market?

Marketing in the ultimate sense is simple: find out what customers want and give it to them. If they don't know what they want, then know them well enough to create something that meets a need they have.

The marketplace, as it's commonly called, was the place where people (customers) gathered together to view what somebody in the community had produced, the latest innovation or product. They would then barter with something that they had that was of value, if both agreed, they would then swap the goods, in what is called *a trade*.

The marketplace used to be mostly local, in a community, town, city or country. But now we are at a turning point in history with a global marketplace at our fingertips! We can choose to open up shop in our local community, in a marketplace of thousands, or from our kitchen table we can focus on a marketplace of billions. The latter sounds more attractive but doesn't necessarily mean that we will have a larger customer-base than the community-based business. However, the internet gives us access to a huge array of different kinds of markets around the globe, of which we may only need a small percentage in order to make a good living. Simply put, a market is a cluster of customers with a common need or dream that they want help with; from the need to be fed, to the goal of climbing a mountain.

The marketplace is one of many ways people engage in exchange. Wikipedia points out that, "in mainstream economics a market is the exchange of any type of good, service or information . The exchange of goods or services for money is a transaction. While parties may exchange goods and services by barter, most markets rely on sellers offering their products or services, including labor, in exchange for money from their customers."

The market is also the place that determines value, the place where the prices of goods and services are established. Market participants consist of all the buyers and sellers of goods or service who influence its price. This influence is a major study of economics and has given rise to several theories and models concerning the basic market forces of supply and demand. There are two roles in markets, buyers and sellers. For a market to be competitive, there must be more than a single buyer or seller. It has been suggested that two people may trade, but it takes at least three persons to have a market, so that there is competition in at least one of its two sides. However, competitive markets, as understood in formal economic theory, rely on much larger numbers of both buyers and sellers. A market with a single seller and multiple buyers is a monopoly. A market with a single buyer and multiple sellers is a monopsony.

Markets vary in form, scale (volume and geographic reach), location, and types of participants, as well as the types of goods and services traded. Examples include:

- Physical retail markets, such as local farmers markets (which are usually held in town squares or parking lots on an ongoing or occasional basis), shopping centers and shopping malls.
- (Non-physical) internet markets
- Ad hoc auction markets
- Labor markets
- International currency and commodity markets
- Stock markets, for the exchange of shares in corporations
- Artificial markets created by regulation to exchange rights for derivatives that have been designed to improve externalities, such as pollution permits (carbon trading).
- Illegal markets such as the market for illicit drugs, arms or pirated products.

What is marketing?

Marketing in the ultimate sense is simple: *find out what customers want and give it to them.* If they do not know what they want, then know them well enough to create something that meets a need they have.

Marketing, in practical terms, is the process of communicating the value of a product or service to new or existing customers. Another definition of marketing is: *the action or business of promoting and selling products or services, including market research and advertising.* It is clearly defining who we are targeting, the market size and all the relevant information that relates to that market and it' environment. This means the ideas, the brand, how you communicate, the design, print process, measuring of effectiveness, market research and the psychology of consumer behavior, all count as part of the bigger picture of 'marketing.' Marketing involves the art of listening to customers and then the identification and creation of new products and/or services.

Businessdictionary.com describes marketing as: "The management process through which goods and services move from concept to the customer. It includes the coordination of four elements called the four P's of marketing:
(1) identification, selection and development of a **product or service**,
(2) determination of its **price**,
(3) selection of a distribution channel to reach the customers **place**, and
(4) development and implementation of a **promotional strategy**."

Understand your market, know your customer

To run a successful business, you need to learn about your customers, your competitors and your industry. *Market research* is the process of analyzing data to help you understand which products and services are in demand, and how to be competitive. *Market research* can also provide valuable insight to help you:
- Reduce business risks
- Spot current and upcoming problems in your industry
- Identify sales opportunities

How to conduct market research

The government offers a wealth of data and information about businesses, industries and economic conditions that can aid in conducting market research. These sources provide valuable information about your customers and competitors:

- Economic Indicators
- Employment Statistics
- Income and Earnings Statements
- Identify Additional Sources of Analysis - Trade groups, business magazines, academic institutions and other third parties that gather and analyze research data about business trends.
- Use Internet and database searches to find information related to your location and industry.

Understand the International marketplace

Today's economy is a globalized marketplace, so it is important to understand the international factors that influence your business. These resources will help you to research potential international markets for your products or services:

Market Research Guide for Exporters: Identifies resources for business owners seeking to sell their products abroad.

- Country Market Research
- Reports on trade issues in countries across the globe.
- BuyUSA.gov Helps U.S. companies find new international business partners.

How do I write a marketing plan?

If you fail to plan you plan to fail. The development of a marketing plan is about defining and refining what your customer really wants and how you are going to deliver.

1. **What are you selling and why are you so special?**
2. **Who are you targeting?**
3. **Who are my competitors?**
4. **How am I going to bring this great idea to market?**
5. **What do I need to sell or secure to be profitable?**
6. **What price would they/you pay?**
7. **How do I set sales targets and develop sales strategies?**
8. **What is my communication and/or branding strategy?**

The Plan

1. What are you selling and why are you so special?

Daniel Priestley in his book, *Entrepreneur Revolution*, says that when he looks at a Rolex he does not see the product as being a watch, but as a conspicuous device that communicates status and high achievement. A person who buys a Rolex does not want to buy a device that tells the time. They could buy a cheaper $20 watch to do that. The desired outcome the customer wants to achieve has more to do with what a Rolex says about the wearer.

So when it comes to identifying what it is that you are selling, try to see beyond your goals and dreams and check again to see what it is that your customer is really wanting to buy. This may have to do with how or where your product or service is delivered. Thinking about what channels you are going to use to deliver your product or service to your customer is also an import and part of your marketing plan. This may even become a part of your *business model* as you expand and multiply.

Starbucks for example, is not only in the business of selling coffee, but also in the business of making it accessible locally and in a friendly environment. In other words, the delivery system for great coffee is as important as the coffee!

Information used to be mostly delivered through soft or hard-covered books, now it can be found using any number of search engines. This is the same information, but a different delivery system. Apple are challenged on a number of key issues in creating something special in the world of technology. Simply put: the look and feel, design flow or usability, value for money, the buying and user experience, and above all, that it is something you love and respect, and are proud to own.

Starbucks

I googled *Starbucks* to see what they think makes them so special and this is what they had to say:

"It happens millions of times each week—a customer receives a drink from a Starbucks barista—but each interaction is unique. It's a connection.

We make sure everything we do honors that connection – from our commitment to the highest quality coffee in the world, to the way we engage with our customers and communities to do business responsibly. From our beginnings as a single store nearly forty years ago, in every place that we've been, and every place that we touch, we've tried to make it a little better than we found it."

The Starbucks Story

"Every day, we go to work hoping to do two things: share great coffee with our friends and help make the world a little better."

— Howard Schultz

This was true when the first *Starbucks* opened in 1971, and it is just as true today. Back then, the company was a single store in Seattle's historic Pike Place Market. From just a narrow storefront, Starbucks offered some of the world's finest fresh-roasted whole bean coffees. The name, inspired by Moby Dick, evoked the romance of the high seas and the seafaring tradition of the early coffee traders.

In 1981, Howard Schultz (Starbucks chairman, president and Chief Executive Officer) had walked into a Starbucks store for the first time. From his first cup of Sumatra, Howard was drawn into Starbucks and joined a year later.

A year later, in 1983, Howard traveled to Italy and became captivated with Italian coffee bars and the romance of the coffee experience. He had a vision to bring the Italian coffeehouse tradition back to the United States, a place for conversation and a sense of community. A third place between work and home. He left Starbucks for a short period of time to start his own, *Il Giornale* coffeehouses, and returned in August 1987 to purchase Starbucks with the help of local investors.

From the beginning, Starbucks set out to be a different kind of company. One that not only celebrated coffee and the rich tradition, but that also brought a feeling of connection.

"Our mission to inspire and nurture the human spirit—one person, one cup, and one neighborhood at a time."

"Today, with more than 15,000 stores in 50 countries, Starbucks is the premier roaster and retailer of specialty coffee in the world. And with every cup, we strive to bring both our heritage and an exceptional experience to life."

Ask yourself the hard questions:

- Why is your idea so special?
- What is it that you are really selling at every level?
- Why is your product or service so cool?
- Why is the way you deliver it so great?
- What is the feedback from those who experienced your idea?
- Looking back in 50 years time, what do you hope people will say?

What business are you really in, and what are you really selling?

Are you selling watches or status? Are you selling iPhones or communication and connection? Are you selling milk or good health? Are you selling travel or lifelong memories? Are you advertising cars or selling safety, eco friendly, engineering and design? Are you selling coffee or intimacy and friendship. Are you advertising clothing or coolness?

2. Who am I targeting?

What is the age, shape and size of my target market?

Whether you come up with an idea and then go in search of a market, or start by identifying a human need; you need to identify and understand who your customer is and what it is they really want. This study will save a lot of time and money wasted in a shotgun approach to reaching your customer.

Generation X

When I started *Global Tribe Extreme Cafe*, I asked a friend heading up a leading advertising company at the time, if they had any research on the youth market? The results of focus groups and the research *Saatchi & Saatchi* had commissioned, gave me a real insight into the mind of my customer, and ignited lots of great ideas. It also sparked the name, *Global Tribe*, when in a section of the research it said, "that this group were like a global tribe searching for the same old stuff — friends, intimacy and a great time!"

Understanding a target group takes time, and even if you think you know them, time spent researching them farther will generally pay off, helping to refine your product or service, or if nothing else, the way you communicate to this group of customers.

I spent countless hours talking to young people or anyone that I thought knew anything about this emerging group. This was a new generation of intelligent customers, who spent more time on the internet than in front of a television. How did these high-tech, high-touch, in-touch customers think and operate? How do you reach a customer that is endlessly on the move like some kind of modern-day global nomad.

This group of highly mobile youth referred to as the *global tribe* were on the one hand, for the first time history, truly global and on the other hand, extremely tribal. They thought globally, but were looking for strong local identity and expression. They were living in an environment of global instability because of the rapid process of globalization.

Ever since Tim Berners-Lee came up with the worldwide web in 1989, and the internet was born, technology has been building like a giant wave. This globalization phenomenon has accelerated the pace of change and forced the world together politically, economically, technologically, and socially, faster than any other time in history. This revolution has empowered the individual and radically changed our global landscape overnight. It is forcing governments to open their markets, and generally become integrated into a new global society. Globalization is an interwoven global marketplace, justice system, economy, and communication network, with a new emerging global culture, especially true of Generation X, Y and Z.

Characteristics of the Global Tribe

A combination of research from leading advertising agencies, *Saatchi & Saatchi* and *Mojo*, painted a picture for me of some of the attitudes and expectations of this new and exciting *global tribe*; and now some years later, many of the characteristics still hold true:

- These *global tribes* think like nomads - they cruise along, taking each day as it comes, they don't hope for too much, they take pleasure where they can, and simply go with the flow. They don't overly believe in anything.

- In an age of moral ignorance and a high level of hypocrisy, realism usually equals having no ideals. The only possible stance for many young people is to be cynical, distant and irreverent.

- In the boredom of mass culture they seek out real adventure, enjoying individual adrenaline pumping, risky adventure sports, team sports, and more social and non-competitive sports.

- These technology nomads integrate technology and nature. Mass communication technology has become a natural part of life, giving access to the world. The internet has granted a greater sense of personal power.

- In a world of fake images and surface values, they expect others to be authentic, be real, be themselves. In a materialistic world, they value the attitude more than the actual thing. Despite living in a world that seems determined to crush self-esteem, they are proud of themselves.

- They have the 'lost child' attitude. They live for the moment because tomorrow may never come. This generation believe they should keep their distance, stay detached, stay as individuals even within a group or a relationship. They do not merge completely with anyone because they believe they will probably get hurt.

- This generation genuinely desire role models of long-term relationships, but these are rare due to parental divorce and family break-ups. They know "sex is dangerous, but often it is still safer than love."

- They find it is not that easy to rebel against parents who have 'been there and done that.' Make no mistake, the digital generation rebel, but their style is subversive rather than confrontational. They love complicating things and pushing the boundaries, infiltrating society rather than invading it.

- Driving forces include the need for identity, self-esteem, self-respect, confidence, empowerment and skill, a feeling of being in control, the freedom to choose, knowledge as power, wisdom, uniqueness, intelligence in humor, and the interactive.

- Within what is sometimes called the *global tribe* there are a myriad of sub-tribes.

- They believe the key to musical creativity is remixing the old and new—recycling fashion. They don't tend to invent new items of clothing or music styles, but they do specialize in refining and remixing existing or past fashion or trends.

- They think alternative, black humor is what's funny. To command a following from this group, any brand big or small, has to have attitude. Consumption of a certain brand or non-brand is a bit like a *tribal* membership.

- Despite grunge-type appearances, they are quite materialistic. They regard promotion, communication, and advertising as art-forms. They are a special effects generation where surreal is real. Both sexes will often list shopping as a favorite recreation.

- They especially like advertising, which ridicules advertising norms, and 'takes the crap' out of conventional baby boomer aspirations, the 'beautiful people,' or stereotypical male or female ideals.

- This generation wants to be entertained, not sold to. They make the following comments: 'I like it, 'cos it's not threatening to me.' 'It's not pushing the product on you.' 'I hate obvious humor.' 'It needs to be subtle and entertaining.' 'slice of life humor is appreciated.' 'don't be funny and stupid, be clever'

All of this research, helped paint a picture for me of the young customer I was attempting to serve. It helped get inside their thinking and understand how they viewed the world—their world view.

There are a different types of customers you will experience:

Loyal Customers: They represent no more than 20 percent of our customer base, but make up more than 50 percent of our sales.

Discount Customers: They shop our stores frequently, but make their decisions based on the size of our markdowns.

Impulse Customers: They do not have buying a particular item at the top of their "To Do" list, but come into the store on a whim. They will purchase what seems good at the time.

Need-Based Customers: They have a specific intention to buy a particular type of item.

Wandering Customers: They have no specific need or desire in mind when they come into the store. Rather, they want a sense of experience and/or community.

If we are serious about growing our business, we need to *focus* our effort on the loyal customers, and merchandise our store to leverage the *impulse* shoppers. The other three types of customers do represent a segment of our business, but they can also cause us to misdirect our resources if we put too much emphasis on them.

3. Who are my competitors?

After being told at school that everyone's a winner, it's a bit of a shock entering the dog eat dog, highly competitive marketplace. You don't get to send your competitors to the principal's office for bullying. Understanding the companies that have a similar idea or concept to yours is the only sensible thing to do. You can learn from their mistakes and improve on what they do. Studying those in a similar field of business will spark valuable ideas, not only relating to your product or service but your business model as well. To be a good player in this often hostile environment does not always mean becoming a Viking. Edward de Bono in his book, *Sur-petition*, talks about finding a higher road as opposed to simply entering the competition. Finding your unique proposition and creating your own new world of possibilities. However, I find that to generate creative ideas you need to create *movement,* so to simulate lateral thinking it is good to study our competitors, simulating progress, while preserving your core concept.

4. How am I going to bring this great idea to market?

We now understand the target customer, so what paths are available to deliver this product or service to them? What will I commit to, and what backup plans can I create?

An extension of, and sometimes as important as a great idea itself, is something that's known as the *business model; defining and describing how and where you bring your product or service to market.* For example, Starbucks not only sells coffee, but a cool space to connect with friends, to snack and do business. If you are not a global brand such as Starbucks, you would be wise to do the same, sell the experience as a part of your product or service.

When it comes to selling homes, my *business model* starts with customers who want cool, beautiful spaces that don't cost the earth. Mostly people find it hard to communicate what they really want, but like purchasing a work of art, they know it when they see it. So *White Cloud Innovations* is passionate about serving our customers with modern day eco-caves. Spaces with the beauty of nature, the design and craftsmanship of Leonardo da Vinci, and the science and engineering of Einstein.

How do I bring my idea to market? What is my business model? Many housing companies advertise themselves as *house builders,* and then work with their customers to construct a home to fit their parcel of land and budget. In my case, I am more of a developer, I purchase the land and build the home with the customer in mind. Each home is in effect my work of art, something that to me is more important than making money. Some companies are driven by extensive market research and this can be very valuable, however, is not the whole story. When it comes to new technology for example, customers have no idea what the next big thing is. They don't know what they don't know! Henry Ford once said, "If I'd asked my customers what they wanted, they would have told me 'a faster horse." Jobs adopted the same philosophy when developing Apple products by asking the question, "what would I want?

Taking your idea to market requires as much creativity and innovation as the product or service you have developed:

- What are the existing channels that could carry your idea to your target customer?
- What could our path to the customer look like?
- Where do our customers go when they want something similar?
- How can we make the connection to our idea a positive experience?
- How can we make our relationship with the customer high-tech as well as high-touch?
- How are we going to approach people in a relational way?
- Are we going to be an online business or do we need to be both retail and online?

5. What do I need to sell or secure in order to be profitable?

This is where we need to earth our *big idea* and get down to specifics. How much of the product or service do I need to sell or secure in order to pay the overheads, the wages, tax, rent, materials and advertising for example? To answer this question, we need a realistic handle on the costs to bring this product or service to market:

- What are the production or service costs?
- To deliver this service, what will it realistically cost me?
- What employees will I need in the first year of operation?
- What price are customers willing to pay?
- What price do my competitors charge?

You need to have a clear view of your gross margin, which is fully explored in PILLAR FIVE: The Accountant. The gross margin is what remains after you divide your gross profit by your net sales (your gross sales minus sold items later returned by customers). The gross margin is a measure of how the selling price of your product compares to its cost. Gross margin = gross profit/net sales

6. What price would they/you pay?

This is what is called the *million dollar question* or *star-gazing*! Getting our head around this question is all important, as it means success or failure. It requires honesty in tension with faith or optimism. Many a great idea has been killed by an overdose of pessimism or died a little while later as a result of poor, but over optimistic financial planning.

It is only after you fully understand your costs that you can even begin to ask this question. This is where you also need to understand your competition and why they have priced their products or services the way they have. This is a critical discussion, set the price too low and you may not cover your production, operating and delivery costs. Set the price too high and you could price yourself off the market. Rush this process and it may come back to bite you.

7. How do I set sales targets and develop sales strategies?

This will be different from one business to another, but these are some of the kinds of questions you may need to address:

- How do I set realistic sales targets?
- How am I going to review results?
- How am I going listen to customers?
- Who's going to do it and when?
- What are you doing for loyal customers?
- What role can network marketing or social media play?

8. What is my communication, feedback and/or branding strategy?

Who do I need to talk to and when? This includes suppliers, customers, media, your network and, most importantly, those working with you. Business is about relationship, and communication is the most important aspect of any relationship. This also goes beyond the obvious to include the kind of messages you want *out there* in order to begin shaping your brand? Messages that create a foot-hold in a customers' thinking.

9. How are we listening to customers?

How we gain and process feedback, is taking what the customer thinks about you seriously.

We need to ask the big questions:

Are we treating our customers with respect?
Are our customers happy?
What do they really want?
Are we really listening?
What processes or systems do we have in place?
In what way do our customers drive the business?

Chapter Twenty Two
What is Social Media Marketing?

Business is a relationship! It's a relationship with interest groups within our local communities or as a result of the Internet, communities anywhere on the planet. In a way the Internet makes the globe local!

The average adult checks their phone 30 times a day, and the average millennial checks their phone more than 150 times a day.

There are now just over 3 billion active Internet users. Nearly 2.1 billion people have social media accounts. 3.6 billion mobile users have access to the internet via smartphones and tablets. Close to 1.7 billion people have active social media accounts.

Conservative estimates show that over 2 billion people in the world use social-media regularly. That means at least 25% of humans on the planet have "Liked" something, Tweeted, watched a video on YouTube, or showed off a photo on Instagram. In only a decade, social-media has gone from something people did mostly for fun, to a marketing essential, and a source of income for millions of professionals.

This has changed the way we do business forever or has it? When this phenomena first emerged I was told that you need to get on board and quickly! I was raising money for our Global Tribe aid programs at the time, based out of Nashville, Tennessee, and it seemed that everybody believed that social-media was the future. So I asked the obvious questions, "how does it work and where are the examples of it working? When, how and where could we use it?" I was told the stories of larger aid agencies that had used it, and that it resulted in huge amounts of money being raised. The stories of crowd-funding and how it had, in some cases, raised millions for truly amazing causes.

Still trying to work it out in my head, I asked more and more questions. The conclusion I came to was that this was indeed a revolution, but it still did not short-circuit the basic principles of business, *to find a need and fill it!* Offering a great product or service that *meets someone's need, serves a person's dream or solves a problem*.

Then there is the time-tested principle of advertising: *word-of-mouth*. **The greatest ad in the world is still *word-of-mouth*; now more powerful than ever as a result of social media.** This revolution means that now instead of our marketplace being the small village we grew up in, our marketplace can be the global village in which we now live, only a few clicks away.

Business is a relationship! It's a relationship with interest groups within our local communities or, as a result of the internet, communities anywhere on the planet. In a way the Internet makes the *globe* local! This is why I named this organization, *Global Tribe*.

Marketing in a digital world

Every single business needs to have a digital footprint these days -- there are no exceptions. While you can always hire a digital marketing firm to handle everything, it is a good idea to have a full understanding of what a digital marketing campaign consists of yourselves.

Along with discussing digital promotion, this course also dives into the creation of digital products. Many businesses - the publishing industry for example - are converting to digital products.

Jeff Bullas, CEO at Jeffbullas.com says, "social media is starting to take off its short pants. It's becoming all grown up. In fact, Facebook is now over 11 years old and heading towards platform puberty and is still the standout leader of the pack."

Google with its Google+ platform (with a development cost of over half a billion dollars) tried to take Mark Zuckerberg on, but it has become an incidental social network that isn't taken seriously by many marketers. They play there, but don't want to work there.

There are even rumors that Google is going to break it up into separate digital products by segmenting the components that got traction… like *Google hangouts* and *photos*.

The emerging trends

The biggest trend over the last 12 months has been the move from earned marketing attention (sometimes called *free*) to "pay to play." Another is the impact of social messaging platforms such as Snapchat and WhatsApp that have become "quasi social networks" in their own right.

It's a social web shift that is driven by a connected generation. If your mom joins Facebook, then maybe it's time to play somewhere else. Teenagers don't want to be dancing with their parents.

In fact the instant services and chat apps now account for three of the top five global social platforms. Facebook tried to buy Snapchat for $3 billion and was snubbed. But then they pulled out $20 billion out of the back pocket and bought WhatsApp. You just have to love deep pockets and a vision of what the future looks like, as it relaxes to mobile, social, and alternative messaging.

What does the social web look like in 2018?

The quick truth is that it can be summed up in one word, *"mobile"*. Smartphone penetration has soared as the devices have become more affordable and the wireless networks more ubiquitous and faster. There are now 7.2 billion people on the planet and of those the following numbers make interesting reading:

- There are just over 3 billion active Internet users.
- Nearly 2.1 billion people have social media accounts.
- 3.6 billion mobile users have access to the internet via smartphones and tablets.
- Close to 1.7 billion people have active social media accounts.

Source: Wearesocial.net

The rise of non-English speaking social networks in China and Russia, such as Qzone, are producing large social networks that exceed Twitter, Instagram and Google+. The traditional social networks as we know them are not the only games in the world-wide social web town!

So what are the social media facts and statistics in 2018 that are worth checking out?

Mobile Social Media facts

The developing world has not had the luxury of fixed wire Internet from poles and wires. To provide access for the aspirational masses, the mobile wireless networks are a fast track to a global world. Putting up a tower rather than build an expensive fixed infrastructure is the way to speed the Internet across the developing world.

As a result, the mobile phone has made the web accessible for almost everyone. In India mobile devices account for 72% of all website traffic. There are 1.65 billion active mobile social accounts globally, with 561 million active mobile social accounts are located in East Asia.

Facebook facts

You may scream at Facebook for its dominance and arrogance, but it cannot be ignored. Tall poppies are easy targets but the reality is that Facebook has cracked the social network code. It's the ultimate beta business. Testing features in real time and snapping up online apps that push the boundaries of user experience in a world that is about digital disruption:

- There are nearly 1.4 billion Facebook users.
- 47% of all Internet users are on Facebook.
- 4.5 billion likes are generated daily.
- Nearly 75% of Facebook's revenue comes from mobile advertising.
- Direct uploads of user videos to Facebook now exceed YouTube.

Twitter facts

- Twitter is an accidental social network, but don't be fooled, it's a great brand awareness facilitator.
- Twitter has 284 million active users at last count.
- 88% of Twitter users are on mobile.
- 500 million tweets per day.

Google+ facts

- Google saw the writing on the wall but turned up to the party a little too late.
- Google+ cost over half a billion to design and develop, but only 363 million users.
- The +1 button is hit 5 billion times per day.

Instagram facts

- This network is owned by Facebook. They saw that social and mobile was a powerful intersection of synergies. They were right!
- Instagram has 300 million users.
- 70 million photos and videos are sent daily.
- 53% of internet users aged 18-29 use Instagram.

Pinterest facts

- Pinterest has made the pinboard a virtual activity. It's female centric and very visual.
- 80% of Internet users on Pinterest are female.
- 70 million users are on Pinterest.
- 88% purchase a product they pinned.

LinkedIn facts

- LinkedIn dominates the professional social network segment. It is one of the oldest having started in 2002. Almost the grandfather of social networks.
- LinkedIn has 347 million registered members.
- Total revenue at the end of 2014 was $643 million (a growth rate of 44% over the previous period).
- There are over 39 million students and recent college graduates on LinkedIn.

Other Social Media facts

Facebook may be the biggest and baddest but there are many other social media facts and networks that should not be forgotten. Both niche and non-English speaking media facts include:

- Viber has over 200 million users.
- There are 639 million users on Qzone. (China)
- 600 million users on Whatsapp.
- Facebook messenger has 500 million users.
- Wechat is close behind with 468 million users. (China)
- Snapchat has been valued at close to $20 billion at the last valuation.
- Snapchat has 100 million monthly users.
- Russia's "VKontake" has 100 million users.
- Social networks will earn $8.3 billion from advertising in 2015.

Sources: Growing social media, Pewinternet.org, LinkedIn.com

What are you going to do?

Social media started with a few players that have now been empowered by another obsessive technology—*Mobile*. The game is changing!

How can you use visual, mobile and messaging in your marketing? Instagram, Snapchat and Whatsapp are disrupting the game. The internet has drastically changed how consumers behave and how businesses market their products and services. Traditional marketing models still apply, but marketers now need a whole new set of skills, as well as up to date knowledge of digital media to create their digital marketing strategies. With

71% of businesses planning to increase their investment in digital marketing in 2016 and beyond, there has been a real surge in demand for Digital Marketers. According to Google Trends, interest in digital marketing has risen dramatically over the past 12 years:

In this ever changing landscape, with such a wide choice of online communications and analytics tools available, the role of the modern day digital marketer can include everything from copy writing, graphic design, analytics, big data science, podcast and video creation, as well as traditional marketing strategy and planning.

What are the experts saying?

We reached out to some of the **top influencers identified in our list below** to ask them for their views on digital marketing. Be sure to follow them to stay up to date on the best content and resources on digital marketing!

Jeff Bullas – CEO at Jeffbullas.com

"There is an elephant in the room for many digital marketers. They love the vanity metrics of traffic, social media sharing and follower growth. They are hooked on the engagement and feedback that cool content provides to the brand. But they often don't work on the last few hard yards. It isn't seen as sexy and it can be boring. It's converting that traffic and engagement into leads and sales. It's time for many social media and content marketers to grow up."

Sam Hurley, Founder of OPTIM-EYEZ

"This saturated, fast-paced digital world in which we live can seem overwhelming for business owners and marketers alike. Aside from the sheer amount of information and data we force ourselves to consume each and every day, there's one precious unit of measurement which we most commonly neglect. Time. To become a successful business owner, brand, solopreneur, marketer… you have to become a master of time.

"Digital marketing is evolving at incredible rates, which only feeds our fixation with shiny new objects such as virtual reality and the newest social media platforms. My advice for this year onward? Focus your time and energy into three key revenue generators that suit your business model (and you!). Become exceptional at nurturing these generators and don't veer off course. Take heed of the new digital trends and adapt, but don't divert. For these three revenue generators, funnel effort into three primary traffic channels (paid, owned and earned) that will gain qualified exposure for your business — exposure that converts into sales. That's all! Test what works and stick with it. Don't waste your time being a jack of all trades."

"Finally; build relationships, be yourself and push your name through social media. I cannot express enough how important this is. Personal branding is absolutely critical for trust, credibility and inbound leads. Spend time on yourself and everything else will follow. Seriously, I'm living proof of this methodology. I've never had to advertise to attract my own clients. My website isn't even live yet! If this seems crazy to you, it's time to alter your approach to business. Concepts of marketing will always remain unchanged. It's only the tools, buzzwords and technologies that form and shift around us…don't be dazzled by them. Digital marketing is fun. Profit as a result (and your continued sanity) is better."

Rand Fishkin – Founder of Moz

"Ad-blocking was part of a huge conversation in 2015, and my guess is that the reaction to this growing technology is going to mimic how entrenched players have reacted to technology leaps in the past — by trying to legislate it away. I anticipate that in either the US or the EU, some form of government action will arise (in the US, most likely due to lobbying AKA our legalized system of bribery) to "protect the interests of publishers and journalists who serve the public good."

Evan Dunn – Digital Marketing Practice Lead at Transform

"The digital media landscape is complex. With new channels, media and technology popping up every month, it's only getting more complex. The most critical component of success in today's marketing universe is a cohesive strategy—a theoretical framework that makes sense of every marketing activity executed by your brand, and provides an architecture for measurement and optimization of every activity. After all, if you're not sure whether an activity is driving ROI, is it really worth doing?

"Today's marketing, whether online or off, must be a scientific art (or an artistic science, either one). It can no longer be gut-driven, dominated by creative, and powered by trendy jargon. Measurement, analytics, statistics, quantification, optimization – these are the stuff of proven strategies. Don't be distracted by flashy ad-tech, although it is sometimes useful. If your digital marketing objective is growing numbers (customers, sales), then your means of accomplishing it must be by analyzing the numbers. Quantitative Marketing is the future of all forms of marketing, including digital."

Michael Brenner CEO of Marketing Insider Group

"10 years ago, you would have found it difficult to find anything labeled *"Digital Marketing"* on the job boards or even listed in the descriptions for openings companies were trying to fill. Now, digital marketing is the hottest job title in all of marketing. Digital marketing skills are in such high demand because we understand how to market to today's always-connected, multi-device consumer. The top digital marketers today combine right and left-brain talents. We are one part content marketers, editors and writers, who understand how to create the kind of content that people actually want to read and share. On the other hand, we are also one part data nerds, who understand how to analyze all the information available to us as we continuously create and promote content across email, search, social and even offline platforms. Today's digital marketer knows how to reach, engage, and convert new customers for our businesses. We defy the old notion that marketing can't be measured. Because we're doing it every day."

Topic analysis

We were interested in seeing which topics were most popular among the top digital marketing influencers, so we analyzed their tweets and blogs from January 1-April19, 2016 and counted mentions of various topics associated with Digital Marketing which we then used to create a topic share voice chart:

It is interesting to note that the most popular topic among the digital marketing influencers is Social Media with a 27% share of voice. Content Marketing was the second most popular debate driver, followed by branding. *Facebook, SEO* and Twitter all received an 8% share of voice, followed by Strategy, Advertising and Analytics. Email Marketing, PPC, LinkedIn and Planning which all received a 3% share of voice followed by Growth Hacking with 2%.

The traits of successful online marketers

When you think of the *"top traits"* of anything, many variables can come into play. Some of the ones I considered for this list include:

- Usefulness and reliability of blog and social media posts
- Advanced knowledge in one or more areas of online marketing
- Size of audience
- Level of engagement on their blog or social media
- Ability to create and sustain a sense of community with their audience
- Awards received - credibility
- Books written
- See the trends early
- Uses of Visual content effectively
- Long-term focus with lots of short-term consistent action

The 7 types of Social Media 'Gurus' you'll meet

Larry Alton Blogger, (writer, business consultant) outlines the different types of players involved in the social media game. "In the social media world, a disproportionately high number of users are actively describing themselves as "gurus." What is a social media guru? That depends on who you ask. The unfortunate truth is that "guru" is an intentionally vague term, and while it sounds both impressive and descriptive, it describes no actual specific function or role. This isn't to say that all social media gurus have no idea what they're doing; on the contrary, most are skilled in the social media world. They just aren't all skilled in the same ways."

Take, for contrasting examples, these seven types of social media "gurus," all of which have some claim to the term:

1. The resume buffer. The resume buffer is probably the least objectively skilled guru on this list. Sometimes straight out of college and sometimes just interested in finding new ways to look more attractive to a potential employer, the resume buffer adopts the title "social media guru" to look good in a professional context. They generally do have a reasonable familiarity with various popular platforms, which is admirable, but they don't have much knowledge about the science of AB tests or the importance of measuring and interpreting analytics. You can tell a resume buffer by asking a few of the right questions—most of the time, resume buffers have no formal experience doing social media work for brands or personalities other than their own.

2. The influencer. The influencer calls themselves a guru because of the large following they have been able to develop. Influencers usually have access to an audience of thousands, accumulated over time by the sheer power of networking or through various online strategies they adopted. Because of their large audience, each post they make is valuable and can sway hundreds to thousands of people toward or away from a separate brand. However, building a large reputation for yourself is no guarantee you'll also be able to do that for someone else (or for a corporate brand). It could be their unique personality that allows them to accumulate such influence.

3. The hard seller. The hard seller calls himself a social media guru because of how much time he spends a day on a given platform. He is in some type of sales role, either serving as a salesman for a specific company or trying to promote himself as a worker. Because of this, he makes a lot of posts and knows how to measure audience responses, but he isn't too familiar with best practices for building relationships with followers. To be successful in the long-term, most businesses require a degree of soft relationship building in addition to some sales experience.

4. The socialite. The socialite is also a "guru" by virtue of the amount of time they spend on various platforms, but instead of hard selling, they are just being themselves. They are intimately familiar with all the parts and functions of each popular platform (and some off the mainstream), but they may not have a wide audience, and may or may not post things that people like. Because of this, they can be said to have a high degree of skill when it comes to the technical use of these platforms, but little skill in relationship building or brand promotion.

5. The marketer. The marketer is a social media guru all about building an audience. Similar to the hard seller, the marketer has a bottom line—get more people to a given website, or attract more followers to a brand. This is distinct because it is a softer, more relationship-focused skillset, and it does not manifest itself through sheer time spent on various platforms. Instead, the marketer usually makes his claim only after doing this work for multiple people or brands, giving him more experience and a more diverse skillset to take advantage of.

6. The writer. The writer uses social media strictly as a means to promote their work. They may be on multiple platforms on a near-constant basis, or a handful of platforms only some of the time, but either way, they spend most of her time trying to promote her writing. This is beneficial, especially if they are skilled at it—a writing-based social media guru can easily rack up hundreds or thousands of followers in a readership, but it also means that their strategies and tactics are dependent on strong content to be successful. If you have strong content already, it could be a perfect match.

7. The brand ambassador. The brand ambassador is the most flexible and useful social "guru" on this list because the main skillset is adapting their skillset for whatever company or brand they are doing work for. For instance, they might focus on networking and building up a large audience for a personal brand, but rely on the power of content marketing for a corporate brand in a specific industry. Brand ambassadors typically call themselves gurus only after they have helped a number of other brands.

The next time a social media guru reaches out to you offering help with your social media campaign, take inventory of what type of social media guru that person is. Being successful in social media requires access to many different skillsets, and not all businesses need the same type of guru to succeed. Know the diverse roles possible in the social media realm, and use those roles to your greatest advantage by finding the *niche experts* you specifically need.

If you're anywhere near the B2B (business to business) marketing world, social selling or recruiting, getting to know LinkedIn is essential. Mastering LinkedIn is essential.

Why? Check out these stats:

- With over 347 million members in over 200 countries and territories, 1 out of every 3 professionals on the planet Earth is on LinkedIn.
- Professionals are signing up to join LinkedIn at a rate of more than two new members per second.
- LinkedIn counts executives from all 2018 Fortune 500 companies as members.
- More than 3 million companies have LinkedIn Company Pages and there are 2.1 million LinkedIn Groups.
- There simply isn't another social network with that kind of community and momentum for business professionals – buyers of business goods and services. With the proclamation of being "all in" on content marketing, LinkedIn serves as an opportunity for social media and content marketers alike. Of course where there's content, there's an opportunity to optimize as well.

While most professionals are already on LinkedIn and see it as a jobs marketplace, many simply haven't taken the time to optimize or maintain their profiles. They also haven't discovered all the ways you can capitalize on LinkedIn as a marketing and social selling tool.

Chapter Twenty Three
What makes a Great Ad?

The saying, 'there's no second chance at making a good first impression," needs to be taken seriously, because once the brain has made a judgment it's hard to reverse it.

Keeping our advertising ideas uncluttered is one of the disciplines of producing a great ad. I made a mental note that, for me, this is true of most great designs: good musicians have a clean sound, great football players work the basics, and elegant art and architecture is minimalist.

If advertisements do not catch your attention within seconds, they have probably failed. To really stand out of the crowd, the idea has to be out of the box, something that makes you laugh, talk about it, or at least make you look twice. What is more, no amount of social media hype will sell something to someone they don't want!

I remember when I was 19 years old, trying to sell my first house. I had built it for a good price, lived in it for a few years and then placed it on the market as we were moving to live in India. The agents had the first go at selling it, with little interest. So I thought I would have a go at selling the property myself before giving it to another agent. I placed an ad in the local paper with a hook in order capture people's attention: *If anyone buys this house, they will get a free trip to Hawaii.* The phone started ringing with a huge number of inquiries. I would like to have told you that the house sold a few weeks later, but it didn't. People came close to buying, but wanted to deal through an agent and not with the owner directly.

Over the years I have been involved in the creation of a multitude of advising stunts from promoting our gym, *Body & Soul*, for a $1 a day, resulting in the gym membership reaching capacity; to doing a handstand on a skateboard in a suit, down the main street of our city in order to get our political party's policy on the six o'clock news.

In order to gain support for our Global Tribe Aid work in Mexico, Haiti, India, and Africa, my friend Wes Campbell, the owner of numerous bands in the US, suggested going on the road to speak and show video at their concerts, raising support and teams of people to go and do aid work around the world. It was a great success, raising millions of dollars and facilitating thousands of volunteers to help build houses. That is until the defining moment, mentioned at the beginning of this book; that starting *enterprise engines* at the heart of these communities was the best way to break people out of poverty, and grow a thriving economy.

In fact the way Wes got the attention of the music world in the US, is a story worth telling. He was trying to introduce his first band, the Newsboys, to one of the largest festivals in America of over 200,000 attendees. They had moved from the gold coast of Australia with no money, and spent a year or more traveling the country in their old van playing every little gig they could talk their way into, clocking up thousands of miles and even more debt. They wanted in, but the emails, phone calls and Oz accent didn't work on the promoters, so they devised a plan to get themselves heard. They decided that because the setup for the festival took a week, they would play to the set-up crew. This meant the set-up crew, management, staging, lighting, and sound guys got to hear them, and after a week of hanging out with the band, the staging crew worked them into a slot at the festival. They were an instant hit and the crowd demanded more, and so for the last 15 years they have played there every year, and mostly as the headline act. To add a twist, some years later, Wes purchased a majority shareholding in the festival.

I was starting a gym in our city called the *The Club,* and working on ideas for advertising. While driving to the coast to go surfing I asked my friend, who was a *Saatchi & Saatchi* advertising guru at the time, what he believed makes a truly great ad. He said without hesitation, *lots of space,* something I have never forgotten. He was referring to print advertising but went on to expand the concept, relating it to all advertising—to keeping-it-simple. The KISS principle: Keep-It-Simple-Stupid. He also said, that an ad campaign is not rocket science, it's common sense. Keeping our advertising ideas uncluttered is one of the disciplines of producing a great ad. I made a mental note that, for me, this is true of most great designs: good musicians have a clean sound, great football players work the basics, and elegant art and architecture is minimalist.

We have to get people's attention amidst huge media noise, and somehow convert that into a trade, their hard-earned money for our idea.

Project: You are selling soccer balls, so generate 10 advertising ideas! Go online and look at the competition, and write a list of advertising possibilities!

Examples:

- **Have a Sale**—This is a common thing to do, but it done well, works well.

- **Do a Live Ad**—This is being used more and more to capture people's attention, as media traffic online today is huge. But in real traffic and on the road, we are more passive and less likely to take notice of sign boards, so beware!

- **Customer Loyalty Schemes**—My Star Alliance, Air New Zealand frequent flyers card was the reason I paid a little more than what was on special with other airlines. The privilege of using their lounges around the world, upgrades, and other comforts helped me stay loyal. The coffee cards often used by cafe owners, reward loyal customers with a free coffee every ten or so coffees. Why spend more on advertising when it cost less to keep existing customers?

Loyal customers are good for our business because they become our best advocates. They recommend you to others, saving you big dollars in advertising costs. A loyal customer's endorsement is more powerful to their friends and family than any advertising campaign.

Project: List your 10 advertising ideas:

1.

2.

3.

4.

5.

6.

7.

8.

9.

10.

Chapter Twenty Four
What is a Brand?

Simply defined, a brand is what your customer thinks of when he or she hears the brand name. It is everything the public thinks it knows about a business, both factual and emotional.

A brand is the intangible sum of the customer's perception concerning the qualities and attributes of a product or service, and the entire culture of the organization. The brand exists in someone's mind, the space owned by your idea or proposition. However, it is critical to NOT rely on what you think they think.

Originally a brand was an identifying mark burned onto livestock or (especially in former times) criminals or slaves with a branding iron. A brand has now become the characteristic's that set a company apart from the pack. A brand is the character and personality of an enterprise. It is more about who we are as opposed to what we do. The feeling someone has as they experience the culture and personality of the company.

Starting out as the name or image branded on an animal, product, or service, the *brand-name, as a* concept has broadened over time to include the *brand image* and *brand culture*. Simply defined, a brand is what your customer thinks of when he or she hears the brand name. It is everything the public thinks it knows about a business, both factual and emotional. A brand is the intangible sum of the customer's perception concerning the qualities and attributes of a product or service, and the entire culture of the organization. The brand exists in someone's mind, the space owned by your idea or proposition.

What comes to mind when you hear the brand name, *Apple?* Cool design that is easy to operate, visually pleasing, cutting edge, intelligent, and the list goes on to describe how you feel about the products and personality of *Apple*.

Brand strategy

A *brand strategy* is how, what, where, when and to whom you plan to communicate your key brand ideas. How you appear in public, where you advertise, your business model, distribution channels and the design of your physical presence, are all included as a part of your brand strategy. Consistent, strategic branding leads to a strong brand equity, which means added value brought to your company's products or services, that allows you to charge more for your brand than what identical, unbranded products command.

The added value intrinsic to brand equity frequently comes in the form of perceived quality or emotional attachment. For example, *Nike* associates its products with star athletes, hoping customers will transfer their emotional attachment from the athlete to the product. For Nike, it's not just the shoe's features that sell the shoe.

Defining your brand is a journey of business self-discovery. It can be difficult, time-consuming and uncomfortable. It requires, at the very least, that you answer the questions below:
- What is your company's mission or mantra?
- What are the benefits and features of your products or services?
- What do your customers and prospects already think of your company?
- What qualities do you want them to associate with your company?

Research, research, research

Do your research. Learn the needs, habits and desires of your current and prospective customers. And do not rely on what you think they think! Know what they think! Market research can give you insight into your market, your competitors, your products, your marketing and your customers. Here are 20 questions market research can help you answer:

1. What are you REALLY selling?
2. WHO is currently buying your product or service?
3. What are these PEOPLE'S LIVES actually like?
4. Why are other people NOT buying it?
5. WHO would be interested in buying it in the future?
6. HOW MANY people like this are there?
7. What general TRENDS are affecting these people's lives at the moment?
8. WHERE would people buy your product or service from?
9. WHEN, WHERE and HOW would they use or consume it?
10. WHY would they buy it? What need are they wanting to satisfy?
11. Who is your real COMPETITION?
12. What IMAGE do people have of your brand vs your competitors?
13. What would be the ideal IMAGE for your brand to have?
14. What do they think about the DIFFERENT ASPECTS of your product or service (name, packaging, features, advertising, pricing...)?
15. What IMPROVEMENTS could be made to your product or service to meet people's needs even better?
16. What is the SINGLE MOST IMPORTANT BENEFIT your brand should be seen to be offering - and why would people believe this to be true?
17. How can you best COMMUNICATE that benefit to the people you are interested in attracting?

18. What is the right PRICE to charge?
19. What other NEW products or services could your brand offer people?
20. So what is your VISION for your brand?
21. And what would be the best ROAD MAP for getting there?

Communication strategy

The secret of good communication is to tailor your approach to the individual. Your customers are all unique personalities and perceive your messages in different ways. Write out the messages that you want to communicate to your customers and then tailor them to reach the different personalities or temperament types.

Most importantly, remember to listen. If you are a big talker, you may have to curb your natural tendency to interrupt or dominate the conversation. To develop a dialogue with your customer, ask open-ended questions and listen to the answers.

The larger you grow, the more detailed your plan needs to be developed, from what must be communicated to staff, to the messages you wish to deliver to your customers.

Project Scenario 1: You believe you have what it takes to be a great professional soccer player, but you know that you need to make enough money during the summer to free yourself up to practice and play soccer full-time during winter. You have an opportunity to purchase cheap soccer balls, which you have decided you will sell in order to free yourself up for the soccer season.

How are you going to do it? BUT you only have one hour.

Project Scenario 2: You did so well at selling soccer balls that you decided to go into business selling soccer balls online. You thought there may be an opportunity to sell them online to a larger market than the small community you live in, so immediately started work on your *Marketing Plan* to sell soccer balls globally.

Develop your marketing plan on the following pages:

Global Tribe Marketing Plan

Question	Answer
1. What are you selling and why are you so special?	
2. Who are you targeting?	
3. Who are my competitors?	
4. How am I going to bring this great idea to market?	

5. What do I need to sell or secure to be profitable? **What Price?**	
6. How do I set sales targets and develop sales strategies?	
7. What is my communication and or branding strategy?	
8. Budget: How much money do you have to promote the product?	

9. Action Plan:	
10. GO	

Pillar Three
The Team

"The bigger the dream, the more important the team!"

Who will help me?

How do I develop my people-skills?

When do I need employees?

Where do I find good workers?

Chapter Twenty Five
Team Up

"Talent wins games, but teamwork and intelligence wins championships."

— Michael Jordan

An economy is not a mindless machine of businesses, regulations and government, it's a *tapestry of relationships*, of empowering or disempowering partnerships, of productive and unproductive people. The ideas, concepts and philosophies of an economy and a community must marry in order to build a sustainable, healthy, thriving nation.

The why

Every startup generally involves a team of people, from the startup advisers to the appointment of the first employees. Most new enterprises begin with the big idea, or the great opportunity; then the inspirational conversations with friends, family and associates begin, hammering the concept into shape. The voices we don't wish to hear are always close by, giving the impossibilities, the cold hard facts, the reasons it will fail. But always remember, *criticism is quality control*, so do not take it personally and always thank others for their input even if it hurts to do so. This is your startup team, made up of people who give formal or informal input in the research and development phase of an idea. Then as your idea takes root, there will be a number of advisers, partners, workers and investors, all involved in creating structure around your idea.

Many members of the team of friends, family, and mentors, that started out *brainstorming* with you as a part of your initial *think tank* may fall away and be replaced by financial partners, employees, empowering companies or people with expertise and experience. Our attitude toward the concept of *Team* is all important and a part of the bigger picture of building healthy entrepreneurs and sustainable businesses. When we disrespect those we partner with in order to create wealth, we are disrespecting ourselves, and are on the road to contracting a terminal sickness known as *greed*.

We really do need to believe in the power and value of partnership, or team, in order to achieve the right kind of success. These kinds of philosophical foundations within our thinking have a huge impact on the new enterprise, often greater than the more technical, operational sides of the business. Good or corrupted character sits beneath the surface of all we think or do. Greed and personal ambition, for example, are among the greatest enemies of building a culture that cares for the needs of others.

The culture

A number of years ago I was partnering with a team of young social entrepreneurs who wanted to serve the young people of their city using a similar model to *Global Tribe*. I remember giving them some advice, that just came out spontaneously, but was news to me as well. I was talking about the importance of building *the culture* of the team as being of more importance than total focus on the wiz-bang programs or the slick look and feel of the place. I told them to check regularly on the culture of genuine care for people. Holding the team accountable, not only to the tasks of their job profiles, but to their attitudes to one another and a general culture of kindness. Culture is shaped by leadership, whether positive or negative, by design or by default. Culture is built by the role models that people are inspired by. In business, a *partnership* can be the legal description of the relationship, a buzz-word, or something that is genuine.

Autumn arrives and the Canadian Geese are on the move south for the winter. By flying in a V formation, a gaggle of geese add at least 72 percent to their flying range compared to each bird flying on its own.

As the lead goose grows weary, it rotates to the back of the V-formation and another goose takes the lead. As each bird flaps its wings, it creates uplift for the bird immediately behind it. The 'V' shape, scientists have now determined is no accident, with aeronautical engineers calculating that the entire gaggle of geese gains an improved energy efficiency and speed of up to 23 percent. Geese teach us that we can fly faster and further in partnership with others than on their own. As these great birds fly, they honk to encourage those up at the front, to keep up their speed and momentum. Above all, the quality to be admired in these incredible birds, is their sacrificial nature. If at any time a goose gets sick or is wounded and falls out of formation, two of the other geese fly down to nurse and protect their sick or injured family member. They tend their friend until they get well or die. They then await another V-train in order to catch up, and connect with their family and friends again.

This is a beautiful picture of a culture of partnership and team spirit. Partnership is a mindset that must be developed. Thinking and productivity is taken to another level in unity with others.

Known as one of the wisest and wealthiest kings who ever lived, Solomon teaches, that allowing ourselves to be woven into positive partnerships gives us greater productivity, provision, protection and power. He taught that, "If one can put one thousand to flight, then two can put ten thousand to flight." Hafford Luccock notes, "No one person can whistle a symphony. It takes an orchestra to play it." Partnership is less of *me* and more of *we*. It requires humility to involve others in the thinking and development process of an idea. Milton Friedman noted, "There is not a single person in the world who can make a pencil; it takes the coordination of thousands of people. The wood may have come from a forest in Washington, the graphite from a mine in South America and the eraser from a Malaysian rubber plantation. Thousands of people cooperate to make a pencil."

When we truly value the thoughts and opinions of others we gain a broader perspective. Andrew Carnegie once said, "I owe whatever success I have attained, by and large, to my ability to surround myself with people who are smarter than I am." A study of Solomon's *wealth creation philosophy,* shows that it came predominately through building strategic trading partnerships. Partnerships that are a win for you and a win for them—a win, win! Nobody is a complete orchestra; no one person is a basketball team, because growing an enterprise is a team sport. Thinking is strengthened when we join forces with others. Solomon says, "Just as iron sharpens iron, friends sharpen the minds of each other." The rough edge of another person may be the very tool that sharpens us. CS Lewis, JRR Tolkien and their friends, in a creative partnership of writers called the Inklings, refined their books such as The Chronicles of Narnia, and The Lord of the Rings. William Wilberforce, one of the great reformers of England, responsible for the abolition of slavery, was strengthened by a band of like-minded friends tagged *the saints* by their contemporaries in Parliament. A partnership that generated a revolution against all odds, as England derived huge economic benefits from slave trading. Wilberforce intentionally "forged strategic partnerships for the common good, irrespective of differences over methods, ideology or religious beliefs."

The skill of great leadership is, more often than not, about instilling a sense of partnership. Max de Pree captures this in his definition of leadership. He states that leadership is more tribal than scientific, more a weaving of relationships than an amassing of information and, in that sense, I don't know how to pin it down in every detail.

Think we, not me
Napoleon Hill, in his book *Think and Grow Rich*, talks about the power of partnership in Henry Ford's business success. He noted that the most rapid strides in the *Ford Motor Company*, and his business empire in general, came after forming strong relationships with Thomas A Edison, Harvey Firestone, John Burroughs and Luther Burbank. Hill says, "No two minds ever came together without thereby creating a third invisible, intangible force which may be likened to a third mind." As a result he built what he called a *mastermind group*, which he defined as "the coordination of knowledge and effort in a spirit of harmony between two or more people for the attainment of a definite purpose. ... [Adding] to his own brain power the sum and substance of the intelligence, experience, knowledge and spiritual forces" of the group.

He believed that because the human mind was a form of energy, a part of it was spiritual in nature.

Throughout the Proverbs of Solomon, he repeats again and again the need for wise advisors: "There is victory in the multitude of counselors," he taught. A Reader's Digest article entitled *"What Good is a Tree?"* revealed that when the roots of certain trees touch, a fungus develops in the soil that somehow reduces competition between them. "This substance works to link the roots of different trees—even of dissimilar species," these trees are designed to share with one another. Whole forests can be linked together, sharing water, nutrients and sunlight. As human beings, we are designed to thrive and succeed through the nurture of partnership.

Mother Teresa puts it this way, "You can do what I cannot do. I can do what you cannot do. Together we can do great things." John Wooden said, "The man who puts the ball through the hoop has ten hands." The ability to partner with the right people is the key to another universe of thinking and achievement.

Chapter Twenty Six
Entrepreneurial Workers

"If I had nine hours to chop down a tree, I'd spend the first six sharpening my axe."

— Abraham Lincoln

"Nothing in the world can take the place of persistence. Talent will not; nothing is more common than unsuccessful men with talent. Genius will not; unrewarded genius is almost a proverb. Education alone will not; the world is full of educated derelicts. Persistence and determination alone are omnipotent."

— Calvin Coolidge

The workers of the future need to posses an Entrepreneurial mindset. This mindset is a set of core characteristics or concepts that give them the X factor. Entrepreneurial workers are optimistic thinkers, idea generators, innovation designers, with a clear vision of the future without allowing a lack of resource or fear to dominate their thinking.

Anna Vial makes an interesting case for future workers needing to become entrepreneurs. She believes that employees will be replaced by entrepreneurs. It turns out that it's not just startups that do not want traditional employees, Google does not want them, small businesses do not want them, agencies don't want them.

Independent Contractors: At one level, she points out that consultants, freelancers and contractors cost 30% less than employees, and without the liabilities. The independent worker has no benefits, no supervision, and you pay-as-you go.

Outsourcing: Specialized jobs, such as software developers, can be done overseas, and in many cases, done over-night while you are asleep. And in most cases, at a fraction of the cost.

Robots: Employees who act like robots, that is just do what they are told, are quickly becoming obsolete. Consider a factory building aircraft. You have a choice of hiring two people at $50,000 per year or buying a robot for $250,000 that will serve you for 15 years, without coffee break, 365 days a year, 24 hours a day and without the personal problems.

No wonder robots are catching on. Today the world's robot population is around 10 million. Many of the manual jobs that humans do are and will increasingly be replaced with robots. In South Korea for instance, there are 347 robots per 10,000 employees.

Intrapreneurs: The term "intrapreneur" dates back to 1992, but it is now that intrapreneurship has become a global phenomenon with companies hiring entrepreneurs-in-residence, holding hackathons, which are company-wide startup competitions; as well as allowing employees to spend 20% of their to work-time on these creative side projects.

Acqui-hires: Company's like Facebook are now purchasing other companies, not because they want their businesses, but purely to acquire their entrepreneurial workers, team or top tech brains.

Sidepreneurs: Workers that sell their creative skills and artistic ability on the side. In this way keeping their bread-and-butter day job, while taking on projects here and there to create extra income and increase their value in the market.

Jack-of-all-trades: This is the entrepreneurial worker who is willing to wear a number of hats. This means gaining skills and experience in a wide range of jobs. This is a shift from the specialist mindset of the past to becoming a generalist. To be a jack-of-all-trades and master-of-none is no longer seen as being a negative thing by small business owners trying to survive and thrive in the new highly competitive, fast changing global marketplace. In the mind of an employer people who gain a broad range of work experience, may not be slackers that can't keep a job, but demonstrating an entrepreneurial attitude.

The entrepreneurial mindset

The way an entrepreneur thinks is their core competency, their primary asset, and sets them apart as creators. This new breed of worker think like a entrepreneur, and have the ability to see a human need or passion and provide for it. They fearlessly create something of value out of very little or nothing. They make the connection between the raw resources and assets at their disposal, and move things around until they work. They take initiative and extreme ownership of the tasks they are given. Their strength is in the way they think, more of an art form or a passion than a skill-set.

Although all of these characteristics may not be possessed, or can be acted on when working for someone else, they are a part of the mindset of an entrepreneur, and can be developed outside of working hours.

Core characteristics

Some of these characteristics overlap conceptually, however form a picture of how entrepreneurs think. In Part One of this book the subject of thinking is also addressed, so I will not go into detail, but give an overview of the entrepreneurial mindset:

Abundance mentality

This is a belief system whispering in the mind, that nature is still a huge untapped resource, which if harvested in a responsible, sustainable manner can provide a prosperous life for all on the planet. This is the mindset that sees the possibilities, for example, the sun raining down trillions upon trillions of tons of life giving photons, linked with innovation in solar energy, could power the earth and our toys for a long time to come.

Visionaries

Entrepreneurs see things that are not, as though they are! They look at an old building and have the ability to imagine what it could become and yield, sometimes within minutes. They are imagineers! They don't start with focusing on the potential problems, their creative juices kick into gear and blind them to the why-not's. Something that has caused many visionaries to go bankrupt or close to it, a good reason to team-up with complimentary mind-sets.

Optimistic thinkers

This mind-set sees all the negatives, and the positives, but chooses to focus on the positive. On fixing the problem, as opposed to fixing the blame; on creative solutions, not navel gazing or the paralysis of analysis. This mind-set is more of an underlying attitude than the ability to see the future, as in a visionary characteristic. This mental toughness is vital when all of hell seems to break loose on your great idea or project.

Team players

Entrepreneurial workers are team players, they connect and communicate with all involved. Team players see themselves in the context of community, where *we* not *me* is the mindset. Team spirit is just that, an invisible force that glues people together into a harmony and cooperation that supersedes the power of the individual. It takes great leadership to achieve this, or the presence of a goal or idea, so strong, that it units people around a common vision. Team players possess a generous spirit where they appreciate and genuinely celebrate other team members gifts, skills or talents. When this mindset becomes the culture of a team they become a force for good. A soccer player who doesn't like passing the ball, and continuously goes it alone, won't last long. Observing teams in any field of endeavor that play together as *one*, is a beauty to behold!

Customer focused

Most successful entrepreneurs and workers are driven by what customers really want. This mind-set has to do with listening, interviewing, observing and surveying what customers are saying, then interpreting what they find into products or services that love their customers. It has to be said that great designers don't always connect with their customers directly. Steve Jobs, the founder of Apple said, that he never conducted focus groups or surveys because the customers don't always know what they want, when they have never seen it before. It seems unusual, but captures your attention when a worker, thinks and acts like the owner. My wife and I were in Auckland, New Zealand, about to check-out of our hotel, when the man taking care of our bags knocked on our hotel room door, then in a humble yet bright tone, he engaged us like he owned the place. He conversed in a natural way, taking interest in where we were traveling and making sure that we had transport to the airport. The sense of ownership he carried was inspiring and made me think, why is this not the norm?

Problem solvers

Business and life in general demands that we solve problems, because problems are the only obstacle between us and success. Entrepreneurial workers don't run from their problems – they face them and slay them, as David did Goliath, they are giant slayers. The courage to solve the problems we face as soon as possible is what this mind-set is all about. Feel the fear, then go into battle regardless!

Risk takers

When we cut loose into the stormy waters of business we can't avoid taking risks, but we must design ways of managing that risks. Risk management is the forecasting and evaluation of financial, social, physical, and environmental risks, together with the implementation of procedures to avoid or minimize the impact. This mind-set is more about calculated risk taking, and managing our risk, than the reckless gung-ho risk-taking some encourage.

Innovators

This is an ability to source the resources needed to turn an idea into reality. To bring the pieces of the jigsaw puzzle together and fit them into place. Innovators create the ideas that add something of value to a customer, thus turning the idea into a profit. They are the pioneers, trailblazers, and developers; the revolutionaries that can inspire action and move mountains. Like the producer of a movie; they cast the vision, develop the business plan, raise the finance, and bring all of the component parts of the project and business ideas together in order to create an enterprise engine and make a profit.

Designers

If the innovator is like the producer of a film, then the designer is the director. Classically, the main areas of design were: painting, sculpture and architecture, which were understood as the major arts, something that has now broadened out to include fashion, movie making, book and song writing to name a few. Although all entrepreneurs are not artisans, this mindset has to do with the creation of something that works. Designing new methods of doing things, new ecosystems, and new business models; living in the workshop of their imagination, they create or redesign the world around them.

Value driven

As already discussed values such as, *placing the customer at the center of our business*, allowing the customer to drive every aspect of the enterprise.

The mission and values messaging that an innovative *shared office company,* called *WeWorks,* have crafted, best illustrates this new entrepreneurial mindset. It reflects the culture they have created and wish to inspire in others:

The WeWorks example (taken from their website)

Create Your life's work

Our mission

To create a world where people work to make a life, not just a living.

Our Story

When we started *WeWork* in 2010, we wanted to build more than beautiful, shared office spaces. We wanted to build a community. A place you join as an individual, 'me', but where you become part of a greater 'we'. A place where success is measured by personal fulfillment, not just by the bottom line. Community is our catalyst.

Our values

Inspired
We do what we love and are connected to something greater than ourselves.

Entrepreneurial
We are creators, leaders, and self-starters. We try new things, we challenge convention, and we are not afraid to fail.

Authentic
We are genuine to our brand, mission, and values. We are not perfect, and we do not pretend to be. We are always honest and as transparent as we can be.

Tenacious
We never settle. We get shit done and we get it done well. Be persistent, and knock down walls— literally if you have to. You have our permission.

Grateful
We are grateful for each other, our members, and to be part of this movement. We do not take success for granted. We are happy to be alive.

Together
We are in this together. This is a team effort. We always look out for one another. We have empathy, we know we are all human, and know we cannot do any of this alone.

Our team

Our mission does not end with the small businesses and entrepreneurs that call us home. We believe in empowering our team to create their own life's work. We move fast and we challenge each other, but we look after each other and care about our culture, which makes working here extremely rewarding. There is a lot of work left for us to do, and we could not do it without a single member of our team.

What the workforce want

Chairman and CEO of *Gallup*, Jim Clifton, in his new book, The Coming Job Wars, says, "If you were to ask me, from all of the world polling *Gallup's* conducted ... Young people simply want a good job. They want to go to work in the morning and be treated with respect and with dignity. Healthy people are the trees on which healthy fruit grow, so finding and looking after these people is of primary importance. Healthy fruit is a byproduct. This vital area is often underestimated in the race to get your product or service to market, and achieve the dream. The bigger the dream, the more important the team! It is easy not to see employees as people, but cogs in the enterprise machine. High-energy work environments are what this new breed of entrepreneurial worker need in order to keep engaged. Miserable employees create miserable customers. Gallup has determined that 28% of the American workforce is engaged, another 53% is not engaged, and a staggering 19% is actively disengaged."

Employers must understand that employees have dreams and ambitions too, and will often work more for a vision or appreciation than for money. Deciding to hire someone is for most businesses, especially startups, one of those do-or-die decisions; because if done too early or if the wrong person is employed, it can cripple the company. On the other hand, the right person is the greatest investment that a business can make, resulting in greater productivity and profitability.

How do I find world-class workers?

You must believe that you can find and attract the best of best—the *A-Team*! Finding the right team to partner with you in growing your business is like discovering gold.

One of the problems with inexperienced entrepreneurs is a lack of understanding of *employment law* and the multitude of laws that relate to this huge responsibility. The legal issues surrounding a new employee are to be found on most government business websites, but are often ignored, resulting in massive future legal costs that can kill a business.

What are employee's rights?

This section provides an overview of the minimum rights and obligations that apply, by law, to employers. Employees can't be asked to agree to less than their minimum rights.

An employee is anyone who has agreed to be employed under a contract of service, to work for some form of payment. This can include wages, salary, and commissions.

A list of some employee rights are listed below, starting with Annual Holidays the employers responsibilities begin to pile up:
- Bereavement leave
- Break entitlements
- Employment agreements
- Employment relationship problems
- Equal pay and equal rights
- Fixed-term employees
- Flexible working arrangements
- Health and safety

- Keeping records
- Minimum pay
- Paying wages
- Penalties
- Public holidays
- Leave - sick and parental leave
- Trial periods
- Unions

This list can change from country to country, so you must do your research and consult your government website and a competent lawyer. Under Pillar Four—The Lawyer, this vital area is covered in greater detail as it relates to law.

The devil you know!

You have heard the saying, "Better the devil you know than the one you don't." Sometimes we can under value those we know, because we know them so well, faults and all. They also know you and how you operate, which can be a big plus and a good head start. On the other hand, employing your friends or family can blow up in your face, and result in long-term friendships ending in tears. It is important to subject friends and family to the same tests and evaluations as you would others, and where practical have someone other than yourself involved in the decision making process.

You should:
- Get a solid handle on what their expectations are.
- Find out where they see their role leading?
- Why do they want the job?
- Where do they see themselves in the next 5 years?

The first question to ask yourself after interviewing them and getting to know them a little bit, is do these new employees past the character, chemistry and competency test?

Character, chemistry and competency test:

Character in a person working for you is like having a toothache, they will get on your nerves, and can become extremely painful and very annoying. Are they honest, reliable, hardworking, positive, and show initiative? Or are they grumpy, lazy, back-stabbing, disloyal, mean-spirited people?

Taking the time to do a background check is all-important. We need to ask the searching questions of the people your prospective employee has given as references. This may help to uncover character flaws that may end up ruining your business. Be careful when asking questions of these people, because most do not like to be negative, they will not voice their concerns loudly for fear that their comments may get back to the prospective employee. This means they may only communicate with what seems like a whisper, hinting at someone's negative character traits, so drill down with direct questions if you hear that whisper.

End your line of questioning with: Would you employ this person again?

If the law of your country allows it, when it comes to the contract stage, only offer the new employee a trial period. A person's chemistry, character or competency is very hard to see, even with the best interview processes. This is not always possible as they may have to leave another job to join your company, making it unattractive or hard for them to make the jump.

Chemistry is more important than many realize, and has to do with how someone connects or fits in with the other people in the team. Will they really be happy long-term with the culture you have developed? For example, an office or working culture with open and honest communication, or the flexible hours you set, or simply the way you choose to operate your meetings.

They do not have to be of the same temperament as you and the others on the team, (opposites do attract and compliment each other), but the marriage needs to work. It is hard to define what chemistry means exactly, but as one friend of mine put it; *"you've got to like the person."* When a chemistry experiment goes bad, it is because you have placed the wrong chemicals together, and it can be explosive. Research reveals one of the major reasons for the failure of a business is the breakdown in a key relationship.

In past I have involved other staff members in social settings, so that the new player can be observed by others on the team. Often in this setting, they let down their guard and show something of who they are, and their ability to mess with the team spirit can become apparent!

Competency is something we can oversee if we like their character and the chemistry fells right. But do they really have the skills or intelligence for the role? Do they have a degree, but no practical experience? What is their track record? Again, it may help to have other staff members or a friend accompany you in the interview process. How many times have you heard it: great character, fantastic chemistry, but hopeless at their job.

Below is a list of questions employers may ask at interviews that you may not have thought about previously. Make it your homework to think about how you would answer these questions:

- If you had the option, would you change your career?
- How do you go about deciding what to do first when given a project?
- What are the most important rewards you expect in your business career?
- Provide an example of how you are a risk taker.
- If you could have any job in the world, what would it be?
- Why do you want to work for us and not for our competitor?
- What did you think of your previous manager/supervisor?
- What did you do in your last job to increase value?
- What are some of the things that bother you?
- Tell me about the last time you felt anger on the job.
- Do you need other people around to stimulate you or are you self-motivated?
- What management style gets the best results out of you?
- How can our company offer you what your previous company could not offer?
- How long do you think it would take before you were making a significant contribution to our business?
- How ambitious are you? Would you compete for my job?
- What do you like and dislike about the job we are discussing?
- Why did you choose a career in… ?
- What do you think is the most important dilemma facing our business today?
- How much does your last job resemble the one you are applying for? What are the differences?

- Why did you decide to join your previous company? Did the job live up to your expectations? Why are you leaving now?
- Explain the organizational structure and hierarchy in your last company and how you fitted into it. Did this suit you?
- Do you prefer to work in a small, medium or large company?
- What interests you about our company, product or service?
- You have not done this sort of job before. How will you cope/succeed?
- Do you consider yourself successful in your career to date?
- What was your greatest success in your professional career? How did you achieve it?
- What has been your biggest failure in your professional career?
- Did you feel you advanced and progressed in your last job?
- How do you handle criticism?
- What would you like to avoid in your next job?
- How did you get on with your previous manager, supervisor, co-workers, and subordinates?
- What will your references say about you?
- Fantasy question! ... what would you do if you won the lottery? Would you come to work tomorrow?

If these people are not in your immediate family or friendship circle, then most countries have websites and agencies that can help you to locate potential entrepreneurial workers, but you must be prepared to take the time out to really look for them, like mining for gold, it is not easy. It is like marriage; there is a lot at stake . It can end in misery or in a romantic friendship that lasts a lifetime.

Chapter Twenty Seven
Team Leaders and Managers

I think Max De Pree best captures the nature of grass-roots leadership in his book, Leadership Is An Art. He defines leadership as—"more tribal than scientific, more a weaving of relationships than an amassing of information, and in that sense, I don't know how to pin it down in every detail."

— Max De Pree

Good leadership or great managers bring all of the pieces of the enterprise engine together in order to build a complete ecosystem. They draw out the best in people and build them into a healthy, functioning community.

For a small business and startups the owner has to be a mixture of both a leader and a manager. This is not ideal, but can be overcome by teaming up with the right staff, mentors, or community of business people. The solution to a lack of management or leadership wisdom is only a question or two away, and begins with an attitude of humility.

In the chapters dealing with *The Manager,* I go into more depth concerning management skills, but for now we will deal with issues that relate to leadership in general and their *people skills. Managers are leaders and need to develop the art of leadership as it applies to their role.*

Grass roots leadership

Leaders are the innovators and entrepreneurs that open the doors of the future and navigate the turbulent uncharted waters of the marketplace or a community. More than any other activity, they have to master and negotiate the stormy waters of a complex web of relationships. Whether an entrepreneur or manager, you will need to develop the art of leadership.

The word *'leadership'* comes from an Anglo-Saxon word that means 'a road way, the path of a ship at sea' (Adair 1990). Leadership is knowing what the next step is, and having the courage, confidence, and commitment to take it.

The definition of insanity is "to keep doing things the same way, but wanting a different result"—something many of us as leaders are guilty of at times. If you always do what you've always done, you will always get what you've always got. It takes strong character and leadership to have the guts to jump the ruts.

Grass-roots leaders challenge people to commit, to climb a little higher, to dig a little deeper, and go a little further, challenging people to focus, give, organize, and develop their skills and character. Grass-roots leaders work the coalface, and at the same time influence people in positions of power. William Wilberforce, who was responsible for the abolition of slavery in England, was a grass-roots leader whose influence extended into the halls of power, a place some may think would disqualify a leader from grass-roots status. But this is the spirit of a people-centered, community building, social entrepreneur.

In my role as politician, I have observed the fact that great leadership has nothing to do with political position, as much as it does political motivation. If a politician is motivated out of a deep love for people, they will have influence through genuinely meeting real peoples' needs instead of a preoccupation many have with programs and processes.

In an excellent little booklet, *The Man Who Changed His Times*, John Pollock gives insights into the grass-roots nature of William Wilberforce's leadership in English politics during the late 1700s and early 1800s. At 28 years of age, on October 28,1787, Wilberforce wrote in his diary, "God Almighty has set before me two great objects, the suppression of the Slave Trade and the reformation of manners." Wilberforce's goal of abolishing the Slave Trade took 46 years to achieve. It was on July 26, 1833, only three days before his death, when the *Bill for the Abolition of Slavery* passed its second reading in the House of Commons. The abolition of slavery throughout the entire British Empire was a mammoth goal when you consider that Britain, 200 years beforehand, was the world's leading slave-trading nation. Wilberforce threatened the economic benefits derived from slave trading—the annual trade of hundreds of ships, the jobs of thousands of sailors, cheap workers for landowners, the businesses of selling slaves in Africa and England. Wilberforce also set out to change England by influencing the moral climate, making goodness fashionable, and restoring respect for the law in all classes."Wilberforce", Pollock said, "touched the world when he made goodness fashionable." "Whatever its faults,19th century British public life became famous for its emphasis on character, morals, and justice, and the British business world famous for integrity."

These kinds of goals will also characterize new generation entrepreneurs, who see themselves as leading community reform; both environmental and economic. Although not all entrepreneurs will be directly involved, this new generation of grass-roots leaders will join forces to initiate change.

Wilberforce was committed to the strategic importance of a band of like-minded friends devoted to working together in chosen ventures. His particular band of associates were tagged *"the Saints"* by their contemporaries in Parliament.

Another characteristic of grass-roots leadership is seen in how Wilberforce 'forged strategic partnerships for the common good irrespective of differences over methods, ideology, or religious beliefs.' This is something modern business now recognizes as the key to the future and their survival.

Entrepreneurs need to be big thinkers, willing to imagine what could happen when we become dangerously honest, ruthlessly loving, and committed to making other people successful. In a book called *Credibility,* Kouzes and Posnet reveal the results of a survey identifying the key characteristics of admired leaders saying, "In virtually every survey we conducted, honesty was selected more often than any other leadership characteristic."

The leaders I have most respected over the years are those who are self-disclosing, who are willing to share their struggles and weaknesses with others.

Chapter Twenty Eight
The Coaching Edge

Your Wisdom + My Wisdom = More Success
One of the essential skills of good leadership or management is seen in the mindset of a coach. They are dangerously honest, masters of giving empowering feedback, know how to frame the hard questions, and tailor their development programs to the individual.

Here are a few quotes that define the art of effective coaching:

"A coach is someone who can give correction without causing resentment."

—John Wooden

"I never cease to be amazed at the power of the coaching process to draw out the skills or talent that was previously hidden within an individual, and which invariably finds a way to solve a problem previously thought unsolvable."

—John Russell

"A good coach will make his players see what they can be, rather than what they are."

—Ara Parasheghian

"The goal of coaching is the goal of good management: to make the most of an organization's valuable resources."

—Harvard Business Review

A guide dog to the blind

When a person is blind, they cannot see the physical world. In the same way someone who has had no business experience is blind to many of the issues and disciplines that are required for success.

Just as guide dogs are the eyes of the person without sight, a coach or mentor are the eyes for someone starting out. But always keep in mind, everyone starts out in the same place - *inexperience!*

We need coaches and mentors who are experienced, intelligent and wise to help us see clearly. When we are blind, we must place faith in someone else because when we don't know what we don't know, and when we can't see want we can't see, we are flying blind.

So when a coach or mentor says, *"make sure that when you price the house you are planning on building, add 40%, then raise the funding for that amount"* — we should listen! Then when we hear similar advice from three of our advisers — *we should, just do it!*

It is at this point that pride can kick in, and we can get overly optimistic and wise in our own eyes and dumb-down what we are hearing. This is because we think we are different and special, when we are not. We need these courageous people in our world, to point out our blind spots and guide us through uncharted waters or unfamiliar territory. It is dangerous to go-it-alone, probably the reason so many businesses needlessly hit the wall.

A great sports team is no different from a great enterprise; they require coaching that develops the players as individuals, at the same time, building them into a team that has a culture of *we, not me*; where every player is pulling in the same direction. Team spirit is a culture that must be developed and is built primarily by the coach.

Great coaches:

1. A Coach is a skilled communicator

One of the amazing discoveries of recent times concerning the human body is that every cell has the ability to communicate with the other cells throughout the body. Communication is not only vital for the health of our bodies, but any organization or community at so many levels and for a variety of reasons.

Positive communication creates: connection, coordination, cooperation, motivation, innovation, collaboration and inspiration:

Connection happens as people *listen* to each other; the reason we have two ears and one mouth. Business and community is an ecosystem of empowering or disempowering relationships and good communication is how and why strong relationships form.

The most effective communicators are skilled listeners, listening with humility, and by asking the right questions. Listening without interruption, taking the time to think and form a response before replying. It takes practice, but penetrates the surface, and says, "I respect your opinion, you and what you have to say is important to me." The ability to draw the best out in people happens in large part when we engage in active listening. People love to be involved, and they feel involved when we respect their ideas. In fact, some of the major breakthroughs and innovations in many fields of endeavor have come the factory floor, because someone in management took the time to listen.

Coordination and cooperation happens with clear and effective communication. The dictionary says, it's the action or process of working together to the same end; the *cooperation between management and workers*: *collaboration*, working together, joint action, combined effort, teamwork, mutual support, partnership, coordination, liaison, association, synergy, unity, understanding, give and take, and compromise.

Our attitude toward leadership, or the coach, and their attitude toward us is all-important in this process, and affects our ability to hear. For our body to function and achieve top performance, the messages coming from the brain (coach) must be unhindered and precise.

Motivation is released when there is an environment of genuine openness and honesty; people somehow feel the criticisms discussed in secret. People long for real community, where leaders with the skill of a great surgeon point out their strengths and are honest about where they can improve. A clear and consistent communication of the vision and mission in any enterprise is the life-blood that energizes people to pull in the same direction. We need to know why before what and how! Communication gives light; people find it hard and cold being left in the dark, so communicate, communicate, communicate!

Innovation, in my experience, happens best in dialogue with the right group of people. Again, in the proverbs of King Solomon, the key to gaining wisdom or developing our ideas was found in what he called, the *multitude of counselors,* something he reinforced again and again. This can feel like entering a tunnel of chaos to begin with, then as you persist the light at the end of the tunnel appears if you listen carefully and honestly to the right people.

Collaboration is the key to innovation that works, and done well, people buy-in as they engage in the process. The huge leap in innovation in the last ten years has come as a result of the internet, the ability to communicate faster, wider and more effectively than ever. This is the platform for greater scientific, business, and educational collaboration, which leads to breakthroughs in every field of endeavor. To be a collaborator requires keeping an *open mind,* which is all important in a highly complex, fast moving marketplace.

Inspiration recharges the human spirit and motivates us to reach new heights of creative expression. It keeps us strong and motivated at the coalface, where pain and stress can take the wind from our sails. To be inspiring means setting a positive example, speaking life-giving words and encouragement that helps us climb a little higher, and walk a little farther.

Leadership comes in many forms and styles, but the skill of new generation leadership is the art of persuasion and the ability to collaborate. This draws the best out in people and gives them a sense of ownership. Artful communication can help a person re-write their DNA, and reprogram their human spirit away from the limiting scripts of the past, scripts that give a multitude of disruptive messages.

2. A Coach is an effective educator

This involves finding articles, books and videos that are tailor made for the person or team you wish to see grow. Classical education dealt with the development of a person's character and intellect, building the whole person. The Latin root of the word education is found in two words: *Educare*, meaning *to rear or bring up.* The other, *Educere*, meaning *to draw out from within; to lead out of.* Greatness needs nurturing, and must be drawn out of a person. The role of a great coach is to *lead out or to draw out* the brilliance that is hidden within.

Everyone is unique, the only one of their kind, so they need to be treated with dignity and care. It is the skill of a great coach to dig for the gold that is planted deep within a person's mind and spirit. This can be done with the skilled use of words, but when it comes to coaching education, often more is "*caught than taught.*" Both motivation and education must go together in order to draw out the gift within. Telling inspiring stories and clearly communicating complex concepts must become the craft of an effective coach. The teachers that inspired me at school were passionate motivators, and educators. Information, understanding and wisdom all grow a deeper root system, communicated with stories and/or the tales of personal experience.

3. Coaches ask probing questions

Voltaire said we should "judge a man by his questions rather than by his answers," and that is never more true than in the role of coaching.

Aristotle trained Alexander the Great with the use of an educator's most valuable tool: probing, searching and truth revealing questions. The most effective coaches are those who develop effective diagnostic abilities, and thus cut through seemingly complicated situations or complex attitudes, and identify the triggers that will really make a difference. They have an insatiable curiosity – asking the questions that open a person up. The mindset of a coach is not about dispensing advice, it is about helping people tap into and act on their intuition and instinct. Leaders understand they need the right information to make the right decisions. The only way to get it is by asking for it. Thoughtful questions open lines of communication with our teams, our contractors, and most importantly, ourselves.

4. A Coach understands people

There are a number of personality studies in existence, from the four personality types known as; A, B, C, and D; to one of the oldest known, the four personality types or temperaments: *sanguine, choleric, melancholic and phlegmatic.* Understanding these personality types are all helpful when it comes to understanding people.

What are the four main temperament or personality types?

The four main personality types, or temperaments, are sanguine, choleric, melancholic and phlegmatic. Choleric and sanguine personalities are typically more extroverted and outgoing, while melancholic and phlegmatic personalities are introverted and reserved.

- **Sanguine** personalities are impulsive and tend to seek out pleasure and social events. People with this personality type can be forgetful and have difficulty finishing tasks.
- **Choleric** personalities tend to be leaders with passion. One negative quality is a tendency for sudden anger or mood swings.
- **Melancholic** personalities are independent and thoughtful, but they may dwell on the negative aspects of the world around them.
- **Phlegmatic** personalities tend towards being relaxed and showing affection. They also can be lazy or passive-aggressive when dealing with issues.

Most people are a mix of two temperaments, and each are unique due to the multitude of environmental, parental and life experiences we have engaged. For those who have never really understood how the different personalities tick, I have placed a full overview of the four main temperaments in the appendix.

5. A Coach needs a sense of humor

By this I do not mean having to be a great joke teller, I mean that it is important to build a fun and a safe environment in which learners can laugh at themselves. An environment that is up tight and on-edge is counter productive, as it heightens the fear of failure and an openness to new ideas. Confidence is increased when someone who believes in you, stands alongside with both encouraging and correcting comments, but with the ability to point out serious issues with a sense of humor or fun in the mix. This is not to be confused with a cynical tone when communicating or when giving feedback, because it can be perceived as a put down.

6. Coaches build individuals into a team

A group of independent players, no matter how skilled, will never consistently beat the team that is playing as a united force. Remember, business is a team sport, and *team* is *we* not just *me*.

A team culture dose not develop overnight. It starts with a generous attitude toward team mates; generous with compliments and generous with a desire to see them succeed. Teams that have fun together, work harder and more effectively because there is a more relaxed, fearless working environment.

7. A good Coach creates a path to success

Hope is the mental and spiritual fuel needed to head off on a long journey into the future. The word hope means *the positive expectation of good*. So setting goals and creating a map is all-important in generating personal motivation and maintaining a *positive expectation of good*. Research shows that by simply setting a goal you are 90% more likely to achieve it. This is due to the function of the *servo-mechanism*.

Maxwell Maltz in his book *Psycho Cybernetics* utilizes a mechanical perspective of your brain and body's activity to create a new system of thinking and behaving. The book was written by a plastic surgeon turned self-help author, Dr. Maxwell Maltz. This book is a cornerstone of the self-help genre and is full of big ideas that can empower you to create a happier, more successful life. The word "Cybernetics" comes from a Greek word which means literally, "the steersman." Servo-mechanisms are designed so that they automatically "steer" their way toward a goal, target, or answer.

Here's the easiest way to get what *Cybernetics* and what a servo-mechanism is all about: think of how a guided missile works. First: you need to set a target (or "goal"). Then, you launch the missile (take action!). From there, the missile uses its mechanical "senses" (whether that's radar or sonar or heat or whatever) to stay on target (they call it "positive feedback"). When it's not on target, it gets "negative feedback" and simply adjusts its course so it gets BACK on track.

"The science of cybernetics does not tell us that "man" is a machine but that man has and uses a machine. Moreover, it tells us how that machine functions and how it can be used."

"Creative striving for a goal that is important to you as a result of your own deep-felt needs, aspirations and talents brings happiness as well as success because you will be functioning as you were meant to function. Man is by nature a goal-striving being. And because man is "built that way" he is not happy unless he is functioning as he was made to function—as a goal-striver. Thus true success and true happiness not only go together but each enhances the other."

"Whatever your definition of happiness may be you will experience happiness only as you experience more life. More living means among other things more accomplishment, the attainment of worthwhile goals, more love experienced and given, more health and enjoyment, more happiness for both yourself and others."

Pathways are a cluster of goals and tasks, sign posts or markers along the way, that lead to the success of a dream, idea or passion. This map will help a person keep on track and reinforce the *believability* of arriving at their destination. This keeps your goal-seeking device working for you, even when you are asleep.

8. Coaches build a culture of discipline

A team of superstars may have the talent, but without discipline they may be inconsistent and fall apart when it really counts.

A culture of discipline is not always easy to develop within a team, but is like the steel running through the foundations of a building. The culture of discipline within a team builds greater self-discipline in an individual because of the environment of discipline that exists within the unit. Lazy individuals can become disciplined due to the influence and positive environment of the team, on the other hand, disciplined individuals as a result of corrupting peer-pressure and poor role-models, can infect a team with a culture of pessimism and laziness.

When it comes to small business, it is vital to set the standard by example, more than by the rule of law. You are the pace-setter, the DNA, the brand, and the best example of how it should be done! Set a high-standard and a high expectation, more than creating an environment of high control in order to build a high-punching them.

Chapter Twenty Nine
Team up with Empowering Companies

"Do what you do best and outsource the rest."

— Peter Drucker

There are of course many *sole traders* and small businesses that may think that this section on building teams do not apply to them, however most sole traders have what are called *empowering-companies*. Companies they rely on as suppliers, or sub-contractors, who should be treated as employees of sorts due to the fact that they perform similar roles as staff, helping to deliver our products or services.

A major part of developing a property (designing, engineering, surveying, permitting, excavation and then the construction of a building) is about the logistics and empowering companies. The contractors and suppliers of a project can make or break you. We can see them as faceless companies, but they are real people, with emotions, thoughts and personalities unique to them! They are self-conscious, and do not spend their days thinking about making you successful.

If the permits take two months longer than expected, the windows don't arrive on time, or the painters are a month late, all your fine tuned planning can go south. Your budgets and best-laid plans are at the mercy of empowering or disempowering companies (people) – they are a partner in your business, as you may be in others. These relationships are as important as staff, and in many cases more important, as they can cost you far more than a few unproductive workers. Trust equity with employees is built over time and is a relationship – not simply a contract. Time spent investing in this relationship can in the end, save time, heartache and tears, not to mention large amounts of money.

The late Peter Drucker got it right when he said, "Effective leadership is not about making speeches or being liked; leadership is defined by results." As in any relationship, sometimes we need to set boundaries, stand our ground, and demand better performance. In most industries we do have options, so we must be careful not to be *Mr Nice Guy* when a contractor is being slack, costing us a lot of money in the process. I have learned this the hard way, they call it *loyalty to a fault,* where you persist with someone way beyond what is reasonable. A builder that thinks they are beyond the rules set by the city, losing a lot of time by having to undo work because of their stubborn refusal to do things the way the council or city wants them to be done.

Do what you do best and outsource the rest

Outsourcing can offer greater budget flexibility and control. Outsourcing allows organizations to pay for the services and business functions they need, when they need them. It also reduces the need to hire and train specialized staff, brings in fresh engineering expertise, and can reduce capital and operating expenses and risk.

"Do what you do best and outsource the rest" has become an internationally recognized business tagline first coined and developed in the 1990s by the legendary management consultant, Peter Drucker. The slogan was primarily used to advocate outsourcing as a viable business strategy. It has been said that Mr. Drucker began explaining the concept of outsourcing as early as 1989 in his Wall Street Journal article entitled "Sell the Mailroom."

From Drucker's perspective, a company should only seek to subcontract in those areas in which it demonstrates no special ability. The business strategy outlined by his slogan recommended that companies should take advantage of a specialist provider's knowledge and economies of scale to improve performance and achieve the service needed.

In 2009, by way of recognition, Peter Drucker posthumously received a significant honor, when he was inducted into the 'outsourcing hall of fame' for his outstanding work in the field.

In business, outsourcing involves the contracting out of a business processes (and operational), and/or non-core functions (e.g. manufacturing, facility management, call center support) to another party (see also business process outsourcing). The concept "outsourcing" came from the American Glossary 'outside resourcing' and it dates back to at least 1981. Outsourcing sometimes involves transferring employees and assets from one firm to another, but not always. Outsourcing is also the practice of handing over control of public services to private enterprise.

Two organizations may enter into a contractual agreement involving an exchange of services, expertise, and payments. Outsourcing is said to help firms to perform well in their core competencies, fuel innovation, and mitigate a shortage of skill or expertise in the areas where they want to outsource.

In the early 21st century, businesses increasingly outsourced to suppliers outside their own country, sometimes referred to as offshoring or offshore outsourcing. Several related terms have emerged to refer to various aspects of the complex relationship between economic organizations or networks, such as offshoring (relocating a business function to a distant country) near-shoring (transferring a business process to a nearby country), crowdsourcing, multi-sourcing, strategic alliances/strategic partnerships, strategic outsourcing and vested outsourcing.

Digital outsourcing

Many think of outsourcing as it relates to manufacturing (e.g. the "made in China" label on the product you buy). However, outsourcing of white collar work has grown rapidly since the early 21st century. The digital workforce of countries like India and China are only paid a fraction of what would be minimum wage in the US. On average, software engineers are getting paid between 250,000 and 1,500,000 rupees ($4,000 to $23,000) in India as opposed to the $40,000-$100,000 in countries like the USA and Canada.

Unlike outsourced manufacturing, outsourced white collar work offers workers the flexibility to choose their working hours, and which companies to work for. With many individuals telecommuting from home, the companies that require this type of work do not need to allocate additional funds for setting up of office space, management salary, and employee benefits as these individuals are contracted workers.*(Wikipedia, the Free Encyclopedia)*

Pillar Four

The Lawyer

"We don't break the laws of the universe, we break ourselves against them."

—Stephen Covey

What legal structure shall I create?

How do I start a company?

What does the law say about tax?

How do I protect my business idea?

Chapter Thirty
Contracts, Tax and other Good Stuff!

In education around the globe, most governments recognize parents as their child's first teacher. The same is true with legal and accounting issues, you need to be your own first accountant and lawyer. You need to know just enough to keep you safe and to fully benefit from their wisdom, able to ask the intelligent questions.

Launching out into the business universe, you must become well versed in the laws of the land that govern businesses, and that may impact your business in a number of ways. Laws range from the practical through to the ridiculous. In Liverpool for example, it is illegal for a woman to be topless except as a clerk in a tropical fish store. Another British law that takes some working out, "It is illegal not to tell the tax man anything you do not want him to know, but legal not to tell him information you do not mind him knowing." In Ohio, it is illegal to get a fish drunk, and in New York, a fine of $25 can be levied for flirting.

My involvement in property was not only about the challenge of constructing buildings on time and on budget, I had to become a lawyer of sorts, to understand the multitude of laws that relate to tax, subdivisions, resource and building consents, contracts, and the list goes on and on. We have laws that govern companies, property, insurance, insolvency, bankruptcy, maritime, intellectual property, copyrights, trademarks, patents, and art. Laws that regulate stocks, banking, company and personal taxes, use of water, environmental-energy, gas, telecoms, consumers, contracts, pollution, trusts, price fixing and laws that even govern space. This list does not stop here, because new laws and regulations are being introduced daily.

I find many business people at war with the law, frustrated at the huge amount of time it takes to comply with the laws that relate to their enterprise. But by refusing to put our *lawyer hat* on, all of our good work in other areas can come crashing down. Not every small business owner has a degree in law, so must do the research and select a good lawyer. However, every entrepreneur must gain a deeper understanding of the laws that relate to their industry, especially employment law. Entrepreneurs must have the mindset of a lawyer.

You are the first laywer

In education around the globe, most governments recognize parents as the child's first teacher. Government education, funding, and schools, are to be a partner with parents in their child's education. Just as the responsibility of a child's education lies with the parents; the same is true with legal and accounting issues, you need to be the first lawyer and accountant. Gaining an understanding in these vital areas gives you the ability to ask the right questions, and oversee intelligently—you can't oversee what you don't understand! Finding the right lawyer, and accountant, is a high priority. The information they give can make you or break you. In the same way many parents leave the entire education of their children in the hands of government, many small businesses leave a huge part of their business exposed by not understanding enough to oversee them properly.

In essence, legal and accounting firms are empowering companies – professionals that can be of greater value to you if you gain a knowledge of what it is they do. Of course you are not able to know it all, otherwise you would not need them, but just enough to keep you safe and to fully benefit from their wisdom. As the result of an income payment I had received, my accountant was informing me that I would have a tax bill of over $50,000. I asked him a few questions and suggested we do this transaction through another legal entity, which resulted in an apology, and by using the tax losses in another company, I did not have to pay a dime. One of the first things I would ask when interviewing a potential lawyer or accountant would be; what is a list of questions you would ask if you where sitting where I am?

What legal structure shall I create?

Most countries have websites that will give you guidance as to what legal structure may be best for your business. Below are a few of the universal legal structures used in many countries, they may use different wording, but the concepts are often the same.

For example, in the USA in 1958, as a result of the great depression, *Small Business America* was a government initiative to help businesses survive and thrive in the hostile business environment of that time. The learning tools and assistance they give is world class, but requires that you take the time and exercise the discipline to used them. The following information can be found on the Small Business Administration website, and applies to US small business, but the principles are often similar globally. www.sba.gov

The information and the forms you must provide the IRS to report your taxes depend on which business structure you choose. Here is a list of the USA business platforms you may choose to use:
1. Sole Proprietorship
2. Limited Liability Company (LLC)
3. Cooperative
4. Corporation
5. Partnership
6. S Corporation

1. Sole proprietorship

A sole proprietorship is the simplest and most common structure chosen to start a business. It is an unincorporated business owned and run by one individual with no distinction between the business and the owner. You are entitled to all profits and are responsible for all your business debts, losses and liabilities.

Forming a sole proprietorship

No formal action is required to form a sole proprietorship. If you are the only owner, this status automatically comes from your business activities. In fact, you may already own one without knowing it. If you are a freelance graphic designer, for example, you are a sole proprietor.

But like all businesses, you need to obtain the necessary licenses and permits. Regulations vary by industry, state and locality. Refer to this Business Licenses and Permits guide www.sba.gov to find what you'll need to run a business.

If you choose to operate under a name different than your own, you will most likely have to file a fictitious name (also known as an assumed name, trade name, or DBA name, short for doing business as).

Sole proprietor taxes

Because you and your business are one and the same, the business itself is not taxed separately—the sole proprietorship income is your income. Learn more about your tax obligations as a sole proprietor.

Advantages of a sole proprietorship

Easy and inexpensive to form: A sole proprietorship is the simplest and least expensive business structure to establish.

Complete control: Because you are the sole owner of the business, you have complete control over all decisions.

Simplified tax preparation: Your business is not taxed separately, so it is easy to fulfill the tax reporting requirements.

Disadvantages of a sole proprietorship

Unlimited personal liability: Because there is no legal separation between you and your business, you can be held personally liable for the debts and obligations of the business. This risk extends to any liabilities incurred because of employee actions.

Hard to raise money: Sole proprietors often face challenges when trying to raise money. Because you cannot sell stock in the business, investors are less likely to invest. Banks are also hesitant to lend to a sole proprietorship because of a perceived lack of credibility when it comes to repayment if the business fails.

Heavy burden: The flip side of complete control is the burden and pressure it can impose. You alone are ultimately responsible for the successes and failures of your business.

Pay your State income taxes

In addition to federal taxes, your business must also pay state and local taxes (income, sales tax, and property tax). As with the IRS, the legal structure of your business determines your state income tax obligations. Learn more in our State and Local Tax Guide. www.sba.gov

2. Limited Liability Company

A limited liability company (LLC) is a hybrid type of legal structure that provides the limited liability features of a corporation and the tax efficiencies and operational flexibility of a partnership.

The "owners" of an LLC are referred to as "members." Depending on the state, the members can consist of a single individual (one owner), two or more individuals, corporations or other LLCs.

Unlike shareholders in a corporation, LLCs are not taxed as a separate business entity. Instead, all profits and losses are "passed through" the business to each member of the LLC. LLC members report profits and losses on their personal federal tax returns, just like the owners of a partnership would.

Forming an LLC

While each state has slight variations to forming an LLC, they all adhere to some general principles:

Choose a business name: There are three rules that your LLC name needs to follow: (1) it must be different from an existing LLC in your state, (2) it must indicate that it is an LLC (such as "LLC" or Limited Company") and (3) it must not include words restricted by your state (such as "bank" and "insurance"). Your business name is automatically registered with your state when you register your business, so you do not have to go through a separate process.

File the "Articles of Organization": The "articles of organization" is a simple document that legitimizes your LLC and includes information like your business name, address, and the names of its members. For most states, you file with the Secretary of State. However, other states may require that you file with a different office such as the State Corporation Commission, Department of Commerce and Consumer Affairs, Department of Consumer and Regulatory Affairs, or the Division of Corporations & Commercial Code.

Create an operating agreement: Most states do not require operating agreements. However, an operating agreement is highly recommended for multi-member LLCs because it structures your LLC's finances and organization, and provides rules and regulations for smooth operation. The operating agreement usually includes percentage of interests, allocation of profits and losses, member's rights and responsibilities and other provisions.

Obtain licenses and permits: Once your business is registered, you must obtain business licenses and permits. Regulations vary by industry, state and locality. Refer to the *Business License and Permit* guide, www.sba.gov, to find a listing of federal, state and local permits, licenses and registrations you will need to run a business.

Announce Your Business: Some states, including Arizona and New York, require the extra step of publishing a statement in your local newspaper about your LLC formation. Check with your state's business filing office for requirements in your area.

LLC Tax Obligations

In the eyes of the federal government, an LLC is not a separate tax entity, so the business itself is not taxed. Instead, all federal income taxes are passed on to the LLC's members and are paid through their personal income tax. While the federal government does not tax income on an LLC, some states do, so check with your state's income tax agency.

Since an LLC is not recognized as a business entity for taxation purposes, all LLCs must file as a corporation, partnership, or sole proprietorship tax return. Certain LLCs are automatically classified and taxed as a corporation by federal tax law.

Learn more about your tax obligations as an LLC: www.sba.gov

Advantages of an LLC

Limited Liability: Members are protected from personal liability for business decisions or actions of the LLC. This means that if the LLC incurs debt or is sued, members' personal assets are usually exempt. This is like the liability protections afforded to shareholders of a corporation. Keep in mind that limited liability means "limited" liability - members are not necessarily shielded from wrongful acts, including those of their employees.

Less record-keeping: An LLC's operational ease is one of its greatest advantages. Compared to an S-Corporation, there is less registration paperwork and their start-up costs are lower.

Sharing of profits: There are fewer restrictions on profit sharing within an LLC, as members distribute profits as they see fit. Members might contribute different proportions of capital and sweat equity. Consequently, it is up to the members themselves to decide who has earned what percentage of the profits or losses.

Disadvantages of an LLC

Limited Life: In many states, when a member leaves an LLC, the business is dissolved and the members must fulfill all remaining legal and business obligations to close the business. The remaining members can decide if they want to start a new LLC or part ways. However, you can include provisions in your operating agreement to prolong the life of the LLC if a member decides to leave the business.

Self-Employment Taxes: Members of an LLC are considered self-employed and must pay the self-employment tax contributions towards Medicare and Social Security. The entire net income of the LLC is subject to this tax.

Combining the benefits of an LLC with an S Corporation

There is always the possibility of requesting S Corporation status for your LLC. An attorney can advise you on the pros and cons. You will have to make a special election with the IRS to have the LLC taxed as an S Corporation using Form 2553. You must file prior to the first two months and fifteen days of the beginning of the tax year in which the election is to take effect.

The LLC remains a limited liability company from a legal standpoint, but for tax purposes it can be treated as an S corporation. Be sure to contact the state's income tax agency where you plan to file your election form. Ask about the tax requirements and if they recognize elections of other entities (such as the S corporation).

3. Cooperative

A cooperative is a business or organization owned by and operated for the benefit of those using its services. Profits and earnings generated by the cooperative are distributed among the members, also known as *user-owners*.

Typically, an elected board of directors and officers run the cooperative while regular members have voting power to control the direction of the cooperative. Members can become part of the cooperative by purchasing shares, though the amount of shares they hold does not affect the weight of their vote.

Cooperatives are common in the healthcare, retail, agriculture, art and restaurant industries.

Forming a Cooperative

Forming a cooperative is different from forming any other business entity. To start up, a group of potential members must agree on a common need and a strategy on how to meet that need. An organizing committee then conducts exploratory meetings, surveys, and cost and feasibility analyses before every member agrees with the business plan. Not all cooperatives are incorporated, though many choose to do so.

If you decide to incorporate your cooperative, you must complete the following steps:
- File Articles of Incorporation
- Create Bylaws
- Create a Membership Application
- Conduct a Charter Member Meeting and Elect Directors
- Obtain Licenses and Permits

Each state will have slightly different laws that govern a cooperative. Consult an attorney, your Secretary of State or State Corporation Commissioner for more information regarding your state's specific laws.

Cooperative taxes

Most businesses must register with the IRS, state and local revenue agencies, and obtain a tax ID number or permit. A cooperative operates as a corporation and receives a "pass-through" designation from the IRS. More specifically, cooperatives do not pay federal income taxes as a business entity. Instead, the cooperative's members pay federal taxes when they file their personal income tax. Members pay federal and state income tax on the margins earned by the cooperative, though the amount of taxation varies slightly by state. Cooperatives must follow the rules and regulations of the IRS's Subchapter T Cooperatives tax code to receive this type of tax treatment.

Some cooperatives, like credit unions and rural utility cooperatives, are exempt from federal and state taxes due to the nature of their operations. Check with your state's income tax agency for information about state taxes.

Advantages of a Cooperative

Less taxation: Like an LLC, cooperatives that are incorporated normally are not taxed on surplus earnings (or patronage dividends) refunded to members. Therefore, members of a cooperative are only taxed once on their income from the cooperative and not on both the individual and the cooperative level.

Funding opportunities: Depending on the type of cooperative you own or participate in, there are a variety of government-sponsored grant programs to help you start. For example, the USDA Rural Development program offers grants to those establishing and operating new and existing rural development cooperatives.

Reduce costs and improve products and services: By leveraging their size, cooperatives can more easily obtain discounts on supplies and other materials and services. Suppliers are more likely to give better products and services because they are working with a customer of more substantial size. Consequently, the members of the cooperative can focus on improving products and services.

Perpetual existence: A cooperative structure brings less disruption and more continuity to the business. Unlike other business structures, members in a cooperative can routinely join or leave the business without causing dissolution.

Democratic organization: Democracy is a defining element of cooperatives. The democratic structure of a cooperative ensures that it serves its members' needs. The amount of a member's monetary investment in the cooperative does not affect the weight of each vote, so no member-owner can dominate the decision-making process. The "one member-one vote" philosophy particularly appeals to smaller investors because they have as much say in the organization as does a larger investor.

Disadvantages of a Cooperative

Obtaining capital through Investors: Cooperatives may suffer from slower cash flow since a member's incentive to contribute depends on how much they use the cooperative's services and products. While the "one member-one vote" philosophy is appealing to small investors, larger investors may choose to invest their money elsewhere because a larger share investment in the cooperative does not translate to greater decision-making power.

Lack of membership and participation: If members do not fully participate and perform their duties, whether it be voting or carrying out daily operations, then the business cannot operate at full capacity. If a lack of participation becomes an ongoing issue for a cooperative, it could risk losing members.

4. Corporation

A corporation (sometimes referred to as a C corporation) is an independent legal entity owned by shareholders. This means that the corporation itself, not the shareholders that own it, is held legally liable for the actions and debts the business incurs.

Corporations are more complex than other business structures because they tend to have costly administrative fees and complex tax and legal requirements. Because of these issues, corporations are generally suggested for established, larger companies with multiple employees.

For businesses in that position, corporations offer the ability to sell ownership shares in the business through stock offerings. "Going public" through an initial public offering (IPO) is a major selling point in attracting investment capital and high quality employees.

Forming a Corporation

A corporation is formed under the laws of the state in which it is registered. To form a corporation, you will need to establish your business name and register your legal name with your state government. If you choose to operate under a name different than the officially registered name, you will most likely have to file a fictitious name (also known as an assumed name, trade name, or DBA name, short for "doing business as"). State laws vary but generally corporations must include a corporate designation (Corporation, Incorporated, Limited) at the end of the business name.

To register your business as a corporation, you need to file certain documents, typically articles of incorporation, with your state's Secretary of State office. Some states require corporations to establish directors and issue stock certificates to initial shareholders in the registration process. Contact your state business entity registration office to find out about specific filing requirements in the state where you form your business.

Once your business is registered, you must obtain business licenses and permits. Regulations vary by industry, state and locality. Refer to our Business License and Permit guide, www.sba.gov, to find a listing of federal, state and local permits, licenses and registrations you will need to run a business.

If you are hiring employees, read more about federal and state regulations for employers.

Corporation taxes

Corporations are required to pay federal, state, and in some cases, local taxes. Most businesses must register with the IRS and state and local revenue agencies, and receive a tax ID number or permit. Unlike sole proprietors and partnerships, corporations pay income tax on their profits. In some cases, corporations are taxed twice – first, when the company makes a profit, and again when dividends are paid to shareholders on their personal tax returns.

Advantages of a Corporation

Limited liability: When it comes to taking responsibility for business debts and actions of a corporation, shareholders' personal assets are protected. Shareholders can generally only be held accountable for their investment in stock of the company.

Ability to generate capital: Corporations have an advantage when it comes to raising capital for their business—the ability to raise funds through the sale of stock.

Corporate tax treatment: Corporations file taxes separately from their owners. Owners of a corporation only pay taxes on corporate profits paid to them in the form of salaries, bonuses, and dividends, while any additional profits are awarded a corporate tax rate, which is usually lower than a personal income tax rate.

Attractive to potential employees: Corporations are generally able to attract and hire high-quality and motivated employees because they offer competitive benefits and the potential for partial ownership through stock options.

Disadvantages of a Corporation

Time and money: Corporations are costly and time-consuming ventures to start and operate. Incorporating requires start-up, operating and tax costs that most other structures do not require.

Double taxing: In some cases, corporations are taxed twice - first, when the company makes a profit, and again when dividends are paid to shareholders.

Additional paperwork: Because corporations are highly regulated by federal, state, and in some cases local agencies, there are increased paperwork and record-keeping burdens associated with this entity.

5. Partnership

A partnership is a single business where two or more people share ownership. Each partner contributes to all aspects of the business, including money, property, labor or skill. In return, each partner shares in the profits and losses of the business.

Because partnerships entail more than one person in the decision-making process, it is important to discuss a wide variety of issues up front and develop a legal partnership agreement. This agreement should document how future business decisions will be made, including how the partners will divide profits, resolve disputes, change ownership (bring in new partners or buy out current partners) and how to dissolve the partnership. Although partnership agreements are not legally required, they are strongly recommended and it is considered extremely risky to operate without one.

Types of Partnerships

There are three general types of partnership arrangements:

General partnerships: assume that profits, liability and management duties are divided equally among partners. If you opt for an unequal distribution, the percentages assigned to each partner must be documented in the partnership agreement.

Limited partnerships: (also known as a partnership with limited liability) are more complex than general partnerships. Limited partnerships allow partners to have limited liability as well as limited input with management decisions. These limits depend on the extent of each partner's investment percentage. Limited partnerships are attractive to investors of short-term projects.

Joint ventures: act as general partnership, but for only a limited period of time or for a single project. Partners in a joint venture can be recognized as an ongoing partnership if they continue the venture, but they must file as such.

Forming a partnership

To form a partnership, you must register your business with your state, a process generally done through your Secretary of State's office. You will also need to establish your business name. For partnerships, your legal name is the name given in your partnership agreement or the last names of the partners. If you choose to operate under a name different than the officially registered name, you will most likely have to file a fictitious name (also known as an assumed name, trade name, or DBA name, short for "doing business as").

Once your business is registered, you must obtain business licenses and permits. Regulations vary by industry, state and locality. Refer to our Business License and Permit guide to learn more. www.sba.gov

Partnership taxes

Most businesses will need to register with the IRS, register with state and local revenue agencies, and obtain a tax ID number or permit.

A partnership must file an 'annual information return' to report the income, deductions, gains and losses from the business's operations, but the business itself does not pay income tax. Instead, the business "passes through" any profits or losses to its partners. Partners include their respective share of the partnership's income or loss on their personal tax returns.

Advantages of a partnership

Easy and inexpensive: Partnerships are generally an inexpensive and easily formed business structure. The majority of time spent starting a partnership often focuses on developing the partnership agreement.

Shared financial commitment: In a partnership, each partner is equally invested in the success of the business. Partnerships have the advantage of pooling resources to obtain capital. This could be beneficial in terms of securing credit, or by simply doubling your seed money.

Complementary skills: A good partnership should reap the benefits of being able to utilize the strengths, resources and expertise of each partner.

Partnership incentives for employees: Partnerships have an employment advantage over other entities if they offer employees the opportunity to become a partner. Partnership incentives often attract highly motivated and qualified employees.

Disadvantages of a partnership

Joint and individual liability: Like sole proprietorships, partnerships retain full, shared liability among the owners. Partners are not only liable for their own actions, but also for the business debts and decisions made by other partners. In addition, the personal assets of all partners can be used to satisfy the partnership's debt.

Disagreements among partners: With multiple partners, there are bound to be disagreements. Partners should consult each other on all decisions, make compromises, and resolve disputes as amicably as possible.

Shared profits: Because partnerships are jointly owned, each partner must share the successes and profits of their business with the other partners. An unequal contribution of time, effort, or resources can cause discord among partners.

6. S Corporation

An S zvorporation (also referred to as an S Corp) is a special type of corporation created through an IRS tax election. An eligible domestic corporation can avoid double taxation (once to the corporation and again to the shareholders) by electing to be treated as an S Corporation.

An S Corp is a corporation with the Subchapter S designation from the IRS. What makes the S Corp different from a traditional corporation (C corp) is that profits and losses can pass through to your personal tax return. Consequently, the business is not taxed itself. Only the shareholders are taxed. There is an important caveat, however: any shareholder who works for the company must pay him or herself "reasonable compensation." Basically, the shareholder must be paid fair market value, or the IRS might reclassify any additional corporate earnings as "wages."

Forming an S Corporation

To file as an S Corporation, you must first file as a corporation. After you are considered a corporation, all shareholders must sign and file Form 2553. Once your business is registered, you must obtain business licenses and permits. Regulations vary by industry, state and locality. Refer to our Business License and Permit guide to learn more.

Combining the benefits of an LLC with an S Corp

There is always the possibility of requesting S Corp status for your LLC. Your attorney can advise you on the pros and cons. You will have to make a special election with the IRS to have the LLC taxed as an S Corp using Form 2553. And you must file it before the first two months and fifteen days of the beginning of the tax year in which the election is to take effect.

The LLC remains a limited liability company from a legal standpoint, but for tax purposes it is treated as an S Corp. Be sure to contact your state's income tax agency where you will file the election form to learn about tax requirements.

Taxes

All states do not tax S Corps equally. Most recognize them similarly to the federal government and tax the shareholders accordingly. However, some states (like Massachusetts) tax S Corps on profits above a specified limit. Other states do not recognize the S Corp election and treat the business as a C corp with all the tax ramifications. Some states (like New York and New Jersey) tax both the S Corp's profits and the shareholder's proportional shares of the profits.

Advantages of an S Corporation

Tax savings: One of the best features of the S Corp is the tax savings for you and your business. While members of an LLC are subject to employment tax on the entire net income of the business, only the wages of the S Corp shareholder who is an employee are subject to employment tax. The remaining income is paid to the owner as a "distribution," which is taxed at a lower rate, if at all.

Business expense tax credits: Some expenses that shareholder/employees incur can be written off as business expenses. Nevertheless, if such an employee owns 2% or more shares, then benefits like health and life insurance are deemed taxable income.

Independent life: An S Corp designation also allows a business to have an independent life, separate from its shareholders. If a shareholder leaves the company, or sells his or her shares, the S Corp can continue doing business relatively undisturbed. Maintaining the business as a distinct corporate entity defines clear lines between the shareholders and the business that improve the protection of the shareholders.

Disadvantages of an S Corporation

Stricter operational processes: As a separate structure, S Corps require scheduled director and shareholder meetings, minutes from those meetings, adoption and updates to by-laws, stock transfers and records maintenance.

Shareholder compensation requirements: A shareholder must receive reasonable compensation. The IRS takes notice of shareholder red flags like low salary/high distribution combinations, and may reclassify your distributions as wages. You could pay a higher employment tax because of an audit with these results.

Chapter Thirty One
The Law

"Lawless are they that make their wills their law."

— William Shakespeare

Choosing and registering your business name is a key step to legally operating your business and potentially obtaining financial aid from the government. Your business name will frame its identity. There are many factors to choosing your business name. Here are some tips to get started:

Register Your Business Name: After you have selected a name for your business, you will need to register it to comply with the law. Learn more about how to register your business name, and thus protect it.

Register With State Agencies: For some businesses, you need to register your business name with state or local government agency. Find out what the requirements are for your state.

Business licenses and permits

To run your business legally, there are certain federal and state licenses and permits you will need to obtain. These resources will help you understand the requirements for your small business:

Federal Licenses and Permits: Certain businesses, like ones that sell alcohol or firearms, require a federal license or permit. Find out which ones impact your business and how you can comply.

State Licenses and Permits: Some states have requirements for specific businesses. Find out what business licenses and permits you need in your state. www.sba.gov

Learn About Business Laws
As a small business owner, you are subject to some of the laws and regulations that apply to large corporations. These resources can help you understand which requirements do apply to your business. www.sba.gov

Advertising and marketing law

Learn the basic rules when it comes to advertising, labeling and marketing your products or services. Marketing and advertising your products or services effectively is key to the success of your business. However, all businesses have a legal responsibility to ensure that any advertising claims are truthful, not deceptive and that your marketing activities do not break the law.

The Federal Trade Commission (FTC) oversees and regulates advertising and marketing law in the United States. These laws can potentially impact many areas of your business, including how you label your products, how you conduct email and telemarketing campaigns, any health and environmental claims you may make, as well as how you advertise to children. Use FTC resources and guides that can help you understand these laws and how they apply to your business.

Truth in advertising and marketing claims: Refer to this guide to learn how you can ensure your promotional activities are truthful and not deceptive. Areas covered include using endorsements in your marketing, advertising to children, "Made in the USA" labels and health and environmental claims.

Industry guides: The FTC has some rules and compliance guides for specific industries including franchises, real estate, clothing manufacturers, and others. Check out this guide for information on laws that could affect your industry or business type.

Telemarketing: Learn how the National Do Not Call Registry and other laws impact your telemarketing efforts and how to comply.

Email SPAM: Planning an email campaign? The law is very specific on what email you can send and to whom.

Finance law

Learn about the financial laws that protect businesses, investors and customers and how you can comply. Antitrust, bankruptcy, and securities laws protect the financial interests of small businesses and individual investors. In this section, you will find an overview on these important laws and how to comply. If your business is facing bankruptcy, you will also find information on this process.

Intellectual property law

Learn how intellectual property law can protect your business interests and find out how to register a trademark or service mark, file a patent or copyright your work.

If you've got a great idea, logo, business name, or even an invention, you need to protect it. The steps involved in filing for patents, trademarks or copyrights are covered in this section, along with additional resources that can help you safeguard your intellectual properties, such as having employees or vendors sign non-disclosure agreements.

Understand intellectual property and how to protect your business—This business guide from *STOPfakes.gov* is an essential starting point for understanding your intellectual property rights and finding the right protection for your business.

Applying for a patent: Learn more about how to apply for a patent through the *USA Patent and Trademark Office* (USPTO).

Registering a trademark or service mark – Find out how to file for trademark or service mark protection for your business name, symbols and logos.

Copyright your work: Books, movies, digital works, and musical recordings are all examples of copyrighted works. Refer to this guide from *US Copyright Office* for more information on what protection copyright affords and the process of copyrighting your work.

Online business law

Whether selling on *eBay*, or operating an e-commerce site, there are several laws that you must comply with, including how and when to collect sales tax.

Collecting sales tax online

If you run a business with a physical storefront, collecting sales tax is straightforward. You charge your customers the sales tax required by the jurisdiction where your business is located. For example, if you operate a retail store in Nashville, Tennessee, you collect both state and local sales taxes from customers buying merchandise at your store.

But suppose you start selling your products online. Does that mean you charge customers the same sales taxes that you do to those who are coming into your store? It depends.

When to collect sales tax online

If your business has a physical presence in a state, such as a store, office or warehouse, you must collect applicable state and local sales tax from your customers. If you do not have a presence in a particular state, you are not required to collect sales taxes.

In legal terms, this physical presence is known as a *"nexus."* Each state defines nexus differently, but all agree that if you have a store or office of some sort, a nexus exists. If you are uncertain whether or not your business qualifies as a physical presence, contact your state's revenue agency. If you do not have a physical presence in a state, you are not required to collect sales taxes from customers in that state.

This rule is based on a 1992 Supreme Court ruling in which the justices ruled that states cannot require mail-order businesses, and by extension, online retailers, to collect sales tax unless they have a physical presence in the state.

State exemptions

Keep in mind that not every state and locality has a sales tax. Alaska, Delaware, Hawaii, Montana, New Hampshire and Oregon do not have a sales tax. In addition, most states have tax exemptions on certain items, such as food or clothing. If you are charging sales tax, you need be familiar with applicable rates.

Determining which sales tax to charge can be a challenge. Many online retailers use online shopping cart software services to handle their sales transactions. Several of these services are programmed to calculate sales tax rates for you.

International online sales

Selling your products online allows for immediate entry into the global marketplace. However, shipping your product overseas presents a few challenges if you have little experience with taxes, duties, customs laws, and consumer protection issues involved with international commerce.

If you are just getting started, the following resources will help you to understand legal and regulatory requirements when shipping overseas:

Export.gov—E-Commerce toolbox: This site brings together information and resources the US Department of Commerce and other US government agencies offer to US businesses interested in using the Internet to export their products.

Electronic Commerce—Selling internationally: A Guide for Business—As members of the Organization for Economic Cooperation and Development, the United States and 28 other countries have signed on to guidelines that help protect consumer information on the Internet.

Privacy law

For many companies, collecting sensitive consumer and employee information is an essential part of doing business. It is your legal responsibility to take steps to properly secure or dispose of it. Financial data, personal information from children, and material derived from credit reports may raise additional compliance considerations. In addition, you may have legal responsibilities to victims of identity theft.

The Federal Trade Commission (FTC) regulates and oversees business privacy laws and policies that impact consumers. Check out the following guides from more information on how you can ensure you are compliant.

Protecting consumer privacy: In general, your online and offline privacy policy is your company's pledge to your customers about how you will collect, use, share, and protect the consumer data you collect from them. While not required by law, the FTC prohibits deceptive practices. Learn more in this FTC guide and read "7 Considerations for Crafting an Online Privacy Policy" to help you develop yours.

Protecting children's privacy online: The law sets out specific guidelines about the online collection of personal information from children under 13.

Using and disposing of consumer and employee credit reports: Does your business use consumer or credit reports to evaluate customers' creditworthiness? Do you consult reports when evaluating applications for jobs, leases, and insurance? Learn more about your responsibilities for handling this data.

Enforcing data security and preventing identity theft: If you keep sensitive personal information about customers or employees in your files, you are required to have a sound security plan in place to collect only what you need, keep it safe, and dispose of it securely. Develop your plan with help from this FTC guide.

Safeguarding sensitive financial data: Do you offer your customers financial products or services, like loans, investment advice, or insurance? Learn how to comply with information-sharing practices to safeguard sensitive data.

Environmental regulations

Laws to protect the environment could impact your small business. Environmental regulations can impact a business at any time. Whether you produce products that could potentially harm the environment, are engaged in agricultural farming, or need to dispose of pollutants or hazardous or non-hazardous waste – you must comply with the law.

Businesses impacted by disasters such as flooding or fire, are also required to implement clean up plans to avoid pollutants entering and damaging the ecosystem.

The Environmental Protection Agency (EPA) and state agencies enforce environmental laws. To find out what laws impact your business and how you can comply, check out the resources below:

EPA environmental laws and regulations: Search laws and compliance guides by topic and industry.

EPA Small Business guide: Learn more about the laws that apply specifically to small businesses.

State environmental laws: For information about federal laws that apply in your state, as well as links to your state government website for state-specific laws.

Regulation of financial contracts

If you are conducting business transactions outside of your state, such as borrowing money, leasing equipment, establishing contracts and selling goods, you need to comply with the Uniform Commercial Code (UCC). UCC consists of uniform rules coordinating and simplifying the sale of goods and other commercial transactions throughout the United States.

Commercial transactions often occur across state lines. Goods, for example, may be manufactured in one state, distributed in another and sold to a customer in a third state. Banking and credit transactions often occur between financial institutions in one state and customers in another state.

For small businesses, UCC comes into effect when borrowing money from an out of state lender or negotiating a lien. Here is what you need to know:

Borrowing money: UCC Filing Statements – The Uniform Commercial Code or UCC, as it relates to lending, is a way for each state to have a consistent method of recording the security of a loan. When banks or Small Business Administration (SBA) lenders make secured loans, or loans with collateral, they file a UCC-1 form with the state where the loan agreement is executed. This filing essentially makes the loan security, or collateral, a matter of public record. Without this filing, a lender could run into difficulties, laying claim to the collateral in case of default. Talk to your lender about the process of filing a UCC-1 form.

Securing liens and the UCC – If your business provides goods or services on credit, Article 9 of the UCC provides a means for you to secure payment from your debtor. If you are in the construction business, the equivalent law is called a construction lien. Visit your state's website for information on filing a lien or finance statement to ensure payment of credit under these laws.

Remember that laws vary from state to state, so you should consult an attorney on matters concerning UCC filings, liens and security agreements.

Chapter Thirty Two
Employment and Labor Law

The workers of the future need to posess an entrepreneurial mindset. This mindset is a set of core characteristics or concepts that give them the X factor. Entrepreneurial workers are optimistic thinkers, idea generators, innovative designers, with a clear vision of the future without allowing a lack of resource or fear to dominate their thinking.

Hiring your first employee or building your business team brings with it a whole new area of compliance– employment and labor law. Labor laws cover everything from preventing discrimination and harassment in the workplace, workplace poster requirements, wage and hour laws and workers compensation regulations. The U.S. Department of Labor oversees federal employment and labor law; however, individual states also have their own specific laws. To help you understand and comply with these laws, refer to the following small business guides and resources.

Find out which Federal Employment Laws Apply to Your Business: This online tool from the Department of Labor—the *"FirstStep Employment Law Advisor"*—can help you determine which laws apply to you and how to comply.

State Labor Laws: Each state has its own laws with which you must comply. This site includes links to your state labor office.

Browse Laws by Category: Get easy-to-understand information about a number of federal employment laws using the "eLaws" online tool from the Department of Labor.

Employment Law Guide: This comprehensive guide describes major employment laws that impact businesses and is designed for those needing "hands-on" information to develop wage, benefit, safety and health, and nondiscrimination policies.

9 Steps to hiring your first employee

These 9 easy steps will guide you through what you need to do when you hire your first employee. US Department of Labor website www.dol.gov

Summary of the major laws of the Department of Labor

The Department of Labor (DOL) administers and enforces more than 180 federal laws. These mandates and the regulations that implement them cover many workplace activities for about 10 million employers and 125 million workers. These things include:
- Wages and Hours
- Workplace Safety and Health
- Workers' Compensation

- Employee Benefits
- Unions and Their Members
- Employee Protection
- Uniformed Services Employment and Reemployment Rights Act
- Employee Polygraph Protection Act
- Garnishment of Wages
- The Family and Medical Leave Act
- Veterans' Preference
- Government Contracts, Grants, or Financial Aid
- Migrant & Seasonal Agricultural Workers
- Mine Safety & Health
- Construction
- Transportation
- Plant Closings & Layoffs
- Posters
- Related Agencies

Workplace safety and health law

Learn more about a variety of tools, guides and training materials that can help you comply with occupational safety and health laws.

As a small business owner, providing workers with a safe and healthy workplace is critical to the wellbeing of your employees and the success of your business – but it is also the law. Under the Occupational Safety and Health Act (OSHA), employers must provide a workplace free from recognized hazards that cause, or are likely to cause, death or serious physical harm to their employees.

The following workplace safety and health resources from the *U.S. Department of Labor's Occupational Safety and Health Administration* will help you understand requirements that apply to your business and how to comply:

Find the Workplace Health and Safety Requirements that Apply to You: Follow this step-by-step guide to pinpoint which OSHA requirements apply to your workplace and how you can comply.

Request an On-Site Consultation Service: Get free advice from trained state government staff at your place of work.

State-Specific Requirements: Some states do operate their own job safety and health programs. Check to see which states have OSHA-approved plans and the standards they mandate.

Training and Educational Programs: Take advantage of a wide selection of training courses and educational programs offered by the Occupational Safety and Health Administration (OSH4) for employers.

Foreign workers and employee eligibility

Be sure to understand all laws and regulations about employee eligibility as you prepare to hire employees.

Hire your first employee

If your business is booming, but you are struggling to keep up, perhaps it is time to hire some help. The nine steps below can help you start the hiring process and ensure you are compliant with key federal and state regulations.

Step one: Obtain an employer identification number (EIN)

Before hiring your first employee, you need to get an employment identification number (EIN) from the U.S. Internal Revenue Service. The EIN is often referred to as an Employer Tax ID or as Form SS-4. The EIN is necessary for reporting taxes and other documents to the IRS. In addition, the EIN is necessary when reporting information about your employees to state agencies. Apply for EIN online or contact the IRS at 1-800-829-4933.

Step two: Set up records for withholding taxes

According to the IRS, you must keep records of employment taxes for at least four years. Keeping good records can also help you monitor the progress of your business, prepare financial statements, identify sources of receipts, keep track of deductible expenses, prepare your tax returns, and support items reported on tax returns.

Below are three types of withholding taxes you need for your business:

Federal income tax withholding
Every employee must provide an employer with a signed withholding exemption certificate (Form W-4) on or before the date of employment. The employer must then submit Form W-4 to the IRS.

Federal wage and tax statement
Every year, employers must report to the federal government wages paid and taxes withheld for each employee. This report is filed using Form W-2, wage and tax statement. Employers must complete a W-2 form for each employee who they pay a salary, wage or other compensation. Employers must send Copy A of W-2 forms to the Social Security Administration by the last day of February to report wages and taxes of your employees for the previous calendar year. In addition, employers should send copies of W-2 forms to their employees by January 31 of the year following the reporting period. Visit SSA.gov/employer for more information.

State taxes
Depending on the state where your employees are located, you may be required to withhold state income taxes.

Step three: Employee eligibility verification

Federal law requires employers to verify an employee's eligibility to work in the United States. Within three days of hire, employers must complete Form I-9, employment eligibility verification, which requires employers to examine documents to confirm the employee's citizenship or eligibility to work in the U.S. Employers can only request documentation specified on the I-9 form.

Employers do not need to submit the I-9 form with the federal government but are required to keep them on file for three years after the date of hire or one year after the date of the employee's termination, whichever is later. Employers can use information taken from the Form I-9 to electronically verify the employment eligibility of newly hired employees by registering with E-Verify. Visit the US Immigration and Customs Enforcement agency's I-9 website to download the form and find more information.

Step four: Register with your State's new hire reporting program

All employers are required to report newly hired and re-hired employees to a state directory within 20 days of their hire or rehire date. Visit the New Hires Reporting Requirements page to learn more and find links to your state's New Hire Reporting System.

Step five: Obtain workers' compensation insurance

All businesses with employees are required to carry workers' compensation insurance coverage through a commercial carrier, on a self-insured basis or through their state's Workers' Compensation Insurance program.

Step six: Post required notices

Employers are required to display certain posters in the workplace that inform employees of their rights and employer responsibilities under labor laws. Visit the Workplace Posters page for specific federal and state posters you will need for your business.

Step seven: File your taxes

Generally, employers who pay wages subject to income tax withholding, Social Security and Medicare taxes must file IRS Form 941, Employer's Quarterly Federal Tax Return. For more information, visit *IRS.gov*.

New and existing employers should consult the IRS Employer's Tax Guide to understand all their federal tax filing requirements. Visit the state and local tax page for specific tax filing requirements for employers.

Step eight: Get organized and keep yourself informed

Being a good employer doesn't stop with fulfilling your various tax and reporting obligations. Maintaining a healthy and fair workplace, providing benefits and keeping employees informed about your company's policies are key to your business success. Step nine outlines additional steps you should take after you've hired your first employee:

Step nine: Set up record-keeping

In addition to requirements for keeping payroll records of your employees for tax purposes, certain federal employment laws also require you to keep records about your employees. The following sites provide more information about federal reporting requirements:
- Tax record-keeping guidance
- Labor record-keeping requirements
- Occupational Safety and Health Act compliance
- Apply Standards that protect employee rights. Complying with standards for employee rights in regards to equal opportunity and fair labor standards is a requirement.

- Following statutes and regulations for minimum wage, overtime, and child labor will help you avoid error and a lawsuit. See the Department of Labor's Employment Law Guide for up-to-date information on these statutes and regulations.

Also, visit the Equal Employment Opportunity Commission and Fair Labor Standards Act.

Chapter Thirty Three
Hiring a Contractor or Employee

"Do unto others as you would have them do unto you."

— Jesus Christ

Independent contractors and employees are not the same, and it is important to understand the difference. Knowing this distinction could save you money on taxes and legal fees. Independent contractors and employees are not the same, and it is important to understand the difference. This distinction will help you determine what your first hiring move will be and affect how you withhold a variety of taxes and avoid costly legal consequences. sba.gov

What is the difference?

An independent contractor:
- Operates under a business name
- Has his/her own employees
- Maintains a separate business checking account
- Advertises his/her business' services
- Invoices for work completed
- Has more than one client
- Has own tools and sets own hours
- Keeps business records

An employee:
- Performs duties dictated or controlled by others
- Is given training for work to be done
- Works for only one employer

Many small businesses rely on independent contractors for their staffing needs. There are many benefits to using contractors over hiring employees:
- Savings in labor costs
- Reduced liability
- Flexibility in hiring and firing

Why does it matter?

Misclassification of an individual as an independent contractor may have a number of costly legal consequences.

If your independent contractor is discovered to meet the legal definition of an employee, you may be required to:
- Reimburse them for wages you should have paid them under the Fair Labor Standards Act, including overtime and minimum wage.
- Pay back taxes and penalties for federal and state income taxes, Social Security, Medicare and unemployment.
- Pay any misclassified injured employees workers' compensation benefits.
- Provide employee benefits, including health insurance, retirement, etc.

Tax requirements
Visit the IRS Independent Contractor or Employee guide to learn about the tax implications of either scenario, download and fill out a form to have the IRS officially determine your workers' status, and find other related resources.

Employment information

There is no single test for determining if an individual is an independent contractor or an employee under the Fair Labor Standards Act.

However, the following guidelines should be taken into account:
- The extent to which the services rendered are an integral part of the principal's business.
- The permanency of the relationship.
- The amount of the alleged contractor's investment in facilities and equipment.
- The nature and degree of control by the principal.
- The alleged contractor's opportunities for profit and loss.
- The amount of initiative, judgment, or foresight in open market competition with others that is required for the success of the claimed independent contractor.
- The degree of independent business organization and operation.
- Whether a person is an independent contractor or an employee generally depends on the amount of control exercised by the employer over the work being done.
- Read Equal Employment Opportunity Laws: Who's Covered? for more information on how to determine whether a person is an independent contractor or an employee, and which are covered under federal laws.

Pre-employment background checks

Before hiring employees, you may want to get more information about candidates to help you make an informed decision. Learn what types of information you can use for background checks.

The following list includes the types of information that employers often consult as part of a pre-employment check, and the laws governing access and use for making hiring decisions:

Credit Reports
Under the Fair Credit Reporting Act (FCRA), businesses must obtain an employee's written consent before seeking an employee's credit report. If you decide not to hire or promote someone based on information in the credit report, you must provide a copy of the report

and let the applicant know of his or her right to challenge the report under the FCRA. Visit the FTC's Bureau of Consumer Protection's website for more information.

Criminal records
To what extent a private employer may consider an applicant's criminal history in making hiring decisions varies from state to state. Because of this variation, you should consult with a lawyer or do further legal research on the laws of your state before exploring whether or not an applicant has a criminal past.

For Federal Bureau of Investigation (FBI) checks, consult these resources:
- FBI Services for Businesses
- FBI Criminal History Checks for Employment and Licensing
- FBI Checks on Employees of Banks and Related Entities
- Lie Detector Tests

The Employee Polygraph Protection Act prohibits most private employers from using lie detector tests, either for pre-employment screening or during the course of employment. The law includes a list of exceptions that apply to businesses that provide armored car services, alarm or guard services, or those that manufacture, distribute, or dispense pharmaceuticals. Even though there is no federal law specifically prohibiting you from using a written honesty test on job applicants, these tests frequently violate federal and state laws that protect against discrimination and violations of privacy.

Medical records
Under the Americans with Disabilities Act, employers cannot discriminate based on a physical or mental impairment or request an employee's medical records. Businesses can, however, inquire about an applicant's ability to perform specific job duties. Some states also have stronger laws protecting the confidentiality of medical records.

Bankruptcies
Bankruptcies are a matter of public record and may appear on an individual's credit report. The Federal Bankruptcy Act prohibits employers from discriminating against applicants because they have filed for bankruptcy.

Military service
Military service records may be released only under limited circumstances, and consent is generally required. The military may, however, disclose name, rank, salary, duty assignments, awards and duty status without the service member's consent.

School records
Under the Family Educational Rights and Privacy Act and similar state laws, educational records such as transcripts, recommendations and financial information are confidential and will not be released by the school without a student's consent.

Workers' compensation records
Workers' compensation appeals are a matter of public record. Information from a workers' compensation appeal may be used in a hiring decision if the employer can show the applicant's injury might interfere with his ability perform required duties.

Required employee benefits
Find out what employee benefit plan managers need to know so your small business complies with federal law. Employee benefits play an important role in the lives of employees

as well as their families. For that reason, the benefits you offer can be a deciding factor for a potential employee's decision to work at your business.

There are two types of employee benefits the employer must provide by law and those the employer offers as an option to compensate employees. Examples of required benefits include Social Security and workers' compensation, while optional benefits include health care insurance coverage and retirement benefits. Both required and optional benefits have legal and tax implications for the employer.

This guide helps employers understand what they need to do to supply employee benefits required by law:

Social Security taxes
Every employer must pay Social Security taxes at the same rate paid by their employees.

The following sites from the *Social Security Administration* can help you comply:
- Information and Resources for Employers
- Social Security: Business Services Online
- Employer W-2 Filling Instructions and Information
- Instructions for Hiring Employees Not Covered by Social Security
- Unemployment Insurance

Businesses with employees may be required to pay unemployment insurance taxes. If your business is required to pay these taxes, you must register with your state's workforce agency, which can be found on our State and Local Tax page.

Workers compensation
Businesses with employees are required to carry Workers' Compensation Insurance coverage through a commercial carrier, on a self-insured basis, or through the state Workers' Compensation Insurance program. Visit the Workers' Compensation page for more information.

Disability insurance
The following states and territories require businesses to provide partial wage replacement insurance coverage to their eligible employees for non-work related sickness or injury:
- California
- Hawaii
- New Jersey
- New York
- Puerto Rico
- Rhode Island

Leave benefits
The majority of common leave benefits offered by employers are not required by federal law, and are offered to employees as part of the employer's overall compensation and benefits plan. These leave benefits include holiday/vacation, jury duty, personal leave, sick leave and funeral/bereavement leave. However, employers are required to provide leave under the Family and Medical Leave Act (FMLA).

Family and medical leave
- The Family and Medical Leave Act (FMLA) entitles employees to have up to 12 weeks of job-protected, unpaid leave during any 12-month period for any of the following reasons:

- Birth and care of the eligible employee's child, or placement for adoption or foster care of a child with the employee.
- Care of an immediate family member (spouse, child, parent) who has a serious health condition.
- Care of the employee's own serious health condition.
- FMLA requires group health benefits to be maintained during the leave as if employees continued to work instead of taking leave.
- FMLA applies to private employers with 50 or more employees, and to all public employers. Visit the Department of Labor's website for more information.

Optional employee benefits

In addition to required employee benefits, businesses can provide optional benefits and incentives that can improve the lives of their employees and families.

This guide will help explain legal and tax implications of these benefits and highlight some common employee incentive programs:

- Health Plans
- Group health plans - Businesses that offer group health plans must comply with a federal law. Visit DOL's Health Benefits Advisor interactive website for a step-by-step guide on how to determine which laws apply to your business.

Affordable Health Care Act
The Affordable Health Care Act aims to lower health care costs for small business owners and expand coverage options for employees. To learn about the Small Business Health Care Tax Credit and find more resources about the law, visit the Health Care and Health Care Reform page.

A small investment in providing incentive programs for your employees can pay large dividends. These programs can help boost morale through engagement and reward, stimulate productivity and encourage group participation in your business success.

The following are just a few of many incentive programs your small business can offer employees:

Flex time: One of the biggest reasons work-at-home business owners enjoy what they do is not necessarily that they are their own boss, but that they can work the hours that work for them. Likewise, offering the opportunity for flexible hours can be a great incentive for attracting and retaining high performing and motivated employees.

Family events: Your business success depends not only on your employees, but also the support of their families. Plan company functions and events that are oriented towards employees and their families such as picnics, movie nights, take your child to work days - the choice is yours and does not need to break the bank.

Project completion perks: Incentivizing employees for goal-oriented project completion is a great way to build a team but also to engage and stimulate your employees to support your business objectives. This can involve recognizing individual achievement or team success. Consider catered lunches, on-site massage therapy, and other perks to keep employees motivated as they work towards a team goal.

Workplace wellness programs: What better way to show your investment in your employees than to help them invest in their wellness? And it does not have to involve a great deal of money or administrative work. Survey your employees' wellness priorities—

whether it's losing weight, quitting smoking, or enhancing the workplace team environment. From there, compile a calendar or schedule of activities. Wellness initiatives can also be tied to incentives and perks. Incentivize employees to quit smoking by offering a prize or bonus to those who quit or look for ways to encourage other healthy lifestyle choices such as introducing a 30-minute lunchtime team walk.

Corporate memberships: Discounted or free corporate memberships can help promote employee wellbeing (e.g. gym memberships) while also enabling and promoting company goals. Recreational or entertainment memberships can act as venues for client entertainment and can be tax deducted.

Writing effective job descriptions
Job descriptions ensure employees understand the roles and responsibilities associated with their position. Job descriptions are an essential part of hiring and managing your employees. These written summaries ensure your applicants and employees understand their roles and what they need to do to be held accountable. www.sba.gov

Job descriptions also:
- Help attract the right job candidates.
- Describe the major areas of an employee's job or position.
- Serve as a major basis for outlining performance expectations, job training, job evaluation and career advancement.
- Provide a reference point for compensation decisions and unfair hiring practices.

Overview
A job description should be practical, clear and accurate to effectively define your needs. Good job descriptions typically begin with a careful analysis of the important facts about a job such as:
- Individual tasks involved
- The methods used to complete the tasks
- The purpose and responsibilities of the job
- The relationship of the job to other jobs
- Qualifications needed for the job

What to avoid
Don't be inflexible with your job description. Jobs are subject to change for personal growth, organizational development and/or evolution of new technologies. A flexible job description encourages employees to grow within their position and contribute over time to your overall business.

Job descriptions typically include:
- Job title
- Job objective or overall purpose statement
- Summary of the general nature and level of the job
- Description of the broad function and scope of the position
- List of duties or tasks performed critical to success
- Key functional and relational responsibilities in order of significance
- Description of the relationships and roles within the company, including supervisory positions, subordinating roles and other working relationships.
- Additional Items for Job Descriptions for Recruiting Situations
- Job specifications, standards, and requirements
- Job location where the work will be performed

- Equipment to be used in the performance of the job
- Collective Bargaining Agreements if your company's employees are members of a union.
- Salary range
- Proper Language in the Job Description

Keep each statement in the job description crisp and clear:
Structure your sentences in classic verb/object and explanatory phrases. Since the occupant of the job is the subject of your sentence, it may be eliminated. For example, a sentence pertaining to the description of a receptionist position might read: "Greets office visitors and personnel in a friendly and sincere manner."

Always use the present tense of verbs.

If necessary, use explanatory phrases telling why, how, where, or how often to add meaning and clarity (e.g. "Collects all employee time sheets on a bi-weekly basis for payroll purposes.")

Omit any unnecessary articles such as "a," "an," "the," or other words for an easy-to-understand description.

Use unbiased terminology. For example, use the he/she approach or construct sentences in such a way that gender pronouns are not required.

Avoid using adverbs or adjectives that are subject to interpretation such as "frequently," "some," "complex," "occasional," and "several."

Employee handbooks

An employee handbook is the most important communication tool between you and your employees. The points below outline how to write one that properly sets expectations for those who work for your small business.

A well-written handbook sets forth your expectations for your employees, and describes what they can expect from your company. It also should describe your legal obligations as an employer, and your employees' rights. This guide will help you write an employee handbook, which typically includes the topics below:

Non-Disclosure Agreements (NDAs) and Conflict of Interest Statements
Although NDAs are not legally required, having employees sign NDAs and conflict of interest statements helps to protect your trade secrets and company proprietary information.

Anti-Discrimination Policies
As a business owner, you must comply with the equal employment opportunity laws prohibiting discrimination and harassment, including the Americans with Disabilities Act. Employee handbooks should include a section about these laws, and how your employees are expected to comply.

Compensation
Clearly explain to your employees that your company will make required deductions for federal and state taxes, as well as voluntary deductions for the company's benefits programs. In addition, you should outline your legal obligations regarding overtime pay, pay schedules, performance reviews, salary increases, time keeping records, breaks and bonuses.

Work schedules
Describe your company's policies regarding work hours and schedules, attendance, punctuality and reporting absences, along with guidelines for flexible schedules and telecommuting.

Standards of conduct
Document your expectations of how you want your employees to conduct themselves including dress code and ethics. In addition, remind your employees of their legal obligations, especially if your business is engaged in an activity that is regulated by the government.

General employment information
Your employee handbook should include an a overview of your business and general employment policies covering employment eligibility, job classifications, employee referrals, employee records, job postings, probationary periods, termination and resignation procedures, transfers and relocation, and union information, if applicable.

Visit the following areas for more information:
- Employment & Labor Laws
- Foreign Workers, Immigration and Employee Eligibility
- Performing Pre-Employment Background Checks
- Terminating Employees
- Unions

Safety and security
Describe your company's policy for creating a safe and secure workplace, including compliance with the Occupational Safety and Health Administration's laws that require employees to report all accidents, injuries, potential safety hazards, safety suggestions and health and safety related issues to management.

Safety policies should also include your company's policy regarding bad weather and hazardous community conditions.

Add your commitment to creating a secure work environment, and your employee's responsibility for abiding by all physical and information security policies, such as locking file cabinets or computers when not in use.

The *Workplace Safety & Health guide* provides information on your legal requirements as an employer.

Computers and technology
Outline policies for appropriate computer and software use, and steps employees should take to secure electronic information, especially any personal identifiable information you collect from your customers. Visit the Information Security page related to privacy for more information on your legal requirements as a business owner.

Media relations
It is a good business practice to have a single point of contact for all media inquiries. Your employee handbook should include a section that explains how your employees should handle calls from reporters or other media inquiries.

Employee benefits
Make sure to detail any benefit programs and eligibility requirements, including all benefits that may be required by law.

This section should also outline your plans for optional benefits such as health insurance, retirement plans and wellness programs.

Leave policies

Your company's leave policies should be carefully documented, especially those you are required to provide by law. Family medical leave, jury duty, military leave, and time off for court cases and voting should all be documented to comply with state and local laws. In addition, you should explain your policies for vacation, holiday, bereavement and sick leave.

What does the law say about tax?

Again, in most countries, this information can be found on their government business development or tax related websites. This has already been covered in part under the types of legal structure available, but is worth covering again independently.

Pay your State income taxes

In addition to federal taxes, in the US, your business must also pay state and local taxes (income, sales tax, and property tax). As with the IRS, the legal structure of your business determines your state income tax obligations. Learn more in SBA State and Local Tax Guide.www.sba.gov

Determine your Federal tax obligations

Your federal tax obligations, the tax you pay to the IRS, is determined by the form of business entity that you establish (e.g. sole proprietorship, partnership, LLC). These taxes include:

Income tax

- Self-employment tax (Social Security and Medicare taxes)
- Estimated tax (a pay-as-you-go tax)
- Employer tax (such as withholding tax)
- Excise tax
- Find the Right Tax Form.

International

Most countries have websites with search engines that make it easier than ever to research law that relates to your business, but many do not do their homework, at great cost at times. For example, if I wish to start or purchase a business in New Zealand I would go to business.govt.nz and find everything I need to know about doing business as it relates to New Zealand:

New Zealand Business law:

Manufacturers and importers:

Retailers
Internet traders
Motor vehicle traders
Financial service providers
Understanding the Fair Trading Act
Understanding the Consumer Guarantees Act

Health and safety:

Health and safety 101
Keeping your business healthy and safe
Creating an H&S culture
H&S advice and WorkSafe visits

The environment:
Resource Management Act for business
Sustainability
Understanding Eco-labels and sustainability claims

Importing and exporting:
Overview of importing & exporting regulations
Importers and customs
Going out of New Zealand for business purposes
What biosecurity means for importers

Employment regulations:
New Zealand employment legislation
Minimum pay
The Employment Relations Act for employers
How does the Privacy Act apply to my business?

Regulatory authorities:
For the environment
For electricity and gas
For importing and exporting
For telecommunications

Pillar Five
The Accountant

"The bottom line of every enterprise is to create a customer loving, profit generating, lifestyle masterpiece."

—A J Walton

What is the bottom-line?

How do you do the accounting?

What about tax?

How do you read financial statements?

How do I develop a cash flow analysis?

Chapter Thirty Four
What is the Bottom Line?

When thinking about the enterprise ecosystem we need to ask ourselves the big philosophical question; "is the bottom line of my business all about making money?"

Although to succeed in business means generating a profit, we must not put the cart before the horse, because to make a profit we must first give the customer exactly what they need or want.

Innovation, when it comes to a new or existing enterprise, should firstly add value to the *customer* in some department of their lives. Value, broadly defined touches on a number of areas in a persons' life: social value, intellectual value, cultural value, spiritual value, and material value. A dominant belief that has taken root in the thinking of many, is that business is purely about making a profit. However, making money is a byproduct, not the first focus. We must first add as much value as possible to someone's life. The more value you create for your customers, the more they will reward you. This includes secondly, adding value to your employees as well, as they can make or break your business. Business is a value add preposition!

This concept of *value-added* must be included in our bottomline thinking, and goes hand in hand with making a profit. Remember also, if we make a profit, we ensure that we add ongoing value to our workers and their families, another vital component in our bottom-line equation.

A speaker I once heard, with the unusual name of Zig Ziggler, put the bottom-line in context when he said, "We will always have what we want in life, if we first help enough people get what they want." The bottomline in business is said to be a profit, however on the same line we must include the goal of helping people get what they want! In order to make a profit we must sell what people want. We must add value to their lives.

In her book, *Secrets of Online Entrepreneurs*, Bernadette Schwerdt gives some good advice: "before starting out in our new venture, we must first ask the big why question, why do I want to go into business? For passion or profit, for lifestyle or to make as much money as I can? What's my vision?"

Bernadette then relays a thought provoking story of a Greek fisherman with a healthy world view:

"There was a boat docked in a tiny Greek village. A man in a business suit complimented the Greek fisherman on the quality of his fish and asked how long it took him to catch them.

'Not very long', answered the fisherman.

'But then, why didn't you stay out longer and catch more?' asked the businessman.

The fisherman explained that his small catch was sufficient to meet his needs and those of his family.

The businessman asked, 'But what do you do with the rest of your time?'

'I sleep late, fish a little, play with my children and take a nap with my wife. In the evening, I go to the village to see my friends, have a few glasses of ouzo, sing a few songs and dance all night...I have a full life.'

The man interrupted, Sir, I have an MBA and can help you. You should fish more, and with the proceeds buy a bigger boat. In no time you could have several boats and eventually you would have a fleet. Then, instead of selling your catch to the middleman, you could sell directly to the customers. You can then leave this little village and move to Athens, London or even New York City! From there you can direct your huge enterprise.'

'How long would that take?' asked the fisherman.

'Twenty, perhaps twenty-five years,' replied the man.

'And after that?'

'Afterwards? That's when it really gets interesting,' answered the businessman laughing. 'When your business gets really big, you can start selling online to an international audience, launch an IPO and make millions!'

'Millions? Really? And after that?'

'After that you'll be able to retire, live in a tiny village near the coast, sleep late, fish a little, play with your children and take a nap with your wife. In the evening you go to the village and visit your friends, have a few glasses of ouzo, sing a few songs and dance all night... you can have a full life.'

Henry David Thoreau said, "Many men go fishing all of their lives without knowing that it is not fish that they are after."

The truth is that if you put your relationships and family first you may end up with both, a great lifestyle and an international business, but not at the expense of your true wealth - family and friends!

To quote WeWorks mission statement again, "To create a world where people work to make a life, not just a living."

Warren Buffett said, "it's kind of crazy to spend your life painting a painting you don't want to look at! I've got to paint my own painting in business, I've built the life I like...

He also says, you don't want to sleep walk through life, the important thing to do, is to take the job you would take if you didn't need a job."

This is the man that, as of 2016, has given away $24.3 billion worth of Berkshire Hathaway stock. The remaining shares are currently worth over $63 billion. (After applying compound interest, the total value would be over $100 billion.)

So what is the bottomline again?

1. Adding real value to a customer.
2. Generating value for yourself and the team—a profit.
3. Creating a lifestyle and serving a need or vision bigger than yourself.

Chapter Thirty Five
How do I do the Accounting?

"I will tell you how to become rich. Close the doors! Be fearful when others are greedy. Be greedy when others are fearful."

—Warren Buffett

Having run a number of organizations and businesses, it has to be said that this has been my area of greatest weakness. In the early days, I never understood what the basics of accounting were, so it was always hard to oversee this vital area of the business ecosystem. www.sba.gov

Estimating startup costs

If you are planning to start a business, it is critical to determine your budgetary needs. Since every business is different, and has its own specific cash needs at different stages of development, there is no universal method for estimating your startup costs. Some businesses can be started on a smaller budget, while others may require considerable investment in inventory or equipment. Additional considerations may include the cost to acquire or renovate a building or the purchase of long-term equipment.

To determine how much seed money you need to start, you must estimate the costs of doing business for the first few months. Some of these expenses will be one-time costs such as the fee for incorporating your business or the price of a sign for your building. Some will be ongoing costs, such as the cost of utilities, inventory, insurance, etc.

While identifying these costs, decide whether they are essential or optional. A realistic startup budget should only include those things that are necessary to start a business.

These essential expenses can be divided into two separate categories: *fixed* and *variable*. Fixed expenses include rent, utilities, administrative costs and insurance costs. Variable expenses include inventory, shipping and packaging costs, sales commissions, and other costs associated with the direct sale of a product or service. The most effective way to calculate your startup costs is to use a worksheet that lists both one-time and ongoing costs.

Using personal finances

Learn how your personal finances can affect your business finances

Starting a business can be a tremendous strain on your personal finances. It takes time before your new venture turns a profit and provides financial support for you and your family. Before starting a business, it is important to get your finances in order.

To get started, write a monthly household budget that accounts for your income and your household expenses. Be as conservative as possible because maintaining your household expenses is vital to the success of your business. Any strain on your personal budget can cause a financial risk to your business.

It is also important to check your personal credit history. Because you have not established a business credit history, lenders and suppliers will use your personal credit history to determine your terms of credit.

Your credit report, which is issued by a credit bureau, determines how potential lenders and suppliers will perceive you. You should know what appears on your credit report because you may find errors to correct. You can get a copy of your personal credit report from one of the three major credit bureaus: Equifax, Experian, or TransUnion.

Preparing financial statements

Understanding financial statements is essential to the success of a small business. They can be used as a roadmap to steer you in the right direction and help you avoid costly breakdowns. Financial statements have a value that goes far beyond preparing tax returns or applying for loans. www.sba.gov

Below you will find information on the two primary financial statements:
- The balance sheet
- The income statement.

What is a balance sheet?
- Assets
- Liabilities and net worth
- Equity

The balance sheet is a snapshot of your business financials: It includes *assets*, *liabilities* and *net worth*. The *bottomline* of a balance sheet must always include (assets = liabilities + net worth). The individual elements of a balance sheet change from day to day and reflect the activities of a business. Analyzing how the balance sheet changes over time will reveal important financial information about a business. It can help you can monitor your ability to collect revenues, manage your inventory, and assess your ability to satisfy creditors and stockholders.

Liabilities and net worth on the balance sheet represent sources of funds: Liabilities and net worth are composed of creditors and investors who have provided cash or its equivalent to your business. As a source of funds, they enable your business to continue or expand operations.

Assets represent the use of funds: A business uses cash or other funds provided by the creditor/investor to acquire assets. Assets include things of value that are owned or due to a business.

Liabilities represent obligations to creditors while net worth represents the owner's investment in the business: Both creditors and owners are investors in the business with the only difference being the timeframe in which they expect repayment.

Assets

Anything of value that is owned or due to the business is included under the asset section of a Balance Sheet.

Current assets:

- Current assets mature in less than one year. They are the sum of:
  - Cash
  - Accounts Receivable (A/R)
  - Inventory
  - Notes Receivable (N/R)
  - Other current assets

Cash: Cash pays bills and obligations. Inventory, receivables, land, building, machinery and equipment do not pay obligations even though they can be sold for cash and then used to pay bills. If cash is inadequate or improperly managed, a business may become insolvent or forced into bankruptcy. Cash includes all checking, money market and short-term savings accounts. Learn more about how to develop a cash flow analysis for your business.

Accounts Receivable (A/R): Accounts receivable are dollars due from customers. More specifically, inventory is sold and shipped, an invoice is sent to the customer, and cash is collected at a later time. The receivable exists for the time period between the selling of the inventory and the receipt of cash. Receivables are proportional to sales. As sales rise, the investment you must make in receivables also increases.

Inventory: Inventory consists of the goods and materials a business purchases to resell at a profit. In the process, sales and receivables are generated. The business purchases raw material inventory that is processed (called work-in-process inventory) to be sold as finished goods inventory. For a business that sells a product, inventory is often the first use of cash. Purchasing inventory to be sold at a profit is the first step in making a profit. Selling inventory does not bring cash back into the business—it creates a receivable. Only after a time lag (equal to the receivable's collection period) will cash return to the business. It is important that inventory is well managed so the business does not keep too much cash tied up in inventory, as this will reduce profits. At the same time, a business must keep sufficient inventory on hand to prevent stockouts (having nothing to sell). Insufficient inventory will erode profits and may result in the loss of customers.

Notes Receivable (N/R): Notes receivable, is a claim due to the business as a result of the business making a loan, such as a promissory note. Notes receivable is usually a claim due from one of three sources: customers, employees or officers of the business.

Customer notes receivable is when the customer borrowed from the business when the customer failed to pay the invoice according to the agreed-upon payment terms. The customer's obligation may have been converted to a promissory note.

Employee notes receivable may be for legitimate reasons, such as a down payment on a home, but the business is neither a charity nor a bank. If the business wants to help an employee, it can co-sign on a loan advanced by a bank.

An officer or owner borrowing from the business is the worst form of note receivable. If an officer takes money from the business, it should be declared as a dividend or withdrawal and reflected as a reduction in net worth. Treating it in any other way leads to possible manipulation of the business stated net worth. Banks and other lending institutions often condemn this practice.

Other current assets: Other current assets consist of prepaid expenses, other miscellaneous and current assets.

Fixed Assets

Fixed assets represent the use of cash to purchase physical assets whose life exceeds one year, such as:
- Land
- Building
- Machinery and equipment
- Furniture and fixtures
- Leasehold improvements

Intangibles

Intangibles are assets with an undetermined life that may never mature into cash. For most analysis purposes, intangibles are ignored as assets and are deducted from net worth because their value is difficult to determine. Intangibles consist of assets such as:
- Research and development
- Patents
- Market research
- Goodwill

Organizational expense

Intangibles are similar to prepaid expenses; the purchase of a benefit that will be expensed at a later date. Intangibles are recouped, like fixed assets, through incremental annual charges (amortization) against income. Standard accounting procedures require most intangibles to be expensed as purchased and never capitalized (include in the balance sheet). An exception to this is purchased patents that may be amortized over the life of the patent.

Other assets

Other assets consist of miscellaneous accounts, such as deposits and long-term notes receivable from third parties. They are turned into cash when the asset is sold or when the note is repaid.

Total assets

Total Assets represent the sum of all the assets owned by or due to a business.

Liabilities and net worth

Liabilities and net worth are sources of cash listed in descending order from the most nervous creditors and soonest to mature obligations (current liabilities), to the least nervous and never due obligations (net worth).

There are two sources of funds:
Current liabilities

Current liabilities are those obligations that will mature and must be paid within 12 months. These are liabilities that can create a business insolvency if cash is inadequate. A satisfied set of current creditors is a healthy and important source of credit for short-term uses of cash (inventory and receivables). A dissatisfied set of current creditors can threaten the survival of the business. The best way to ensure creditors will be satisfied is to keep their obligations current.

Current liabilities consist of the following obligation accounts:
- Accounts Payable (A/P)
- Accrued expenses
- Notes Payable (N/P)
- Current portion of Long-Term Debt (LTD)

Proper matching of sources and uses of funds requires that short-term (current) liabilities must be used only to purchase short-term assets (inventory and receivables).

Accounts payable (A/P): Accounts payable are obligations due to trade suppliers who have provided inventory, goods or services used in operating the business. Suppliers generally offer terms (just like you do for your customers), since the suppliers' competition offer payment terms. Whenever possible, you should take advantage of payment terms because this will keep your costs down. If the business is paying its suppliers in a timely fashion, days payable will not exceed the terms of payment.

Accrued expenses: Accrued expenses are obligations owed, but not billed such as wages and payroll taxes, or obligations accruing. These expenses can also be paid over a period of time such as interest on a loan.

Accruals include wages, payroll taxes, interest payable and employee benefits accruals such as pension funds. As a labor-related category, it should vary in accordance with payroll policy. For example, if wages are paid weekly, the accrual category should seldom exceed one week's payroll and payroll taxes.

Notes payable (N/P): Notes payable are obligations in the form of promissory notes with short-term maturity dates of less than 12 months. Often, they are payable upon demand. Other times they have specific maturity dates (30, 60, 90, 180, 270, 360 days maturities are typical). Notes payable include only the principal amount of the debt. Any interest owed is listed under accruals.

The proceeds of notes payable should be used to finance current assets (inventory and receivables). The use of funds must be short-term so that the asset matures into cash prior to the obligation's maturation. Proper matching would indicate borrowing for seasonal swings in sales, which cause shifts in inventory and receivables, or to repay accounts payable when attractive discount terms are offered for early payment.

Non-current liabilities
Non-current liabilities are those obligations that will be payable in the following year. There are three types of non-current liabilities, only two of which are listed on the balance sheet:
- Non-current portion of Long-Term Debt (LTD)
- Notes Payable to Officers, Shareholders, or Owners
- Contingent Liabilities

Non-current portion of long-term debt is the principal portion of a term loan not payable in the coming year. Subordinated officer loans are treated as an item that lies between debt and equity. Contingent liabilities listed in the footnotes are potential liabilities, which hopefully never become due.

Non-current portion of long-term debt (LTD): Non-current portion of LTD is the portion of a term loan that is not due within the next 12 months. It is listed below the current liability section to demonstrate that the loan does not have to be fully liquidated in the coming year. LTD provides cash to be used for a long-term asset purchase, either permanent working capital or fixed assets.

Notes payable to officers, shareholders or owners: Notes payable to officers, shareholders or owners represent cash that the shareholders or owners have put into the business. For tax reasons, owners may increase their equity investment beyond the initial business capitalization by making loans to the business rather than purchasing additional stock. Any return on investment to the owners can therefore be paid as tax-deductible interest expense rather than as non-tax-deductible dividends.

When a business borrows from a financial institution, it is common for the officer loans to be subordinated or put on standby. The subordination agreement prohibits the officer from collecting his or her loan prior to the repayment of the institution's loan. When on standby, the loan will be considered as equity by the financial institution. Notes receivable officer are considered a bad sign to lenders, while notes payable officer are considered to be reassuring.

Contingent Liabilities: Contingent Liabilities are potential liabilities that are not listed on the balance sheet. They are listed in the footnotes because they may never become due and payable. Contingent liabilities include lawsuits, warranties and cross Guarantees.

If the business has been sued, but the litigation has not been initiated, there is no way of knowing whether or not the suit will result in a liability to the business. It will be listed in the footnotes because, while not a real liability, it does represent a potential liability which may impair the ability of the business to meet future obligations. Alternatively, if the business guarantees a loan made by a third party to an affiliate, the liability is contingent because it will never become due as long as the affiliate remains healthy and meets its obligations.

Total liabilities: Total liabilities represent the sum of all monetary obligations of a business and claims creditors have on its assets.

Equity

Equity is represented by total assets minus total liabilities. Equity or net worth is the most patient and last to mature source of funds. It represents the owners' share in the financing of all the assets.

Income statement

The income statement, also known as the profit and loss statement, includes all income and expense accounts over a period of time. This financial statement shows how much money the business will make after all expenses are accounted for. An income statement does not reveal hidden problems, like insufficient cash flow. Income statements are read from top to bottom and represent earnings and expenses over a period of time.

Chapter Thirty Six
Developing a Cash Flow Analysis

Cash flow is the movement of money in and out of your business — cash is King!

For small businesses, cash is king. You need it to start, operate, and expand your operations, but many small business owners often have trouble managing and maintaining cash. Inaccurate cash flow analysis—or lack of available cash—can affect the everyday operations of your business and your eligibility to receive a loan. sba.gov

Cash flow is the movement of money in and out of your business.

The process includes:

- **Inflow** which comes from operations such as the sale of goods and services, loans, lines of credit, and asset sales.
- **Outflow** which occurs during operations such as business expenditures, loan payments, and business purchases. It's crucial to balance these two figures and maintain a reasonable balance of cash at all times. An effective cash flow system will help you manage funds to cover operational costs and bills and help you foresee potential problems in the future.

Profit and loss statements and income statements can be used to determine projections for future cash flow trends of your business. These financial documents are instrumental in making cash flow projections. However, a cash flow statement serves an important and independent purpose - it accounts for non-cash items and expenses to adjust profit figures. Cash flow analysis statements display not only changes over time, but also available net cash.

Cash flow analysis statements are generally separated into three parts:

Operating activities: This section evaluates net income and loses of a business. By assessing sales and business expenditures, all income from non-cash items is adjusted to incorporate inflows and outflows of cash transactions to determine a net figure.

Investment activities: This section reports inflows and outflows from purchases and sales of long-term business investments such as property, assets, equipment, and securities. For example - if your bakery business purchases an additional piece of kitchen equipment, this would be considered an investment and accounted for as an outflow of cash. If your business then sold equipment that was no longer needed, this would be considered an inflow of cash.

Financing activities: This section accounts for the cash flow trends of all money that is related to financing your business. For example: if you received a loan for your small business, the loan itself would be considered an inflow of cash. Loan payments would be considered an outflow of cash, and both would be recorded in this part of the cash flow analysis statement.

Breakeven analysis

Breakeven analysis: How to know when you can expect a profit

Breakeven analysis is used to determine when your business will be able to cover all its expenses and begin to make a profit. It is important to identify your startup costs, which will help you determine your sales revenue needed to pay ongoing business expenses.

For instance, if you have $5,000 of product sales, this will not cover $5,000 in monthly overhead expenses. The cost of selling $5,000 in retail goods could easily be $3,000 at the wholesale price, so the $5,000 in sales revenue only provides $2,000 in gross profit. The breakeven point is reached when revenue equals all business costs.

To calculate your breakeven point, you will need to identify your fixed and variable costs. Fixed costs are expenses that do not vary with sales volume, such as rent and administrative salaries. These expenses must be paid regardless of sales, and are often referred to as overhead costs. Variable costs fluctuate directly with sales volume, such as purchasing inventory, shipping, and manufacturing a product. To determine your breakeven point, use the equation below:

Breakeven point = fixed costs/ (unit selling price – variable costs)

Borrowing money for your business

After you have developed a cash flow analysis and determined when your business will make profit, you may decide you need additional funding. Borrowing money is one of the most common sources of funding for a small business, but obtaining a loan isn't always easy. Before you approach a lender for a loan, you will need to understand the factors the bank will use to evaluate your application.

The following outlines some of the key factors a lender uses to analyze a potential borrower. www.sba.gov
- Types of Financing
- Ability to Repay
- Credit History
- Equity Investment
- Collateral
- Management Experience

Questions your lender will ask

Types of financing

There are two types of financing: *equity financing and debt financing*. When looking for money, you must consider your company's debt-to-equity ratio. This ratio is the relation between dollars you have borrowed and dollars you have invested in your business. The more money owners have invested in their business, the easier it is to obtain financing.

If your firm has a high ratio of equity to debt, you should probably seek debt financing. However, if your company has a high proportion of debt to equity, experts advise that you should increase your ownership capital (equity investment) for additional funds. This will prevent you from being over-leveraged to the point of jeopardizing your company's survival.

Equity financing

Equity financing (or equity capital) is money raised by a company in exchange for a share of ownership in the business. Ownership accounts for owning shares of stock outright or having the right to convert other financial instruments into stock. Equity financing allows a business to obtain funds without incurring debt, or without having to repay a specific amount of money at a particular time.

Most small or growth-stage businesses use limited equity financing. Equity often comes from investors such as friends, relatives, employees, customers, or industry colleagues. The most common source of equity funding comes from *venture capitalists*. These are institutional risk takers and may be groups of wealthy individuals, government-assisted sources, or major financial institutions. Most specialize in one or a few closely related industries.

Debt financing

Debt financing means borrowing money that must be repaid over a period of time, usually with interest. Debt financing can be either short-term, with full repayment due in less than one year, or long-term, with repayment due over a period greater than one year. The lender does not gain an ownership interest in the business, and debt obligations are typically limited to repaying the loan with interest. Loans are often secured by some or all of the assets of the company. In addition, lenders commonly require the borrower's personal guarantee in case of default. This ensures that the borrower has a sufficient personal interest at stake in the business.

Loans can be obtained from many different sources, including banks, savings and loans, credit unions, commercial finance companies, and SBA-guaranteed loans. State and local governments have many programs that encourage the growth of small businesses. Family members, friends, and former associates are all potential sources, especially when capital requirements are smaller.

Traditionally, banks have been the major source of small business funding. The principal role of banks includes short-term loans, seasonal lines of credit, and single-purpose loans for machinery and equipment. Banks generally have been reluctant to offer long-term loans to small firms. SBA's guaranteed lending programs encourage banks and non-bank lenders to make long-term loans to small firms by reducing their risk and leveraging the funds they have available.

Ability to repay

The ability (or capacity) to repay the funds you receive from a lender must be justified in your loan package. Banks want to see two sources of repayment—cash flow from the business as well as a secondary source such as collateral. The lender reviews the past financial statements of a business to analyze its cash flow.

Generally, banks are more comfortable offering assistance to businesses that have been in existence for a number of years and have a proven financial track record. If the business has consistently made a profit and that profit can cover the payment of additional debt, it is likely that the loan will be approved. If however, the business is a start-up or has been operating marginally and has an opportunity to grow, it is necessary to prepare a thorough loan package with a detailed explanation including how the business will be able to repay the loan.

Credit history

When a small business requests a loan, one of the first things a lender looks at is personal and business credit history. So before you even start the process of preparing a loan request, you want to make sure you have good credit.

Get your personal credit report from one of the credit bureaus, such as *TransUnion, Equifax or Experian*. You should initiate this step well in advance of seeking a loan. Personal credit reports may contain errors or be out of date, and it can take three to four weeks for errors to be corrected. It is up to you to see that corrections are made, so make sure you check regularly on progress. You want to make sure that when a lender pulls your credit report, all the errors have been corrected and your history is up to date.

Once you obtain your credit report, check to make sure that all personal information, including your name, Social Security number and address is correct. Then carefully examine the rest of the report, which contains a list of all the credit you obtained in the past such as credit cards, mortgages, student loans and information on how you paid that credit. Any item indicating that you have had a problem in paying will be toward the top of the list. These are the credits that may affect your ability to obtain a loan.

If you have been late by a month on an occasional payment, this probably will not adversely affect your credit. But it is likely that you will have difficulty in obtaining a loan if you are continuously late in paying your credit, have a credit that was never paid, have a judgment against you, or have declared bankruptcy in the last seven years.

A person may have a period of bad credit as a result of divorce, medical crisis, or some other significant event. If you can show that your credit was good before and after this event and that you have tried to pay back those debts, you should be able to obtain a loan. It is best if you write an explanation of your credit problems and how you have rectified them, and attach this to your credit report in your loan package.

Each credit bureau has a slightly different way of presenting your credit information. Contact the bureau you used for more specific information how to read your credit report. If you need additional help in interpreting or evaluating your credit report, ask your accountant or a local banker.

Equity investment

Do not be misled into thinking that a start-up business can obtain all financing through conventional or special loan programs. Financial institutions want to see a certain amount of equity in a business.

Equity can be built up through retained earnings or by the injection of cash from either the owner or investors. Most banks want to see that the total liabilities or debt of a business is *not more* than four times the amount of equity. So if you want a loan for your business, make sure that there is enough equity in the company to leverage that loan. Owners usually must put some of their own money into the business to get a loan. The amount of financing depends on the type of loan, purpose and terms. Most banks want the owner to put in at least 20 to 40 percent of the total request.

Having the right debt to equity ratio does not guarantee your business will get a loan. There are a number of other factors used to evaluate a business, such as net worth, which is the amount of equity in a business, which is often a combination of retained earnings and owner's equity.

Collateral

When a financial institution gives a loan, it wants to make sure it will get its money back. That is why a lender usually requires a second source of repayment called collateral. Collateral is personal and business assets that can be sold in case the cash generated by the small business is not sufficient to repay the loan. Every loan program requires at least some collateral. If a potential borrower has no collateral, he/she will need a co-signer who has collateral to pledge. Otherwise it may be difficult to obtain a loan.

The value of collateral is not based on market value; rather, it is discounted to take into account the value that would be lost if the assets had to be liquidated quickly.

The bank will calculate your collateral coverage ratio as part of the loan evaluation process. This ratio is calculated by dividing the total discounted collateral value by the total loan request.

Management experience

Managerial expertise is a critical element in the success of any business. In fact, poor management is most frequently cited as the reason businesses fail. Lenders will be looking closely at your education and experience as well as that of your key managers. To strengthen your management skills, SBA offers a wide range of free, online training courses. You can also get management advice from counselors at your local SCORE office.

Questions your lender will ask

Before you apply for a loan, you need to think about a variety of questions:

- Can the business repay the loan? (Is cash flow greater than debt service?)
- Can you repay the loan if the business fails? (Is collateral sufficient to repay the loan?)
- Does the business collect its bills?

- Does the business pay its bills?
- Does the business control its inventory?
- Does the business control expenses?
- Are the officers committed to the business?
- Does the business have a profitable operating history?
- Does the business match its sources and uses of funds?
- Are sales growing?
- Are profits increasing as a percentage of sales?
- Is there any discretionary cash flow?
- What is the future of the industry?
- Who is your competition and what are their strengths and weaknesses?

Small Business America financial assistance eligibility

SBA have funds for startup's, check out their website: sba.gov

The types of businesses that are eligible for financial assistance from the SBA, must:
- Operate for profit
- Be engaged in, or propose to do business in, the United States
- Have reasonable owner equity to invest
- Use alternative financial resources, including personal assets, before seeking financial assistance

Chapter Thirty Seven
What About Tax?

Imagine a world where there where no taxes—great! But no roads, no free education, no parks, no emergency medical care, no police, no defense force, no care for those in poverty, and the list goes on. Yes, I have issues with the way our taxes are spent at times, but without your tax money, there would be chaos. Our taxes contribute to making our communities a healthy, thriving, safe place.

Is it a business or a hobby?

Has your hobby become more than a pastime? Are you making a profit? Confused about what you can and can't deduct when it comes to hobby-related expenses and losses?

As a rule, any income you earn from a hobby must be reported on your tax return. However, how you report the income and any associated expenses depend on whether the activity is a hobby or a business.

For more information visit IRS.gov's guidance on determining whether an activity is a business or a hobby.

www.sba.gov

Obtain your Federal Business Tax ID

One of the key responsibilities for many new businesses or businesses that are restructuring is obtaining an Employer Identification Number (EIN) from the IRS.

An EIN is a unique nine-digit number that identifies your business for tax purposes. It's like a Social Security number but is meant for business related items only.

An EIN can be used to open a business bank account, file your tax returns, and, in some instances, apply for business licenses. It's helpful to apply for one as soon as you start planning your business. This will ensure there are no delays in getting the appropriate licenses or financing that you may need to operate.

Who needs an EIN?
An EIN is needed by any business that retains employees. However, non-employers are also required to obtain one if they operate as a corporation or partnership. Sole proprietors are not required to obtain an EIN.

As your business grows, be sure to visit the IRS website and its resources for a complete list of who needs an EIN.

How to apply for an EIN
The simplest way to apply for your EIN is online via the IRS EIN Assistant. As soon as your

application is complete and validated, you will be issued an EIN. There is no charge for this service.

Determine your Federal Tax obligations:

Your federal tax obligations, the tax you pay to the IRS, is determined by the form of business entity that you establish (e.g. sole proprietorship, partnership, LLC). These taxes include:
- Income tax
- Self-employment tax (social security and Medicare taxes)
- Estimated tax (a pay-as-you-go tax)
- Employer tax (such as withholding tax)
- Excise tax

Find the right tax form
The forms you use to report your taxes depends on how your business is organized. Find out which forms you need to file:

- Sole Proprietorship
- Partnership
- Corporation
- S Corporation
- Limited Liability Company (LLC)

Pay your State income taxes

In addition to federal taxes, your business must also pay state and local taxes (income, sales tax, and property tax). As with the IRS, the legal structure of your business determines your state income tax obligations. Learn more in our State and Local Tax Guide.

Determine your State tax obligations

In addition to federal business taxes, your business must pay certain state and local taxes. The most common types of tax requirements for small business are income taxes and employment taxes.

Income Taxes
Your state income tax obligation is determined by the legal structure of your business. For example, LLCs are taxed separately from the owners, while sole proprietors report their personal and business income taxes using the same form.

Employment Taxes
In addition to federal employment taxes, if you have employees you are also responsible for paying certain state employment taxes such as workers' compensation insurance and unemployment insurance taxes. The following states/territories also require a business to pay for temporary disability insurance:
- California
- Hawaii
- New Jersey
- New York
- Rhode Island
- Puerto Rico

Determine when the tax year starts

A tax year is an accounting period for which you must report your taxable income and business expenses. The law requires you to operate according to a consistent tax year. The most common is to follow a calendar year. However, businesses can also report based on a fiscal tax year (any 12-month period ending on the last day of any month, except December) and a short tax year.

Here are some guidelines for choosing the right tax year for your small business:

Calendar tax year

This is a standard method used by many business owners and is determined by your business structure. For example, sole proprietors, partnerships, and LLCs generally adhere to a calendar tax year. As a rule, if any of the following apply, the IRS requires that you must adopt the calendar year:
- You keep no books or records
- You have no annual accounting period
- Your present tax year does not qualify as a fiscal year
- You are required to use a calendar year by a provision of the Internal Revenue Code or the Income Tax Regulations

If you file your first tax return using the calendar tax year and you later begin business as a sole proprietor, become a partner in a partnership, or become a shareholder in an S Corporation, you must continue to use the calendar year unless you get IRS approval to change it or meet one of the exceptions listed in the instructions to Form 1128, *Application To Adopt, Change, or Retain a Tax Year.*

Fiscal tax year

Many corporations and larger firms operate on a fiscal tax year basis. For small businesses that might not have the accounting expertise on-hand to keep everything reconciled, a calendar tax year is easier to manage. But there are exceptions where it may make sense to consider a fiscal year. For example, if you operate a seasonal business, reporting income by calendar year could split your season and give a distorted view of income and expenses.

Likewise, if your business shows most of its expenses in one year and income in another, you may want to consider a fiscal tax year so that both periods are included in the same 12-month set.

Short tax year

Technically, a short tax year (less than 12 months) is not an annual accounting period; instead, it applies to businesses that did not exist for the entire tax year or those that changed their tax year period during the year.

Even if you (a taxable entity) were not in existence for the entire year, a tax return is required for the time you were in existence. Requirements for filing the return and figuring the tax are generally the same as the requirements for a return for a full tax year (12 months) ending on the last day of the short tax year.

Changing your tax year

Once you have adopted a tax year, you may need to get IRS approval to change it. Typically, businesses that change their legal structure may wish to shift from a calendar year to a fiscal year method. In these cases, you will need to file Form 1128, Application to Adopt, Change, or Retain a Tax Year.

Chapter Thirty Eight
The Bank

"Financial peace isn't the acquisition of stuff. It's learning to live on less than you make, so you can give money back and have money to invest. You can't win until you do this."

— Dave Ramsey

Business loan application checklist

Small Business Administration (SBA) is not the only source for small-business loans. State and local economic-development agencies—and numerous nonprofit organizations—provide low-interest loans to small business owners who may not qualify for traditional commercial loans.

When it comes to applying for these loans, the good news is that most of these other lenders require the same kinds of information. Of course, each loan program has specific forms you need to fill out. But for the most part, you will need to submit the same types of documentation.

Here are the typical items required for any small business loan application:

Loan application form
Forms vary by program and lending institution, but they all ask for the same information. You should be prepared to answer the following questions. It is a good idea to have this information prepared before you fill out a bank or finance company application:
- Why are you applying for this loan?
- How will the loan proceeds be used?
- What assets need to be purchased, and who are your suppliers?
- What other business debt do you have, and who are your creditors?
- Who are the members of your management team?

Personal background
Either as part of the loan application or as a separate document, you will likely need to provide some personal background information, including previous addresses, names used, criminal record, educational background, etc.

Resumes
Some lenders require evidence of management or business experience, particularly for loans that can be used to start a new business.

Business plan
All loan programs require a sound business plan to be submitted with the loan application. The business plan should include a complete set of projected financial statements, including profit and loss, cash flow and balance sheet.

Here are some resources for preparing your business plan for investment:

Personal credit report
Your lender will obtain your personal credit report as part of the application process. However, you should obtain a credit report from all three major consumer credit rating agencies before submitting a loan application to the lender. Inaccuracies and blemishes on your credit report can hurt your chances of getting a loan approved. It is critical you try to clear these up before beginning the application process.

Business credit report
If you are already in business, you should be prepared to submit a credit report for your business. As with the personal credit report, it is important to review your business' credit report before beginning the application process.

Income tax returns
Most loan programs require applicants to submit personal and business income tax returns for the previous three years.

Financial statements
Many loan programs require owners with more than a 20 percent stake in your business to submit signed personal financial statements.

You may also be required to provide projected financial statements either as part of, or separate from your business plan. It is a good idea to have these prepared and ready in case a program for which you are applying requires these documents to be submitted individually.

The following forms may be used to prepare your projected financial statements:

- Balance Sheet
- Income Statement
- Cash Flow
- Bank Statements

Many loan programs require one year of personal and business bank statements to be submitted as part of a loan package.

Accounts receivable and accounts payable
Most loan programs require details of a business's most current financial position. Before you begin the loan application process, make sure you have accounts receivable and accounts payable documents in hand.

Collateral

Collateral requirements vary greatly. Some loan programs do not require collateral. Loans involving higher risk factors for default require substantial collateral. Strong business plans and financial statements can help you avoid putting up collateral. In any case, it is a good idea to prepare a collateral document that describes cost/value of personal or business property that will be used to secure a loan.

Legal documents

Depending on a loan's specific requirements, your lender may require you to submit one or more legal documents. Make sure you have the following items in order, if applicable:
- Business licenses and registrations required for you to conduct business
- Articles of Incorporation
- Copies of contracts you have with any third parties
- Franchise agreements
- Commercial leases
- Other documents that may relate

Keeping good records is essential for running a successful business, but even more critical when applying for a loan. Make sure required documents are orderly and accurate. All information you provide will be verified by your lender and the organization guaranteeing the loan. False or misleading information will result in your loan being denied. Finally, make sure you keep personal copies of all loan packages.

Financial projections for a business plan

For the purpose of launching a new enterprise, we have chosen to cover this topic again as it relates to securing finance.

Financial projections

You should develop the Financial Projections section after you have analyzed the market and set clear objectives. Only then can you allocate resources efficiently. The following is a list of the critical financial statements to include in your business plan packet: www.sba.gov

Historical financial data

If you own an established business, you will be requested to supply historical data related to your company's performance. Most creditors request data for the last three to five years, depending on the length of time you have been in business.

The historical financial data to include are your company's income statements, balance sheets, and cash flow statements for each year you have been in business (usually for up to three to five years). Often, creditors are also interested in any collateral that you may have that could be used to ensure your loan, regardless of the stage of your business.

Prospective financial data

All businesses, whether startup or growing, will be required to supply prospective financial data. Most of the time, creditors will want to see what you expect your company to be able to do within the next five years. Each year's documents should include forecasted income statements, balance sheets, cash flow statements, and capital expenditure budgets. For the first year, you should supply monthly or quarterly projections. After that, you can stretch it to quarterly and/or yearly projections for years two through five.

Make sure that your projections match your funding requests; as creditors will be on the lookout for inconsistencies. It is much better if you catch mistakes before they do. If you have made assumptions in your projections, be sure to summarize what you have assumed. This way, the reader will not be left guessing.

Finally, include a short analysis of your financial information. Include a ratio and trend analysis for all of your financial statements (both historical and prospective). Since pictures speak louder than words, you may want to add graphs of your trend analysis (especially if they are positive).

Next, you may want to include an Appendix to your plan. This can include items such as your credit history, resumes, letters of reference, and any additional information that a lender may request.

Pillar Six
The Manager

"Managers are the enterprise clock builders, the architects of the business engine. Building the clock means robust systems of feedback, evaluation and action. Good managers are responsible for making sure a company's many moving parts are well oiled, and all doing their part to make the business machinery run smoothly."

—AJ Walton

What makes a great manager?
How do I empower the team?
What operational systems do I need in place?
What are the key disciplines of Management?

Chapter Thirty Nine
Building the Clock

"A leader builds a team of strong individuals, rather than acting as a genius with 1000 helpers on whom everything depends."

— Jim Collins

Great entrepreneurs are not always great managers, and are often especially weak at administration. Something that, in the end, can lead to the down-fall of a new business. Creating systems for organizing people, communications, filing, and the list goes on, can be neglected, causing chaos and conflict. These tasks can be tedious and boring, but must be done in order for the clock to function.

Clock building is primarily about management and leadership, and is the ability to coordinate people in order to achieve the goals and objectives of the company, utilizing available recourses efficiently and effectively.

Today, a lot is written about leadership and entrepreneurship, however the subject of management is often neglected. Steven Covey points out that, "the problem with a lot of the existing management systems, is that they are based on the old military model, and are not working for a new generation of young employees."

The word management comes from the French word for housekeeping, ménagerie, derived from ménager ("to keep house"), also encompasses taking care of domestic animals. It has to be said, that there are a lot of domestic animals that would be easier to manage than certain people. Managing can be like herding cats at times!

Wikipedia defines, "Management as forecasting, planning, organizing, staffing and generally building the ecosystems of the entire operation. Leading, empowering and directing the organization toward achieving the vision, dream and goals of the owner or board. According to Henri Fayol, "to manage is to forecast and to plan, to organize, to command, to co-ordinate and to control."

Built to last

Jerry Porras and Jim Collins in their book, *Built to Last,* write about what builds long-lasting, visionary companies. They studied the habits of 18 exceptional companies that had been in existence between 40 and 180 years; companies such as *Disney, Boeing, Sony, IBM, Ford, 3M, Hewlett-Packard, General Electric, Walt-Mart, Motorola and Marriott.*

Built to Last is a philosophical blueprint based on extensive research into the development of some of the United States' most successful corporations. In essence, *Built to Last* is an analysis of how visionary companies should operate.

In their research, Jim Collins and Jerry Porras made a surprising discovery: the visionary companies they studied weren't a platform for a charismatic leader to make his or her mark or a vehicle to bring an amazing product to the world. It was not about creating a product or a leader; *the company itself was the ultimate creation.* Great managers build the business clock so that everyone can engage in what they call; *Clock Building, not Time Telling.*

Collins says, "Imagine that you met a remarkable person who could look at the sun or the stars and, amazingly, state the exact time and date. Wouldn't it be even more amazing still if, instead of telling the time, that person built a clock that could tell the time forever, even after he or she were dead and gone? Having a great idea or being a charismatic visionary leader is 'time telling'; building a company that can prosper far beyond the presence of any single leader and through multiple product life cycles is clock building.'"

Time tellers see themselves as the center of the universe, they build a reliance on themselves, often without realizing it. They see themselves as the chief, with an army of helpers. Take the time teller or chief out of the equation, and expect utter chaos and catastrophe.

Leaders who are clock builders see the big picture. They have a "quarter century perspective" and focus on long term success. Porras and Collins explain the importance of building an organization's "core value system" instead of relying on great product ideas, charismatic leaders, and paying too much attention to profit.

1. Building the clock is a manager mindset

Management, like leadership, is an art-form and a mindset, strengthened by developing leadership skills and strengths in areas of personal weakness. Managers need an entrepreneurial mindset in order to design the systems that take labor and other resources from a lower level of productivity to higher place.

Management does not need to be seen from an enterprise point of view alone, because management is an essential function to improve one's life and relationships at every level. Good management starts with self-management.

In, *Another Way of Thinking,* Mary Parker Follett (1868–1933), allegedly defined management as "the art of getting things done through people". She described management as philosophy, not a set of rules.

Just as leaders are often required to develop management skills, especially in smaller businesses or startups, managers must develop leadership thinking as a part of a balanced mindset. To say, *'that's not me,"* is a copout. The way a manager thinks is their primary asset, and sets them apart as clock creators.

The following material is from Wikipedia, and helps define the effect that our mindset can have on our thinking, and can override objectivity when it comes to the development of productive systems:

A mindset is defined as, "the established set of attitudes held by a person, for instance, the region seems stuck in a medieval mindset."

"In decision theory and general systems theory, a mindset is a set of assumptions, methods, or culture held by one or more people. This phenomenon is also sometimes described as, collective mindsets, groupthink, an attitude, or a paradigm, and it is often difficult to counteract its effects upon analysis and the decision making processes."

Fixed mindset and growth mindset

According to Carol Dweck, individuals can be placed on a continuum according to their implicit views of "where ability comes from".

Dweck states that, "there are two categories (*growth mindset* versus *fixed mindset*) that can group individuals based on their behavior, specifically their reaction to failure. Those with a "fixed mindset" believe that abilities are mostly innate or intuitive and interpret or define failure as the lack-of-necessary-basic-abilities, while those with a "growth mindset" believe that they can acquire any given ability provided they invest effort or study." Dweck argues that the growth mindset "will allow a person to live a less stressful and more successful life."

In a 2012 interview, Dweck defined both fixed and growth mindsets: "In a fixed mindset, students believe their basic abilities, their intelligence, their talents, are just fixed traits. They have a certain amount and that's that, and then their goal becomes to look smart all the time and never look dumb. In a growth mindset, students understand that their talents and abilities can be developed through effort, good teaching and persistence. They don't necessarily think everyone's the same or anyone can be Einstein, but they believe everyone can get smarter if they work at it."

Abundance mindset and scarcity mindset

The *abundance mentality,* or abundance mindset, is a concept in which a person believes there are enough resources and successes to share with others. It contrasts it with the *scarcity mindset*, which is founded on the idea that, if someone else wins or is successful in a situation, that means you lose; not considering the possibility of all parties winning in a given situation, at the same time. The reality is, when everyone in an economy is working and producing, the pie is increasing in size so that everyone can have a piece of the pie, as opposed to trying to steal pie form others. The abundance mentality arises from having a high self-worth and security, and leads to the sharing of profits, recognition and responsibility.

Productive mindset and defensive mindset

According to Chris Argyris (2004), there are two dominant mindsets in organizations: the *productive mindset* and the *defensive mindset.* The productive mindset seeks out valid knowledge that is testable. The productive reasoning mindset creates informed choices and makes reasoning transparent. There is a commitment to objective facts or truth, and the input of others, even if it's not what they want to hear.

The defensive mindset, on the other hand, is self-protective and self-deceptive. When this mindset is active, people or organizations only seek out information that will protect them. Truth can be shut out when it is seen as threatening. The defensive mindset may lead to learning based on false assumptions or prevent learning altogether (Argyris, 2004).

The Manager mindset

This mindset should include the entrepreneurial mindset as already mentioned in an earlier chapter. This mindset may not come naturally for a manager with a more methodical way of thinking, but will deepen their understanding and appreciation of entrepreneurs and/or entrepreneurial workers. It will also add to their thinking ability, giving them an edge other managers often do not possess.

As a part of their wiring, managers are good analysts, or critical thinkers, that can see the inconsistencies and problems within systems, and the people working for them. Managers however must always go beyond identifying the problem or fixing the blame, to fixing the problem. They are the designers of systems that produce constancy, the architects of environments that inspire productivity and innovation, the coaches that empower the team and the creators of effective training processes. Great managers make sure the vision is clear and concise, they get personal engagement, maintain lines of communication, handle toxic employees, admit their mistakes, understand the power of gratitude, and make work fun.

2. Building the clock means designing operational ecosystems

Management involves identifying the mission, objectives, procedures, rules and the coordination of the human capital to contribute to the success of the enterprise.

I had named this Pillar, *Operations,* until somewhere in the middle of my research I realized that great organizations are about great people and wise managers, not perfectly crafted systems or operations manuals. Having said this, if a manager is truly wise, then they focus on building the organization into a well crafted precision clock with systems and structures that cause the enterprise to last or operate beyond themselves. They build and maintain every component part of this living breathing growing ecosystem.

Ecosystems

A simple definition of an ecosystem is, "a community of living things and the environment in which they live."

The word was first coined in 1930 by Roy Clapham, to denote the physical and biological components of an environment and their relationship to each other as a unit. The term is now used more broadly to describe many other kinds of eco-systems as well. In the same way, every enterprise is an ecosystem of relationships, experience, information and issues that relate to any given subject, decision or problem. Business is a mental, social and spiritual ecosystem.

Ecosystem definitions:
- A community of plants, animals and microorganisms, along with their environment, that function together as a unit. An ecosystem can be as large as a rain forest or as small as a rotting log.
- A biological system consisting of many organisms that exist in mutual dependence with the other organisms in the system.

- A complex system of interaction between living organisms and their non-living environment.
- A complex set of relationships of living organisms functioning as a unit and interacting with their physical environment.
- Now, what does clock-building look like?

Jim Collins shares three steps you can take to leave a lasting legacy:

1. Build a system that can be great beyond any single leader or great idea

The leader or manager is a clock-builder, not just a time teller—he or she is building a system that can prosper beyond his or her presence.

A leader builds a team of strong individuals, rather than acting as a "genius with 1000 helpers" on whom everything depends.

If any individual leader were to disappear tomorrow, our discipline would remain as strong as ever; we have built a culture of discipline, as distinct from having a larger-than-life disciplinarian at the helm.

2. Create catalytic mechanisms

We have *red flag mechanisms* that bring brutal facts to our attention, and force us to confront those facts, no matter how uncomfortable. We set in place powerful mechanisms that stimulate progress—mechanisms designed to force us to continually improve. Our mechanisms are designed so that people who hold power – and who might want to ignore the brutal facts – cannot easily subvert the mechanisms.

3. Manage for the quarter century

No matter what short-term pressures we face, we build for long-term greatness; we manage not for the quarter, but for the quarter century. In a world of short-term thinking great leaders measure their success, as much by how their organization performs in the hands of a successor, as by how it fares during their own personal reign.

A good example was *Disney* vs. *Columbia Pictures*. Walt Disney was a *time-teller* and *built the clock!* Walt showed he was a *time-teller* buy personally creating many of Disney's masterpieces himself, but he also developed many processes that would ensure his company created happiness for a long time after his days at the company. He established art classes for all the animators, instituted the "You Make Happiness" training program for all Disney employees, etc., which helped him build the Disney clock. Alternatively, Harry Cohn, at Columbia Pictures, was too busy creating a name for himself. As mentioned in the book, *Good to Great,* he became the first person in Hollywood to assume the titles of president and producer. However, he did little to prepare Columbia for the days when he would no longer be around, and sadly the company went into disarray after he passed away.

3. Building the clock is empowering the team

Good management needs to understand how good teams operate. When forming teams managers must create a balance so that there is a diverse set of skills, personalities and perspectives.

You may think it's easier to manage a group of people who are likely to get along, but truly effective teams invite many viewpoints and use their differences to be creative and innovative. Here, your task is to develop the skills needed to steer those differences in a positive direction.

Selecting and Developing the Right People
Finding great new team members, and developing the skills needed for your team's success is another important part of team formation.

We need to take the advice of Jim Collins and Jerry Porras from their book, *Good to Great*, where they found that the leaders of the GREAT companies, did not start out casting vision or setting strategy, they first got the right people on the bus, then the wrong people off the bus, and the right people in the right seats — and then they figured out where to drive it.

In essence they first asked WHO, then HOW, WHEN and WHERE, getting the wrong people off the bus and the right people on board.

Delegating effectively
Those in management roles must be able to determine the next steps for every situation, and to delegate related tasks to employees as needed. Having the right people with the right skills is not sufficient for a team's success. Managers must also know how to get the job done efficiently. Some managers, especially those who earned their positions based on their technical expertise, can try to do most of the work themselves. They think that, because they're responsible for the work, they should do it themselves to make sure it is done right.

Effective managers recognize that by assigning work to the right people (not just those with the most time available), and clearly outlining expectations, teams can accomplish much more. However it is often difficult to trust others to do the job properly. As a manager, remember that when your team members have the right skills, training and motivation, you can usually trust them to get the work done right.

Understanding team dynamics and encouraging good relationships
Understanding how people tick and keeping them informed and focused is key in building the enterprise clock, as the cogs in this machine have emotions, ambitions, blind-spots and any number of other personal issues

Motivating people
Another necessary management skill is motivating and inspiring others. It is one thing to motivate yourself, but it is quite another to motivate someone else. The key thing to remember is that motivation is personal. We are all motivated by different things, and we all have different levels of personal motivation. So, getting to know our team members on a personal level allows us to motivate people in a more personalized way. Managers must be able to connect human and business resources together in an established system and coordinate staff in such a way that the company's goals can be reached quickly and efficiently.

Understanding the power of gratitude is all important in this process. Have you ever worked in a company where the salary or the job was not that amazing, but you stayed because you simply loved your manager? Now think about the best managers you ever had the chance to work with. What did they have in common? Gratitude and personal encouragement. Saying, "Thank you" or "well done," to an employee who successfully completed a task is a powerful motivator—even better than money.

Managing discipline and dealing with conflict
Sometimes, despite your best efforts, there are problems with individual performance. As

a manager, you have to deal with these issues promptly. If this is not done quickly and graciously, like a cancer, it will grow and could become lethal. Like a judge who is honest and fair, all the facts need to be researched and the evidence clear before coming to a conclusion and/or holding a meeting.

If you do not discipline, you risk negative impacts on the rest of the team as well as your customers, as poor performance typically impacts customer service, and it hurts the team and everything that the team has accomplished. It's very demotivating to work beside someone who consistently fails to meet expectations, so if you tolerate it, the rest of the team will likely suffer.

Team performance will also suffer when differences between individual team members turn into outright conflict, and it's your job as team manager to facilitate a resolution. However, conflict can be positive when it highlights underlying structural problems—make sure that you recognize conflict and deal with its causes, rather than just suppressing its symptoms or avoiding it.

Communicating
An element that's common to all of these management skills is effective communication. This is critical to any position you hold, but especially important as a manager. You need to let your team know what's happening and keep them informed as much as possible. Communication ties the entire ecosystem together and is the oil of the enterprise, keeping people united and pulling in the same direction. Even the cells of our body communicate with each other constantly.

Planning, making decisions, and problem solving
Those in management roles must hone the ability to action plan, to make the tough decisions, and review for the future. Without a clear plan and good communication, conflict and confusion can demotivate a team and create unrest. Planning gives people a map in order to keep on track.

4. Building the clock means the development of disciplines

"God has entrusted me with myself. No man is free who is not master of himself. A man should so live that his happiness shall depend as little as possible on external things. The world turns aside to let any man pass who knows where he is going."

— Epictetus

Ten years after the worldwide bestseller *Good to Great,* Jim Collins returns with another groundbreaking work, this time to ask: Why do some companies thrive in uncertainty, even chaos, and others do not? Based on nine years of research, buttressed by rigorous analysis and infused with engaging stories, Collins and his colleague, Morten Hansen, catalogues the principles for building a truly great enterprise in unpredictable, tumultuous, and fast-moving times.

Great by Choice distinguishes itself from Collins's prior work by its focus, not just on performance, but also on the type of unstable environments faced by leaders today.

With a team of more than twenty researchers, Collins and Hansen studied companies that rose to greatness —beating their industry indexes by a minimum of ten times over fifteen years—in environments characterized by big forces and rapid shifts that leaders could not predict or control.

The study results were full of provocative surprises, such as:

The best leaders were not more risk taking, more visionary, or more creative than the comparisons; they were more disciplined, more empirical, and more paranoid.

Innovation by itself turns out not to be the trump card in a chaotic and uncertain world; more important is the ability to scale innovation and to blend creativity with discipline.

Following the belief that leading in a "fast world" always requires "fast decisions" and "fast action" is a good way to get killed.

The great companies changed less in reaction to a radically changing world than the comparison companies.

Starting with 20,400 companies, their rigorous research identified seven 10X companies including *Amgen, Biomet, Intel, Microsoft, Progressive Insurance, Southwest Airlines, and Stryker*. These 10X (companies beat their industry index by at least 10 times) and they did it during chaotic environments.

For example, in the chaotic airline environment from 1972 to 2002 filled with fuel shocks, deregulation, labor strife, air-traffic-control strikes, interest-rate spikes, hijackings (including 9-11), recessions, and multiple bankruptcies, *Southwest Airlines* had a stock return 63 times better than the general stock market.

How did the 10x companies achieve such astounding results in such uncertain environments? Collins and Hansen's extensive research reveals three core behaviors that set the 10X companies apart from their comparison companies:

The first behavior is FANATIC DISCIPLINE. Discipline is "consistency of action, consistency of values, consistency with long-term goals, consistency with performance standards, consistency of method, consistency over time." It is not the same as measurement, hierarchical obedience, or adherence to bureaucratic rules. "For a 10Xer, the only legitimate form of discipline is self-discipline, having the inner will to do whatever it takes to create a great outcome, no matter how difficult. True discipline requires the independence of mind to reject pressures to conform in ways incompatible with values, performance standards, and long term aspirations." Discipline means relentless, unbending focus on the mission.

The authors compared *Fanatic Discipline* to a 20 Mile March. Imagine you start in San Diego with a goal to march all the way to Maine. Your goal is to march 20 miles per day, every day, regardless of the weather. You don't do less (you have ambition to achieve), and you do not overreach and do more (you have self-control to hold back). 10X companies identify what their 20-mile march is and stick to it regardless of the whether.

Collins and Hansen observe, "The 20 Mile March creates two types of self-imposed discomfort: (1) the discomfort of unwavering commitment to high performance in difficult conditions, and (2) the discomfort of holding back in good conditions." For example, despite all of the chaos in Southwest Airlines' environment, they generated a profit for 30 consecutive years. However, they were self-disciplined, to "hold back in good times so as not to extend beyond its ability to preserve profitability and the Southwest culture."

Management disciplines:
A - G
Accuracy

Achieving Goals	Focus	Professionalism
Adaptability	Genuine	Product Management
Administrative	Goal-oriented	Project Management
Analytical Ability	Goal Setting	Process Management
Assertiveness		Public Speaking
Budget Management	**H - M**	Punctuality
Business Management	Hiring	Research
Business Storytelling	Honesty	Responsibility
Collaboration	Influencing	Qualitative Skills
Communication	Innovation	Sales
Conflict Management	Interpersonal	Scheduling
Conflict Resolution	Leadership	Staffing
Coordination	Legal	Strategic Planning
Critical Thinking	Listening	Strategic Thinking
Decision Making	Logical Thinking	Success
Delegation	Logistics	**T - Z**
Development	Microsoft Office	Tactfulness
Diplomacy	Motivation	Teaching
Discipline		Team Building
Division of Work	**N - S**	Team Manager
Dynamic	Negotiating	Team Player
Emotional Intelligence	Networking	Teamwork
Empathy	Nonverbal Communication	Technical Knowledge
Empowerment	Obstacle Removal	Technology
Energetic	Organizing	Time Management
Engagement	Patience	Training
Execution	Persuasion	Uncertainty Removal
Facilitating	Planning	Writing
Finance	Presentation	Verbal Communication
Financial Management	Productivity	Vision
Flexibility	Problem Solving	

The second behavior is EMPIRICAL CREATIVITY. What is essential is that creativity and discipline exist together. "Intel's founders believed that *innovation without discipline leads to disaster.*" In fact, Intel's #1 core value is not innovation or creativity, it is discipline. Collins and Hansen observe, "The great task, rarely achieved, is to blend creativity intensity with relentless discipline so as to amplify the creativity rather than destroy it."

But the key is not just creativity alone...it's EMPIRICAL, well researched, well thought out, well implemented CREATIVITY.

The Third Behavior is PRODUCTIVE PARANOIA. Collins and Hansen make it clear: "The only mistakes you can learn from are the ones you survive". The idea of Productive Paranoia is not for leaders to walk around scared, afraid to make decisions and suspiciously paranoid about their employees. Rather, the authors note that leaders in the 10X companies constantly ask "What If." They state, "The 10X winners in our research always assumed that conditions can – and often do – unexpectedly change, violently and fast. They were hypersensitive to changing conditions, continually asking, 'What if?'"

Being careful, curious, or taking the time to stop and think ahead, needs to become our discipline. Employ some *Red* thinking; STOP and think, long and hard!

5. Building the clock is the art of leadership

Instead of getting bogged down in the day to day decisions of running the business, they keep their heads up and focus on aligning the company around the great idea, core purpose, and core values, and become an "architect of leadership" – someone who builds great leaders around them, rather than being a great chief in charge of a 1000 slaves.

As mentioned earlier, Max De Pree defines the nature of leadership in his book *Leadership Is An Art* as, "more tribal than scientific, more a weaving of relationships than an amassing of information, and in that sense, I don't know how to pin it down in every detail."

Levels of Leadership

At this point it is important to understand the different levels of Leadership that exist. Management comes in many different forms or styles and is, in most cases, a form of leadership.

Level one: Lifestyle leadership

Who we are speaks to people louder than words, in fact sometimes our actions speak so loudly people can not hear what we are saying. Mother Teresa, Nelson Mandela and many of the admirable leaders throughout history, had a lifestyle of loving generosity, real compassion and a gracious tone. It is the small acts of kindness that give a person beauty, authority and respect. Research suggests that on average, we deeply influence eight people during our life time. The way we live our lives gives a mix of both positive and negative leadership, the challenge is to make our influence 80% positive.

Level two: Educational leaders

The ideas that have shaped our world have been formed by what I call, educational leadership. Educational leaders create ideas that, for whatever reason, catch on and take root in the thinking of a person, a group, and a nation or can even go global, thus influencing behavior and forming culture for negative or for good. Communism, Capitalism, Islam, Christianity, Atheism, and Evolution, are all examples of the *educational leader's* powerful destructive or constructive leadership.

Level three: Entrepreneurial leadership

Entrepreneurial leadership is seen in the influence their innovation has in the marketplace on others, or the way they go about their business: Eco-friendly, profit-sharing, or innovative breakthroughs, where the patients are setup legally so that others can use their *intellectual capital* free of charge. The way certain companies construct their business model and build the clock—gives leadership.

Entrepreneurs see the future of an idea, how they can dig it out of the ground or plant it in a marketplace environment where it can grow. They then use their powers of persuasion to sell the idea to investors, banks and their friends, or network for sweat equity. They also engage people and companies that can help develop and refine their product or service. All this and more takes entrepreneurial leadership.

Level four: Clock building leaders

Management, as already mentioned, is about giving leadership to the designing of business ecosystems, and finding innovative new ways of empowering and rewarding workers. Managers develop leaders, empower leaders, and lead leaders. They give leadership to teams, customers, subcontractors and other suppliers. They must also give leadership to those higher up the chain and in the board room.

They have to lead designers in the development of a new world and rapid innovation. Managers are the enterprise clock builders, the architects of the business machine. Building the clock means robust systems of feedback, evaluation and action. Good managers are responsible for making sure a company's many moving parts are well oiled, and all doing their part to make the business machinery run smoothly. They are the *manager-preneurs* of the company clock.

Level five: Meta leaders

Meta leadership is about leading 21st century organizations that have not just one ecosystem, but multiple ecosystems as in nature: Earth is an ecosystem in which the living and non-living worlds interact through four major subsystems: the atmosphere, hydrosphere, geosphere (the soil and the extreme upper portion of the continental crust), and biosphere.

Meta leaders also go beyond the confines of their own organizations to achieve a higher goal. A good example would be Bill and Melinda Gates, great leaders in business, building the *Microsoft* empire, but launching from there to have influence on governments around the world, not-for-profits and other cultures, in order to help those in poverty.

Meta leaders know the art of leading across the complex systems and relationships of business, government, not-for-profits, and cultures in order to bring them all on board. Empowering them to work together for their own interests, and the interest of the meta leaders organization or idea. Meta leadership also extends to understanding and dealing with intergenerational gaps, gender issues, race discrimination, and many other tribal groupings and interest groups.

What is the difference between leadership and meta-leadership?

Meta-leadership incorporates insights from the research of Warren Bennis, Daniel Goleman, Ronald Heifetz, Robert Thomas, and others; but is distinct in that it is focused on cross-cutting leadership that generates connectivity among disparate stakeholders. "Leadership refers to the recognized or expected span of authority that a person has in his or her formal role."

Meta-leadership is leadership employing influence over authority. "Meta-leaders seek to influence and activate change well above and beyond established lines of their decision-making and control. These leaders are driven by a purpose broader than that prescribed by their formal roles, and are therefore motivated and capable of acting in ways that transcend usual organizational confines." These leaders may be grass-roots or in positions of power in business, not-for-profits or government, but they have earned a respect beyond the walls of their own organization and to often further an ultraistic agenda beyond their position.

6. Building the clock is about people, people, people!

Leading and developing people's raw talent and releasing the giant slayer within is the art of great leader-managers. It is also one of the huge, but intangible payoffs of the role, the satisfaction of empowering someone is rewarding. This people focus, and coaching edge is management at its best. Growing and developing a person is not something that the person may enjoy at the time, but if they are wise and teachable, they will appreciate it in the long-run.

Strategic plans built around people and their strengths, and weaknesses, work better than the old military model of organization—do it or else! This was something I learned in my role as a political leader while developing party policy. As I read the policies on education put forward by our opposition party, I thought, this is really good, so why where teachers so upset? Upon discussing this with teacher friends of mine, I realized that the policy did not fit who teachers were as people, and they did not feel anyone had really listened to them. It was not so much a policy problem, but a lack of understanding of their audience, and a lack of a sound process, whereby teachers could engage, be heard, and feel that at least they were consulted.

7. Building the clock is about working your strategy

We have already talked about strategy, but this is an example of how Jack Ma, one of China's leading entrepreneurs, developed his strategy to take *Alibaba* from ground-zero to become a global leader. A strategy that is run like clock-work by an army of outstanding leader-managers.

What is the iron triangle?

Alibaba's iron triangle strategy is a combination of *e-commerce, logistics* and *finance*. Author Duncan Clark, who has worked closely with Jack Ma, explains the iron triangle very well in his book *Alibaba, the House that Jack Ma Built.*

E-commerce

In e-commerce, the Alibaba operates Taobao, Tmall and Juhuasuan. Taobao is a platform where a large number of Chinese merchants list their products, with 9 million storefronts run by small traders or individuals. Alibaba doesn't charge a fee for setting up your storefront, but makes money by providing advertising services to merchants. Tmall is more like a "glitzy" high end mall, which sells brands like Apple and Zara, Clark writes, and Juhuasuan is a group-buying website. Between the three sites, Alibaba earns over $10 billion a year in revenue, nearly 80 percent of its total sales and has over one billion products for sale. Many of the nine million small business merchants were driven to the Alibaba platform due to government taxation on the commercial property they controlled. This was a way for these entrepreneurs to access the global marketplace and lower their overheads—a true win-win.

Logistics

"In logistics, Alibaba owns a 48% stake in 'China Smart Logistics,' or '*Cainiao*.' The rest of the company is owned by logistics players that are together called 'Three Tongs, One Da'. They are Shentong, Yuantong, Zhongtong and Yunda, all from a town called Tonglu close to Alibaba's headquarters in Hangzhou," writes Clark. The scale at which it operates is mind blowing.

On an average day however, they deliver 30 million packages, and expect to generate more than 100 million packages a day by 2020. On Single's Day 2015, orders placed on Alibaba's websites generated 464 million packages, requiring more then 1.7 million couriers and four hundred thousand vehicles to deliver the goods.

Cainao is not your typical logistics company, they partner with Alibaba in the daily nightmare of high-speed, on target product delivery. Although Alibaba has invested in their company, the most import asset is the trust equity they have built with each other. *Cainiao* is essentially a large data platform which links a network of logistics partners, warehouses and consumers. The company recently raised an undisclosed amount of funding at a $7.7 billion valuation.

Finance

The third corner of the triangle is finance. Alibaba's payment platform, Alipay is like PayPal in the United States. But it claims to be much bigger. Its systems, which run on top of e-commerce data from Alibaba's ecommerce platforms, can process nearly 85,000 payments every second. On an average day it processes 180 million transactions. (PayPal does about 13.7 million transactions a day). Alipay also gives micro-loans to small and medium size enterprises, based on a system which combines credit ratings with the shopping history of a person. It also operates a money market fund for nearly 281 million customers. By far the most popular online payment tool in China, Alipay handles more than three-quarters of a trillion dollars a year in online transactions. As a form of escrow, Alipay diffuses trust throughout Alibaba's e-commerce empire. The customers know that when they pay with Alipay their accounts will only be debited when they have received and are satisfied with the products they have ordered. Alipay is the largest asset of a company, controlled personally by one person, Jack Ma, which has been valued by one analyst at $45 billion.

The trust between the customer and Alibaba is seen by the huge response to Alibaba's Yu'e Bas online mutual fund. Launched in 2013, offering higher rates than the banks, as much as two percentage points higher, they allowed their customers to make withdrawals at any time, without penalty. By 2014, Yu'e Bas had attracted over $93 billion from 80 million investors. The inflow was so huge that in only ten months Yu'e Bas was ranked the fourth largest money manager in the world.

Jack's mantra for his company is, and is known by heart by every Alibaba employee:
- Customers First
- Employees Second
- Shareholders Third

In Alibaba, leaders make sure people not only see the vision, they live and breathe it. The team learn to embrace change at a number of levels: the continuous evolution of products and services, the continuous, ever-changing job descriptions, and the rotation of their jobs.

Alibaba devolves a lot of autonomy to its business units, in an effort to maintain a relatively *flat management hierarchy* and minimize the temptation to blame, instead of demonstrating extreme ownership.

What is a flat organizational/management structure?

An organizational structure in which most middle-management levels and their functions have been eliminated, thus bringing the top management in direct contact with the frontline salespeople, shop floor employees, and customers.

Despite their breadth, flat organizations can benefit from most of the advantages enjoyed by small companies, such as faster response time to changing conditions and customer preferences.

Pillar Seven
The Innovator

"We cannot predict the future. But we can create it."

— Jim Collins

The Why?

How do I get started?

How do I write a business plan?

Where do I find investors?

Is it better to buy into a franchise?

Chapter Forty
The Innovator

"Entrepreneurial innovators are the backbone of every thriving economy, the economic engine and lifeblood of healthy communities, and a prosperous nation."

— A J Walton

Innovation is the ability to source the resources needed to turn an idea into reality. To bring all of the pieces of the jigsaw puzzle together and fit them into place. Innovators create the ideas that add something of value to a customer, thus turning the idea into a profit. Innovators are the pioneers, trailblazers, and developers, the revolutionaries that can inspire action and move mountains. Like the producer of a movie, they cast the vision, develop the business plan, raise the finances, and bring all of the component parts of the project or business idea together in order to create the enterprise engine and make a profit.

Focusing on the development of entrepreneurs is the best way to break communities out of poverty, and the best way to ensure young people become productive, enjoying wealth creation, a job, and a healthy life style.

Entrepreneurial innovators are the backbone of every thriving economy, the economic engine and lifeblood of healthy communities and a prosperous nation.

Innovation is what we do with opportunity

Like many great entrepreneurs, my son Ben was struggling at school, but already had many of the characteristics that would make him an outstanding entrepreneur. He was good with people, he loved to help those in need and he really listened to what others had to say—he was teachable. The reasons that boys have had trouble learning within mainstream education has been well researched, but there were not many answers. As Ben's dad, I was thinking through the options as to what Ben's path to earning a living might look like.

About that time Global Tribe was becoming involved in Mexico, I was leading teams of volunteers to build homes for the poor near the US border, and thought that it would be an amazing experience for Ben (12) and his sister Rebecca (10) to travel to Mexico with me, and help in building a home. For both of them this was the beginning of a desire to help those trapped in poverty.

The seed was planted, and it was there that Wes, a close friend, invited Ben to travel and work on the road with the bands he managed. I was discussing Ben's issue with school, and brain storming with Wes over a possible solution, when out of the blue he said, "that we all had problems with school, so send him to Nashville and we'll give him some real-life schooling on the road."

So when Ben turned 16, I took him out of school and sent him to North America for three months, a trip that opened the door and set him on a path. Of course, this path was not without years of hard work on the road, and countless confrontations and character building experiences. It also has to be noted, that he had the best coaches and mentors in the business, Wes and his brother Steve, two of the greatest speech makers on the planet. If anyone could shape his work ethic, people, and management skills they could, and did – something I will always be grateful for.

I remember being on the bus one day and overhearing Steve offer Ben his first business opportunity, to manage a week long Christmas production out on the west coast of America. From that platform he started GT Pro and has built it up to become a very successful business.

Most enterprise startups come out of an existing job or another business. In fact in my country of New Zealand, around half of all entrepreneurs will start their new business in the same industry as their present job. You do not need a flashy office or lots of space; 69% of new businesses in the U.S. start at home, and 59% of established businesses are home-based.

Innovation

Innovation is best defined by Ian Hunter in his book, *Imagine*, as the process of generating wealth from new ideas—taking what resides in your imagination and converting it into a reality— a customer loving, profit generating, lifestyle masterpiece.

Collins and Porras in their book, *Built to Last*, write about what builds long-lasting, visionary companies. They studied the habits of eighteen exceptional companies that had been in existence between 40 and 180 years; companies such as *Disney, Boeing, Sony, IBM, Ford, 3M, Hewlett-Packard, General Electric, Walmart, Motorola and Marriott.* In their introduction they say "The only reliable source of stability is a strong inner core and the willingness to change and adapt everything except that core." They dedicate a chapter to this concept, "Preserve the core, stimulate progress."

Collins and Porras go on to observe, "Those who built the visionary companies wisely understood that it is better to understand 'who you are' than 'where you are going' for where you are going will almost certainly change." This is why so much time and space in this book is dedicated to *The Entrepreneur, their thinking* and their identity. These lessons are as relevant to any new enterprise startup as they are to large visionary companies.

Every enterprise has its own design, its own DNA, its own personality. The core DNA is not about the great idea that an entrepreneur gives birth to, it is about who they are, their style and culture. Business architects must preserve the core concept, culture and success style, while stimulating progressive thinking as to what that may look like in the 21st century.

One of the interesting and unexpected discoveries Collins and Porras encountered was that by far the clearest characteristic of the extraordinary companies versus their comparison companies was the difference in their *core ideology*, their core values and sense of purpose that went beyond just making money. The truly visionary companies were more ideologically driven and less purely profit-driven.

Their book is all about branding, yet it does not mention branding once. It does however talk about the importance of having a core ideology (purpose + core values), and ensuring that the entire organization is focused on living up to its ideology. It also discusses how visionary companies aim for both profits and purpose, but profit maximization is not the primary focus.

Collins and Porras point out "Profitability is a necessary condition for existence and a means to more important ends, but it is not the end in itself for many of the visionary companies. Profit is like oxygen, food, water, and blood for the body; they are not the point of life, but without them, there is no life."

Profit was not the *why* of these great businesses, but they adhered to a wider definition of what the bottom line includes.

Remember the big three bottom line items:

1. **Adding real value to a customer.**
2. **Generating value for yourself and the team = a profit.**
3. **Creating a lifestyle, and serving a need or vision bigger than yourself.**

Chapter Forty One
The Why

To start with, we need a moment of extreme honesty and brutal feedback from those who won't lie to us. This could save a lot of heartache and tears, not to mention a lot of money. We need to focus on why we want to go into business, because hidden motives can blind us to the truth about ourselves and our abilities.

Is entrepreneurship for you?

Starting your own business can be an exciting and rewarding experience. It can offer numerous advantages such as setting your own schedule and making a living doing something you enjoy. But, becoming a successful entrepreneur requires thorough planning, creativity and hard work.

Consider whether you have the following characteristics and skills commonly associated with successful entrepreneurs:

Comfortable with taking risks: Being your own boss also means you are the one making tough decisions. Entrepreneurship involves uncertainty. Do you avoid uncertainty in life at all costs? If yes, then entrepreneurship may not be the best fit for you. Do you enjoy the thrill of taking calculated risks? If yes then read on.

Independent: Entrepreneurs have to make a lot of decisions on their own. If you find you can trust your instincts — and you are not afraid of rejection every now and then — you could be on your way to being an entrepreneur.

Persuasive: You may have the greatest idea in the world, but if you cannot persuade customers, employees and potential lenders or partners, you may find entrepreneurship to be challenging. If you enjoy public speaking, engage new people with ease and find you make compelling arguments grounded in facts, it is likely you're poised to make your idea succeed.

Able to negotiate: As a small business owner, you will need to negotiate everything from leases to contract terms to rates. Polished negotiation skills will help you save money and keep your business running smoothly.

Creative: Are you able to think of new ideas? Can you imagine new ways to solve problems? Entrepreneurs must be able to think creatively. If you have insights on how to take advantage of new opportunities, entrepreneurship may be a good fit.

Supported by others: Before you start a business, it is important to have a strong support system in place. You will be forced to make many important decisions, especially in the first months of opening your business. If you do not have a support network of people to help you, consider finding a business mentor. A business mentor is someone who is experienced, successful and willing to provide advice and guidance.

The why — 20 questions before starting

Still think you have what it takes to be an entrepreneur and start a new business? Great! Now ask yourself these 20 questions to help ensure you have thought about the right financial and business details:

1. Why am I starting a business?
2. What kind of business do I want?
3. Who is my ideal customer?
4. What products or services will my business provide?
5. Am I prepared to spend the time and money needed to get my business started?
6. Where will my business be located?
7. How many employees will I need?
8. What types of suppliers do I need?
9. How much money do I need to get started?
10. Will I need to get a loan?
11. How soon will it take before my products or services are available?
12. How long do I have until I start making a profit?
13. Who is my competition?
14. How will I price my product compared to my competition?
15. How will I set up the legal structure of my business?
16. What taxes do I need to pay?
17. What kind of insurance do I need?
18. How will I manage my business?
19. How will I advertise my business?
20. What differentiates my business idea and the products or services I will provide from others in the market?

10 steps to starting a business

Starting a business involves planning, making key financial decisions and completing a series of legal activities. These 10 easy steps can help you plan, prepare and manage your business. www.sba.gov

Step 1: Write a Business Plan
Use tools in this book to create a business plan. This written guide will help you map out how you will start and run your business successfully.

Step 2: Get Business Assistance and Training
Take advantage of free training and counseling services, from preparing a business plan and securing financing, to expanding or relocating a business.

Step 3: Choose a Business Location
Get advice on how to select a customer-friendly location and comply with zoning laws.

Step 4: Finance Your Business
Find government-backed loans, venture capital and research grants to help you get started.

Step 5: Determine the Legal Structure of Your Business
Decide which form of ownership is best for you: sole proprietorship, partnership, Limited Liability Company (LLC), corporation, S Corporation, nonprofit or cooperative.

Step 6: Register a Business Name ("Doing Business As")
Register your business name with your state government.

Learn which tax identification number you will need to obtain from the IRS and your state revenue agency.

Step 7: Register for State and Local Taxes
Register with your state to obtain a tax identification number, workers' compensation, unemployment and disability insurance.

Step 8: Obtain Business Licenses and Permits
Get a list of federal, state and local licenses and permits required for your business.

Step 9: Understand Employer Responsibilities
Learn the legal steps you need to take to hire employees.

Step 10: Find Local Assistance
Contact your local Small Business Administration, SBA office, to learn more about how SBA can help.

Startup resources

There are a number of available programs to assist startups, micro businesses, and underserved or disadvantaged groups. The following resources provide information to help specialized audiences start their own businesses:
- Environmentally—Friendly "Green" Business
- Home-Based Business
- Online Business
- Self Employment
- Minority Owned Business
- Veteran Owned Business
- Woman Owned Business

You can save money when starting or expanding your business by using government surplus. From commercial real estate and cars, to furniture, computers and office equipment, find what you need for your business in one place.

Franchise businesses

Want to be your own boss, but not willing to take on the risk of starting your own business from scratch? Franchising can be a great alternative if you want to have some guidance in the start-up phase of the business.

What is Franchising?

A franchise is a business model that involves one business owner licensing trademarks and methods to an independent entrepreneur. Sometimes, franchises are referred to as chains.

There are two primary forms of franchising:

Product/Trade Name Franchising
Franchisor owns the right to the name or trademark and sells that right to a franchisee.

Business Format Franchising
Franchisor and franchisee have an ongoing relationship, and the franchisor often provides a full range of services, including site selection, training, product supply, marketing plans and even assistance in obtaining financing.

Before Investing in a Franchise

Before you decide to franchise, you need to do your research. You could lose a significant amount of money if you do not investigate a business carefully before you buy. By law, franchise sellers must disclose certain information about their business to potential buyers. Make sure you get all the information you need first before entering into this form of business. To learn more about franchising opportunities, visit *Federal Trade Commission Bureau of Consumer Protection.*

The decision to purchase a franchise involves many factors. To help you explore if franchising is right for you, consider the following questions:

Do you know how much you can invest?
What are your abilities?
What are your goals?

Franchising Strategy

You need a strategy before investing in a franchise. Doing your homework about the franchise first will help you gain a solid understanding of what to expect as well as the risks that could be involved.

Be a detective in addition to the routine investigation that should be conducted prior to any business purchase, and to contact other franchisees before deciding to invest. You can obtain a *Uniform Franchise Offering Circular* (UFOC), which contains vital details about the franchise's legal, financial, and personnel history, before you sign a contract.

Know what you are getting into. Before entering into any contract to buy a franchise, you should make sure that you would have the right to use the franchise name and trademark, receive training and management assistance from the franchisor, use the franchisor's expertise in marketing, advertising, facility design, layouts, displays and fixtures and do business in an area protected from other competing franchisees or franchises.

Watch Out for Possible Pitfalls
The contract between the two parties usually benefits the franchisor far more than the franchisee. The franchisee is generally subject to meeting sales quotas and is required to purchase equipment, supplies and inventory exclusively from the franchisor.

Seek professional help. The tax rules surrounding franchises are often complex, and an attorney, preferably a specialist in franchise law, should assist you to evaluate the franchise package and tax considerations. An accountant may be needed to determine the full costs of purchasing and operating the business as well as to assess the potential profit to the franchisee.

Blogs
Over 50 blog articles covering franchise tips and best practices are available from SBA.

Buying a business

Using the same principles shown in this book concerning startups, research the business you are looking at, do not focus on what they have turned over in the past, look at this opportunity going forward.

Chapter Forty Two
The BIG Plan!

"If you want your life to be a magnificent story, then begin by realizing that you are the author and every day you have the opportunity to write a new page."

— Mark Houligan

What is a business plan?

Every business starts somewhere, and at this pregnancy/birthing stage it is easy to lose the baby, as giving birth is often a do-or-die experience. The process of developing a start-up or business plan creates confidence and helps you avoid problems before they arrive in real-time.

Before starting to develop your plan, it is good to gain an overview of what the business plan is all about, and ask a few questions concerning your idea and resources. The primary value of your business plan will be to create a written outline that evaluates all aspects of the economic viability of your business venture, including a description and analysis of your business prospects. Preparing and maintaining a business plan is important for any business regardless of its size or nature... but it will not ensure your success. If you maintain a correct assessment of the changing economics of your business, your plan will provide a useful roadmap as well as a financing tool. But if you have miscalculated the potential, then your business plan could become a roadmap leading to failure.

Keep in mind that creating a business plan is an essential step for any prudent entrepreneur to take, regardless of the size of the business. This step is too often skipped, but we have made it easy for you by providing this ready format to build your plan as you progress through this course.

Be aware now, that most start-up entrepreneurs are reluctant to write down their business plan. It is, therefore, strongly recommended that you complete each segment of the plan as you progress through this course.

If you wish to attract investors and/or need to communicate to the bank, you will need to develop a business plan. However, if you do not need investors it is wise to go through this process anyway, it will save you time and money and help clarify your thoughts. If nothing else it will help you to have a deeper understanding of the intricate details of your business.

Do not expect that all of your plan's initial assumptions will be correct. Instead, look at your business plan as an ongoing assessment that you will frequently review and change to conform to actual operating experiences. For example, your cash flow projection should be updated frequently to ensure ongoing liquidity (not running out of cash).

Your business plan will become your roadmap to chart the course of your business. But at the outset, you cannot predict all of the changing conditions that will surface. It is important that you periodically review and update your plan after you have opened your business in order to stay on top of these changing conditions.

Why prepare a business plan?

The business plan enables the entrepreneur to analyze and evaluate the project, to identify any existing or foreseeable obstacles and constraints, and to find solutions. It obliges the entrepreneur to take a step back, check the feasibility of the project and adopt whatever measures become necessary. It also allows him/her to direct the company in line with the expected results and adapt a strategy to achieve them.

As for possible partners, such as investors, bankers or public administrators, they will generally read the business plan before even meeting the person initiating the project.

A study of firms found that 85% were still in business after three years, if they had developed a business plan at the outset.

Your business plan represents the final product of all your reflection, market research and planning. It is your map for business success, clearly identifying where you are now, where you are going, and how you plan to get there. This living document generally projects 3-5 years ahead and outlines the route a company intends to take to grow revenues. The business plan is only useful if you use it. In normal circumstances, and without a plan, fifty percent of new businesses fail in the first two years. Failure is often attributed to a lack of planning. To enhance your success, use your plan! A comprehensive, well-constructed business plan can prevent a business from a downward spiral.

It helps to focus ideas and serves as a feasibility study of the business's chances for success and growth. The finished report serves as an operational tool to define the company's present status and future possibilities. It can help you manage the business and prepare you for success.

It is a strong communication tool for your business. It defines your purpose, your competition, your management and personnel. The process of constructing a business plan can be a strong reality check. Planning is very important if a business is to survive. By taking an objective look at your business you can identify areas of weakness and strength. You will realize needs that may have been overlooked, spot problems and nip them before they escalate, and establish plans to meet your business goals.

Eight steps to a great business plan

Start-up entrepreneurs often have difficulty writing out business plans. A business plan is an essential roadmap for business success. This discipline is going to help you in many ways so do not skip this planning tool! To make it easier, here are eight steps that will produce a worthwhile plan:

- Set time aside to prepare your business plan.
- Focus and refine your concept based on the information you have collected.
- Gather all the data you can on the feasibility and the specifics of your business concept.
- Outline the specifics of your business, using a "what, where, why, how" approach.
- Include your experience, education and personal information.
- Use clear language and realistic projections.
- You may wish to enhance your presentation with bar charts, pie charts and graphics.
- Share a draft of your plan with trusted advisers. Use their feedback to improve the plan.

Who should write the business plan?

You, the owner of the business, should write the plan. It does not matter if you are using the business plan to seek financial resources or to evaluate future growth, define a mission, or provide guidance for running your business—you are the one that knows the most about the business.

There are a number of software packages in addition to this article that can assist you in the formatting process: *Business Plan Pro, Palo Alto Software* are only two of many available.

Consultants can be hired to assist you in the process of formulating a business plan, but in reality you must do the majority of the work. Only you can come up with the financial data, the purpose of your business, the key employees, and management styles to mention a few items. You may still choose to use a consultant, but realize that you will still need to do most of the work, so why not tackle the plan yourself? If you need further help in one area, then seek the assistance of the consultant.

Does your plan include the following necessary factors?

1. **A sound business concept:** The single most common mistake made by entrepreneurs is not selecting the right business initially. The best way to learn about your prospective business is to work for someone else in that business before beginning your own. There can be a huge gap between your concept of a fine business and reality.

2. **Understanding your market:** A good way to test your understanding is to test-market your product or service before your start. Do you think you have a great kite that will capture the imagination of kite fliers throughout the world? Then craft some kites and try selling them first.

3. **A healthy, growing and stable Industry:** Remember that some of the great inventions of all time, like airplanes and cars, did not result in economic benefit for many of those who tried to exploit these great advances. For example, the cumulative earnings of all airlines since Wilbur Wright flew that first plane are less than zero. Success comes to those who find businesses with great economics and not necessarily great inventions or advances to mankind.

4. **Capable management:** Look for people you like and admire, who have good ethical values, have complementary skills and are smarter than you. Plan to hire people who have the skills that you lack. Define your unique ability and seek out others who turn your weaknesses into strengths.

5. **Able financial control:** You will learn later the importance of becoming qualified in accounting, computer software and cash flow management. Most entrepreneurs do not come from accounting backgrounds and must go back to school to learn these

skills. Would you bet your savings in a game where you do not know how to keep score? People mistakenly do it in business all the time.

6. **Financial management skills:** Build a qualified team to evaluate the best options for utilizing retained earnings.

7. **A consistent business focus:** As a rule, people who specialize in a product or service will do better than people who do not specialize. Focus your efforts on something that you can do so well that you will not be competing solely on the basis of price.

8. **A mindset to anticipate change:** Do not commit yourself too early. Your first plan should be written in pencil, not in ink. Keep a fluid mindset and be aggressive in making revisions as warranted by changing circumstances and expanding knowledge.

Formulate (and reformulate) your business plan
Donald N. Sull, associate professor of management practice at the London Business School, in an article in the MIT Sloan Management Review, offers some practical suggestions for managing inevitable risks while pursuing opportunities.

Here is a capsulation of his suggestions on how to formulate (and reformulate) your business plan:
- Be flexible early in the process and keep it fluid.
- Don't commit too early. Expect your first plan to be provisional and subject to revision.
- Ask yourself if your experience or expertise gives you the right to an opinion on your specific opportunity.
- Identify your potential deal killers: variables that are likely to prove fatal to the venture.
- Clearly identify what you see as the key drivers of success. What are you betting on here?
- Raise only the amount of money required to finance the next experiment or evaluation you envision, with a cushion for contingencies.
- Delay hiring key managers until initial rounds of experimentation have produced a stable business model.
- At some point, take the plunge and test your product or service on a small scale in the real world through customer research, test marketing, or prototypes.
- Test and refine your business model before expanding your operations.

How to conduct a SWOT analysis

A SWOT Analysis is a method for examining the *Strengths, Weaknesses, Opportunities,* and *Threats* facing a business. It can give you insight into your company's position in the competitive arena. When carrying out a SWOT analysis to determine how you rate against a competitor, the following guides should be used:

Strengths
Consider your company's strong points. This should be both from your own and your customers' points of view. Don't be modest; be realistic.
- What distinct advantages does your company offer?
- Why do customers say they enjoy doing business with you?
- Is there anything you currently offer that cannot be copied by a competitor, now or in the future?

Weaknesses
Evaluate your company's weaknesses, not only from your perspective, but also from the perspective of your competitors. It is sometimes difficult to think about and discuss your weaknesses, but it is best to be realistic now and face any unpleasant truths as soon as possible.
- What does your company do that can be improved?
- What does your company do poorly?
- What should be avoided?
- What do your competitors do better than you?
- Do competitors have a particular market or segment locked up?

Opportunities
Next consider the areas in your market that offer you room to grow. Opportunities can come from changes in technology and markets on both a broad and narrow scale changes in government policy related to your industry, changes in social patterns demographics and customer lifestyle changes and local events such as the closing of a store near you.
- What and where are the interesting opportunities in your market?
- What are the important trends occurring in your local area as well as across the nation?
- What do you anticipate happening in the future that may represent an opportunity?

Threats
Although we do not like to think about them, we all face threats in our businesses. Many times they are out of our control, such as a downturn in the economy, a shift in market demographics, or perhaps a new mega-corporation opening in your local area. It is critical to think about and be prepared for such events.

- What are the obstacles that your company faces?
- What is your competition doing that could take business away from you or stunt your company's growth?
- Are the required specifications for your products or services changing?
- Is the changing technology threatening your position in the market?
- Do you have cash flow problems that could keep your company from acquiring new technology, staff or equipment?

Chapter Forty Three
Developing a Business Plan

"By failing to prepare, you are preparing to fail."

— Benjamin Franklin

Armed with your SWOT analysis and an overview of why and how, let's begin. The Business Plan format can take a number of forms and different styles, but must have the following basic information presented in a systematic way, showing all of the factors critical to your business purpose, goals and success.

The importance of planning should never be overlooked. For a business to be successful and profitable, the owners and the managing directors must have a clear understanding of the firm's customers, strengths and competition. They must also have the foresight to plan for future expansion. Whether yours is a new business or an existing business in the process of expanding, money is often an issue. Taking time to create an extensive business plan provides you with insight into your business. This document can serve as a powerful financing proposal.

The business plan

1. **The Executive Summary**
2. **The Product or Service**
3. **The Market or Customer**
4. **The Marketing Plan**
5. **The Competition**
6. **Operations**
7. **The Management Team**
8. **Personnel**
9. **Financial Data**
10. **Supporting Documentation**
11. **Summary**
12. **Resources**

The business plan summary

1. The executive summary

The first page of your business plan should be a persuasive summary that will entice a reader to take the plan seriously and continue reading. The Executive Summary should follow the cover page, and not exceed two pages in length.

The summary should include:
- A brief description of the company's history.
- The company's objectives.
- A brief description of the company's products or services.
- The market in which the business will compete in.
- A persuasive statement as to why and how the business will succeed, discussing the business competitive advantage.
- Projected growth for the company and the market.
- A brief description of the key management team.
- A description of funding requirements, including a time-line and how the funds will be used.

2. The product or service

It is important for the reader to thoroughly understand your product offering or the services you currently provide or plan on providing. However, it is important to explain this section in layman's terms to avoid confusion. Do not overwhelm the reader with technical explanations or industry jargon that he or she will not understand.

It is important to discuss the competitive advantage your product or service has over the competition. Or, if you are entering a new market, you should answer why there is a need for your offering.

If appropriate, discuss any patents, copyrights and trademarks the company currently owns or has recently applied for and discuss any confidential and non-disclosure protection the company has secured.

Discuss any barriers that you face in bringing the product to market, such as government regulations, competing products, high product development costs, the need for manufacturing materials, etc.

Areas that should be covered in this section include:
- Is your product or service already on the market or is it still in the research and development stage?
- If you are still in the development stage, what is the roll-out strategy or timeline to bring the product to market?
- What makes your product or service unique? What competitive advantage does the product or service have over its competition?
- Can you price the product or service competitively and still maintain a healthy profit margin?

3. The market or customer

Investors look for management teams with a thorough knowledge of their target market. If you are launching a new product, include your marketing research data. If you have existing customers, provide an analysis of who your customers are, their purchasing habits, their buying cycle.

Customer profile

This section of the plan is extremely important, because if there is no need or desire for your product or service, there will not be any customers. If a business has no customers, there is no business.

This section of the plan should include:
- A general description of your market.
- The niche you plan on capitalizing on and why.
- The size of the niche market. Include supporting documentation.
- A statement and supporting documentation as to why you believe there is a need for your product or offering by this market.
- What percentage of the market do you project you can capture?
- What is the growth potential of the market? Include supporting documentation.
- Will your share of the market increase or decrease as the market grows?
- How will you satisfy the growth of the market?
- How will you price your goods or services in the growing competitive market?

4. The marketing strategy

Once you have identified who your market is, you will need to explain your strategy for reaching the market and distributing your product or service. Potential investors will look at this section carefully to make sure there is a viable method to reach the target market identified at a price point that makes sense.

Analyze your competitors' marketing strategies to learn how they reach the market. If their strategy is working, consider adopting a similar plan. If there is room for improvement – work on creating an innovative plan that will position your product or service in the minds of your potential customers. The most effective marketing strategies typically integrate multiple mediums or promotional strategies to reach the market. The following are some promotional options to consider. For more in-depth information on these media, see the article called *Create a Promotional Package*. www.sba.gov

- TV
- Radio
- Print
- Web
- Direct mail
- Trade shows
- Public relations
- Promotional materials
- Telephone sales
- One-on-one sales
- Strategic alliances

If you have current samples of marketing materials or strategies that have proved successful, make sure you include them with your plan.

Developing an innovative marketing plan is critical to your company's success. Investors look favorably upon creative strategies that will put your product or service in front of potential customers. Spend time developing this section.

Once you have identified how you will reach the market, discuss in detail your strategy for distributing the product or service to your customers. Will you mail order, personally deliver, hire sales reps, contract with distributors or resellers, etc.?

5. The competition

Understanding your competition's strengths and weaknesses is critical for establishing your product's or service's competitive advantage. If you find a competitor is struggling, you need to know why, so you do not make the same mistake. If your competitors are highly successful, you will want to identify why. You will also want to explain why there is room for another player in the market.

Specific areas to address in this section are:
Identify your closest competitors. Where are they located? What are their revenues? How long have they been in business?

Define their target market:
- What percentage of the market do they currently have?
- How do your operations differ from your competition? What do they do well? Where is there room for improvement?
- In what ways is your business superior to the competition?
- How is their business doing? Is it growing? Is it scaling back?
- How are their operations similar to yours and how do they differ?

Are there certain areas of the business where the competition surpasses you? If so, what are those areas and how do you plan on compensating? Analyzing your competitors should be an ongoing practice. Knowing your competition will allow you to become more motivated to succeed, efficient and effective in the marketplace.

6. Operations

Now that you have had an opportunity to really sell your idea and wow potential investors, the next question on their mind is how will you implement the idea. What resources and processes are necessary to get the product to market? This section of the plan should describe the manufacturing, R&D, purchasing, staffing, equipment and facilities required for your business.

You will want to provide a roll-out strategy as to when these requirements need to be purchased and implemented. Your financials should reflect your roll-out plan. In addition, describe the vendors and sub contractors you will need to build the business. Do you have current relationships or do you need to establish new ones? Who will you choose and why?

7. The management team

For most investors the experience and quality of the management team is the most important aspect they evaluate when investing in a company. Investors must feel confident that the management team knows its market, product and has the ability to implement the plan. In essence, your plan must communicate management's capabilities in obtaining the objectives outlined in the plan. If this area is lacking, your chances for obtaining financing are bleak.

If your team lacks in a critical area, identify how you plan on compensating for the void. Whether it is additional training required or additional management staff needed, show that you know the problem exists, and provide your options for solutions.

When preparing this section of the business plan you should address the following six areas:

Personal history of the principals:
- Business background of the principals
- Past experience -- tracking successes, responsibilities and capabilities
- Educational background (formal and informal)

Personal data:
- Age, current address, past addresses, interests, education, special abilities.
- Reasons for entering into a business.
- Personal financial statement with supporting documentation.

Work experience:
- Direct operational and managerial experience in this type of business.
- Indirect managerial experiences.

Duties and responsibilities:
- Who will do what and why.
- Organizational chart with chain of command and listing of duties.
- Who is responsible for the final decisions?

Salaries and benefits:
- A simple statement of what management will be paid by position.
- Listing of bonuses in realistic terms.
- Benefits (medical, life insurance, disability).

Resources available to your business:
- Insurance broker(s)
- Lawyer
- Accountant
- Consulting group(s)
- Small Business Association
- Chambers of Commerce
- Local colleges and universities
- Federal, state, and local agencies
- World Wide Web (various search engines)
- Banker

8. Personnel

The success of a business can often be measured by its employees. Seventy percent of consumers will go elsewhere if they do not receive prompt and courteous service.

You must consider the following questions in completing this section of the business plan:
- What are your current personnel needs (full or part-time)? How many employees do you envision in the near future and then in the next three to five years?
- What skills must your employees have? What will their job descriptions be?
- Are the people you need readily available and how will you attract them?

- Will you be paying salaries or hourly wages?
- Will there be benefits? If so, what will they be and at what cost?
- Will you pay overtime?

9. Financial data

At the heart of any business operation is the accounting system. It is important to have a certified public accountant establish your accounting system before the start of business. At times there is a tendency to do it yourself. Remember that an incredible number of businesses fail due to managerial inefficiencies. Leave it to the trained professional to help you in the area of accounting and legal matters. If your business cannot afford a public accountant to establish your books, then you are undercapitalized. You need to secure additional resources before starting.

One of the first steps to having a profitable business is to establish a bookkeeping system which provides you with data in the following four areas:

Balance Sheet - indicates what the cash position of the business is and what the owner's equity is at a given point (the balance sheet will show assets, liabilities and retained earnings).

Break-Even Analysis - this is based on the income statement and cash flow. All businesses should perform this analysis without exceptions. A break-even analysis shows the volume of revenue from sales that are needed to balance the fixed and variable expenses.

Income Statement - also called the profit and loss statement, is used to indicate how well the company is managing its cash, by subtracting disbursements from receipts.

Cash Flow - this projects all cash receipts and disbursements. Cash flow is critical to the survival of any business.

If the goal of your business plan is to obtain financing, you will be required to generate financial forecasts. The forecasts demonstrate the need for funds and the future value of equity investment or debt repayments. This exercise is critical in obtaining capital for your business. To obtain capital from lending institutions you must demonstrate the need for the funding and your ability to repay the loan.

The forecast that you generate should cover a three to five-year period. This is a period in which realistic goals can be established and attained without much speculation. Forecasts should be broken down in monthly increments.

Projections and forecasts are an integral part of your financial portfolio. Carefully and accurately state your assumptions. Honesty is the best policy! Over-optimism and over-inflation can lead to failure. For more help, review the tools *Conduct a Sales Forecast* and prepare a *Balance Sheet*. www.sba.gov

10. Supporting documentation

You must include any documents that lend support to statements made in the body of your company's business plan. The following is a list of some items for your consideration. Please be aware that this list is not complete and may vary depending on the stage of development of your business:

- Resumes
- Credit information, include in Appendix
- Quotes or Estimates
- Letters of Intent from prospective customers
- Letters of Support from credible people who know you
- Leases or Buy/Sell Agreements
- Legal Documents relevant to the business
- Census/Demographic data

11. Summary

The completed business plan should be bound. For internal purposes three-ring binders work well. Additions and changes can easily be placed in the binders. For the business plan that is to be circulated to a lender and/or investor, many types of appropriate folders and binders can be purchased at office supply stores.

Once the business plan is completed, it should become an operational tool to measure the success of the business. This plan should be updated as milestones are reached. Often companies will spend enormous time, energy and financial resources to complete this arduous task just for the purpose of obtaining additional capital. The companies that shelve the business plan after its completion and presentation to lenders lose out on the real value of this useful tool in the growth and development of small and large businesses.

12. Resources

Books and Websites, etc

Chapter Forty Four
Imagineering

"Innovation is best defined, as the process of generating wealth from new ideas—taking what resides in your imagination and converting it into a reality."

— Ian Hunter

How to make your business plan stand out

The following tips can help you clarify what your business has to offer, identify the right target market for it and build a niche for yourself.

One of the first steps in business planning is determining your target market and why they would want to buy from you.

For example, is the market you serve the best one for your product or service? Are the benefits of dealing with your business clear and are they aligned with customer needs? If you are unsure about the answers to any of these questions, take a step back and revisit the foundation of your business plan.

Be clear about what you have to offer

Ask yourself: Beyond basic products or services, what are you really selling? Consider this example: Your town probably has several restaurants all selling one fundamental product—food. But each is targeted at a different need or clientele.

One might be a drive-thru fast food restaurant, perhaps another sells pizza in a rustic Italian kitchen, and maybe there is a fine dining seafood restaurant that specializes in wood-grilled fare. All these restaurants sell meals, but they sell them to targeted clientele looking for the unique qualities each has to offer. What they are really selling is a combination of product, value, ambience and brand experience.

When starting a business, be sure to understand what makes your business unique. What needs does your product or service fulfill? What benefits and differentiators will help your business stand out from the crowd?

Do not become a 'Jack of all Trades'—learn to strategize

It's important to clearly define what you are selling. You do not want to become a jack-of-all trades and master of none because this can have a negative impact on business growth. As a smaller business, it's often a better strategy to divide your products or services into manageable market niches. Small operations can then offer specialized goods and services that are attractive to a specific group of prospective buyers.

Identify your niche

Creating a niche for your business is essential to success. Often, business owners can identify a niche based on their own market knowledge, but it can also be helpful to conduct a market survey with potential customers to uncover untapped needs. During your research process, identify the following:

- Which areas your competitors are already well-established.
- Which areas are being ignored by your competitors.
- Potential opportunities for your business.

Project: Start imagineering using the template provided. Develop a business plan for your soccer ball business. You have already done a marketing plan, so now develop the business plan.

Use a business plan layout that works for you

Again, this is just one of may different formats or templates. However, they all generally have the same basic content, they are just worded or ordered differently. The different headings suit some plans more than others, depending on the audience. If the words under some of the headings do not work, then use another description that works for you.

Contents:
1. The Executive Summary
2. The Product/Service
3. The Market
4. The Marketing Plan
5. The Competition
6. Operations
7. The Management Team
8. Personnel
9. Financial Data
10. Supporting Documentation
11. Summary
12. Resources

Appendix

Green businesses

The explosion of organic and eco-friendly products on retail store shelves is more than just a passing fad. It is big business. This reality presents opportunities for environmentally minded entrepreneurs ready to start their own small business. Successful green businesses not only benefit the environment, but also use green business practices as a means to market their products. If you are thinking of starting a green business, consider the following tips:

Find your niche
The eco-friendly lifestyle continues to catch on with consumers which presents many growth possibilities for businesses. Production of food, cosmetics and cleaning supplies are growing areas within organic trade. To be successful, look for opportunities that match your interests.

Get certified
To differentiate your product or service as environmentally sound, consider obtaining certification from an independent, third-party. Being certified means that you can include their "ecolabel" on your product's label and other marketing materials. This ecolabel is important for attracting "green" customers, and can strengthen the value of your brand.

Investigate the following organizations and programs for certification opportunities:

Domestic certification

Products: Green Seal sets product standards and awards its label to a wide variety of products:
Agriculture, Manufacturing and Electricity: Certified by Scientific Certification Systems

Buildings: The U.S. Green Building Council certifies new and existing buildings using the Leadership in Energy and Environmental Design (LEED) Green Building Rating System

Chlorine-free products: Certified by the Chlorine Free Products Association

Energy efficient products: Certified by the U.S. Government's ENERGY STAR Program

Organic produce: Certified by the U.S. Department of Agriculture's National Organic Program

Renewable energy: Certified by the Center for Resource Solution's Green e-Certification Program

Wood products: Criteria set by Forest Stewardship Council; certified by Scientific Certification Systems

International certification

The European Union *Eco-Label* Program encourages businesses to market products and services that are kinder to the environment to European consumers.

Canada's EcoLogo Label program certifies products from the United States and Canada in more than 120 categories.

Germany's Blue Angel program provides ecolabeling for a wide variety products.

Japan's EcoMark Program provides product certification and ecolabeling for several product types.

Taiwan's Green Mark and Energy Label programs provide certification and ecolabeling for green and energy efficient products.

Eco-Label resources
The Global Eco labeling Network is a nonprofit association of third-party, environmental performance labeling organizations to improve, promote and develop the "ecolabelling" of products and services.

The Collaborative Labeling and Appliance Standards Program (CLASP) is an international organization that helps broker national policies for energy efficiency standards and labels for appliances, equipment, and lighting products.

Practice what you preach
The most successful green businesses do not just sell the green lifestyle. They live it. Selling green means being green, and this helps build your brand and image as socially responsible. Before you start your business, consult the Small Business Guide for Energy Efficiency.

Join Industry Partnerships

StartUP checklist

Top ten do's and don'ts

The top ten do's

- Prepare a complete business plan for any business you are considering.
- Use the business plan templates.
- Complete sections of your business plan as you proceed through the course.
- Research (use search engines) to find business plans that are available on the Internet.
- Package your business plan in an attractive kit as a selling tool.
- Submit your business plan to experts in your intended business for their advice.
- Spell out your strategies on how you intend to handle adversities.
- Spell out the strengths and weaknesses of your management team.
- Include a monthly one-year cash flow projection.
- Freely and frequently modify your business plans to account for changing conditions.

The top ten don'ts

- Be optimistic (on the high side) in estimating future sales.
- Be optimistic (on the low side) in estimating future costs.
- Disregard or discount weaknesses in your plan. Spell them out.
- Stress about long-term projections. Better to focus on projections for your first year.
- Depend entirely on the uniqueness of your business or the success of an invention.
- Project yourself as someone you're not. Be brutally realistic.
- Be everything to everybody. Highly focused specialists usually do best.
- Proceed without adequate financial and accounting know-how.
- Base your business plan on a wonderful concept. Test it first.
- Pursue a business not substantiated by your business plan analysis.

Government websites:

USA - SBA.gov

New Zealand - http://www.business.govt.nz

Singapore - http://www.enterpriseone.gov.sg

Australia - http://www.becaustralia.org.au

The Four Human Temperaments

by Dr. D. W. Ekstrand

There are "reasons" for everything we do as human beings, though it is often difficult for us to understand why we think like we think, feel like we feel, or act like we act in life. Many of the answers for human behavior can be found in people's temperaments or personalities.

The study of the human personality goes all the way back to the famous Greek physician Hippocrates (460-370 BC), the "father of medicine" — he was born during the prophetic ministries of Nehemiah and Malachi, or some 450 years before the birth of Christ. Hippocrates' work has been researched extensively and is used as a dynamic diagnostic tool in both psychology and psychiatry to this day. A generic explanation of human "temperaments" or "personalities" is that all of us have been born with genetically inherited "behavioral tendencies" that are as much a part of our DNA as is the color of our hair; all of us are made up of DNA combinations passed on to us through our parents and ancestors. This fact is important because it helps us to more fully understand our basic behavioral disposition.

Even though much of our human personality is inherited, it should also be noted, much of it has also been influenced and shaped by our unique environments. Most scientific research on human behavior suggests that about 50% of the variations in human personality are determined by genetic factors — so our human behavior is shaped equally by our environment and by our DNA. Thus, all of us as human beings have been hard-wired by our Creator, and we have all been impacted by the world around us.

Furthermore, according to the scientific analysis all human personalities are commonly divided up into four major categories (with the exception of those with severe mental disorders), and these four types are further broken down into two categories — Extroverts and Introverts:

Extroverted Personalities: The *Choleric* and *Sanguine* personality-types are more "outgoing," more sociable, and more comfortable in a crowd, even standing out in a crowd.

Introverted Personalities: The *Melancholy* and *Phlegmatic* personality-types are more shy and "reserved" and feel anxious about being in crowd, especially at being singled-out in a crowd.

It should be noted that all human beings have a degree of each of these four personality types within them, though each person will definitely test out higher in one, with another being a close second. No individual possesses one personality type only, and most of us have a very strong secondary temperament. All four personality types have general strengths and weaknesses with which people must contend, and no one personality type is better than any other. All four have both good and bad qualities, and all four are needed to make this world a better place.

Of all the relationships we have in life, marriage is by far the most important. A good relationship between a husband and a wife makes for a happy home. A marriage shadowed by bitterness, fighting and other unpleasantness leaves its scars on not only the couple, but also on their children and those around them. Good marriages are not just accidents — they are the result of hard work and understanding. In general, marriages between two people with the "same personality type" have the greatest potential for clashing, and anyone married to a S*anguine* or *Choleric* is in for a challenge; this is mainly due to the tendencies of these two personality types to require excessive attention and control, respectively. Thus pretty much all marriages will have fairly significant challenges. Most often "opposites do attract"—*Sanguine* individuals tend to marry Melancholy ones, and *Cholerics* favor *Phlegmatics*; though such situations are not always the case, they do appear to be the most common. It should be noted that there is no such thing as "the ideal combination," we are all fallen human beings with foibles and shortcomings.

Following is a brief description of each of the four temperaments or personalities — at the end of each description I have listed the two primary characteristics for that temperament. By identifying the two temperaments that best describe who you are as a person, you should be able to identify your *"strongest characteristic"*—be it predominantly extroversion, introversion, organizational, or relational. Aside from the Extrovert-Introvert continuum that was described above on the previous page, there is the Organizational-Relational continuum—Cholerics and Melancholies are more "organizational," whereas the Sanguines and Phlegmatics are more "relational." With that said, let's look at a description of the four temperaments, beginning with the "sanguine."

A. Sanguine—The Sanguine temperament is fundamentally impulsive and pleasure-seeking. Sanguines are frequently referred to as "the talkers." They are expressive in personality… desire influence, and being enthusiastic with people… in expressing thoughts with excitement… and being the center of attention. The Sanguine is sociable and charismatic, generally warm-hearted, pleasant, lively, optimistic, creative, compassionate, and outgoing; he is the life of the party, humorous, enthusiastic, and cheerful; he easily attracts others and makes friends; he inspires others to work and join in the fun. He is sincere at heart, always a child, creative and colorful, possesses energy and enthusiasm, loves people, is a great volunteer, thrives on compliments, and doesn't hold grudges. The Sanguine likes to talk a lot… struggles with completing tasks… is chronically late… and tends to forget his obligations… he bases his decisions primarily on feelings. Sanguine types can be great parents, because they love to have fun; but their homes are often frenzied and disorganized, and the only time you find everyone silent is when they are sleeping! Sanguine people usually possess high amounts of energy, so they often seem restless and spontaneous. This type of personality loves the life of luxury and impressing others… they are big spenders… they love to travel the world and indulge in rich, comfortable living… and they will do almost anything to satisfy their always present need to be absorbed by something meaningful and exciting. They are impulsive and often find it difficult to control their cravings; as such, people with this temperament are more susceptible to smoking, alcohol, drugs, gambling and taking risks; sadly, they are most susceptible to chemical imbalances, addictions and mood disorders. These people feel bored if they are not absorbed by something intriguing and adventurous.

The Sanguine is very poor at tolerating boredom; for the most part he will try to avoid monotony and that which is routine at all costs; routine jobs and boring companions annoy him and irritate him. In addition to the characteristics listed below, the Sanguine is essentially described as being relational and an extrovert:

- Is self-composed, seldom shows signs of embarrassment, perhaps forward or bold.
- Is eager to express himself before a group; likes to be heard.
- Prefers group activities; work or play; not easily satisfied with individual projects.
- Is not insistent upon acceptance of his ideas or plans; compliant and yielding.
- Is not good in details; prefers activities requiring pep and energy.
- Is impetuous and impulsive; his decisions are often (usually) wrong.
- Is keenly alive to environment, physical and social; likes curiosity.
- Tends to take success for granted; is a follower; lacks initiative.
- Is hearty and cordial, even to strangers; forms acquaintanceship easily.
- Tends to elation of spirit; not given to worry and anxiety; is carefree.
- Seeks wide and broad range of friendships; is not selective; not exclusive in games.
- Is quick and decisive in movements; pronounced or excessive energy output.
- Turns from one activity to another in rapid succession; little perseverance.
- Makes adjustments easily; welcomes changes; makes the best appearance possible.
- Is frank, talkative, sociable, expresses emotions readily; does not stand on ceremony.
- Has frequent fluctuations of mood; tends to frequent alterations of elation and depression.

B. Choleric—The Choleric temperament is fundamentally ambitious and leader-like. The Choleric is the strongest of the extroverted temperaments, and is sometimes referred to as a "Type A" personality or "the doer" (or "the driver"); he is a hard driving individual known for accomplishing goals… he has a lot of aggression, energy, and/or passion, and tries to instill it in others. Dominant in personality, Cholerics desire control, and are best at jobs that demand strong control and authority, and require quick decisions and instant attention. The Choleric is the most insensitive of the temperaments; they care little for the feelings of others; feelings simply don't play into the equation for them. Most Cholerics are men, and born leaders who exude confidence; they are naturally gifted businessmen, strong willed, independent, self sufficient, they see the whole picture, organize well, insist on production, stimulate activity, thrive on opposition, are unemotional and not easily discouraged. They are decisive, must correct wrongs when they see them, and compulsively need to change things. They systematize everything, are all about independence, and do not do well in a subordinate position. They are goal oriented and have a wonderful focus as they work; they are good at math and engineering, are analytical, logical and pragmatic; and are masters at figuring things out. They are skeptical and do not trust easily; they need to investigate the facts on their own, relying on their own logic and reasoning. If they are absorbed in something, do not even bother trying to get their attention. Negatively, they are bossy, domineering, impatient, can't relax, quick tempered, easily angered, unsympathetic, enjoy arguments, too impetuous, and can dominate people of other temperaments, especially the Phlegmatic types. Many great charismatic military and political figures were Cholerics. They like to be in charge of everything… they are workaholics who thrive on control and want their way… they are highly independent people, and have very little respect for diplomas and other credentials. They set high standards, are diligent and hard-working, are rarely satisfied, and never give up their attempts to succeed. Choleric women are very rare, but strangely are very popular people. Cholerics have the most trouble with anger, intolerance and impatience; they want facts instead of emotions; and should you get your feelings hurt, it's your problem, not theirs. The Choleric does not have many friends (though he needs them), and he has a tendency to fall into deep sudden depression and is much prone to mood swings. In addition to the characteristics listed below, the Choleric is essentially described as being organizational and an extrovert...

- Is self-composed; seldom shows embarrassment, is forward or bold.
- Is eager to express himself before a group if he has some purpose in view.
- Is insistent upon the acceptance of his ideas or plans; argumentative and persuasive.
- Is impetuous and impulsive; plunges into situations where forethought would have deterred him.
- Is self-confident and self-reliant; tends to take success for granted.
- Exhibits strong initiative; tends to elation of spirit; seldom gloomy; prefers to lead.
- Is very sensitive and easily hurt; reacts strongly to praise or blame.
- Is not given to worry or anxiety; they are seclusive.
- Is quick and decisive in movement; pronounced or excessive energy output.
- Has marked tendency to persevere; does not abandon something readily regardless of success.
- Is characterized by emotions not freely or spontaneously expressed, except anger.
- Makes best appearance possible; perhaps conceited; may use hypocrisy, deceit, disguise.

C. Phlegmatic — The Phlegmatic temperament is fundamentally relaxed and quiet, ranging from warmly attentive to lazily sluggish. Phlegmatics are referred to as "the watchers" — they are best in positions of unity and mediation, and solid in positions that desire steadiness. The Phlegmatic is most often a female who tends to be easygoing, content with herself, calm, cool and collected, tolerant of others, well-balanced, sympathetic, kind, unassuming, keeps emotions hidden, is happily reconciled to life, not in a hurry, has many friends, avoids conflict, inoffensive, quiet but witty, agreeable and intuitive... though they are very peaceful, patient and adaptable, they tend to be reluctant, indecisive and a worrier. They are wonderful at gathering facts, classifying them, and seeing the relationship between them; basically, they are good at generalizing, seeing the bigger picture, and reading between the lines. They are accepting, affectionate, frequently shy, and often prefer stability to uncertainty and change. Because they are fearful, indecisive and hesitant of things in life, they have a compromising nature. Phlegmatics often worry about everything. They want to know other people's deepest feelings and strive to build intimate attachments with just about everyone in their lives. They are interested in cooperation and interpersonal harmony, and this is why they preserve their family ties and friendships. They could be described as considerate, charitable, sympathetic, trusting, warm, calm, relaxed, consistent, rational, curious, and observant — this makes them good administrators. Phlegmatic men and women strive for greater self-knowledge, and seek to contribute to society at large. On the negative side, they are often selfish, self-righteous, judge others easily, resist change, stay uninvolved, dampen enthusiasm, and can be passive-aggressive. In large part, the Phlegmatic temperament is deemed to be a neutral temperament. In addition to the following characteristics, the Phlegmatic is essentially described as being relational and an introvert.

- Is deliberative; slow in making decisions; perhaps overcautious in minor matters.
- Is indifferent to external affairs.
- Is reserved and distant.

- Is slow in movement.
- Has a marked tendency to persevere.
- Exhibits a constancy of mood.

D. Melancholic— The Melancholic temperament is fundamentally introverted and thoughtful. Melancholies are often referred to as "the thinkers." Their analytical personalities desire caution and restraint, and they are best at attending to details and analyzing problems too difficult for others. They tend to be deep-thinkers and feelers who often see the negative attributes of life, rather than the good and positive things. They are self-reliant and independent and get wholly involved in what they are doing. Melancholies can be highly creative in activities such as art, literature, music, health-care and ministry, and can become preoccupied with the tragedy and cruelty in the world; they long to make a significant and lasting difference in the world. Melancholies usually have a high degree of perfectionist tendencies, especially in regards to their own lives or performance. They are serious, purposeful, analytical, musical, artistic, talented, creative, self-sacrificing, conscientious, idealistic, philosophical, and are genius prone. They are also very "introspective" and hold themselves to a very high standard — one that can rarely be achieved. They tend to be highly organized, schedule oriented, economical, tidy, neat, detail conscious, finish what they start, like charts, graphs, figures and lists, see the problems and are able to identify creative solutions with ease. Sadly, many Melancholies are also victims of deep bouts of depression that come from great dissatisfaction, disappointment, hurtful words or events. Melancholy personalities are people who have a deep love for others, while usually holding themselves in contempt. In short, melancholies take life very seriously (too much so sometimes) and it often leaves them feeling blue, helpless or even hopeless. Because they are deeply caring people, they make great doctors, nurses, social workers, ministers, and teachers. This comes from a deep sense of what others are feeling or experiencing and the inward need to reach out and do something in order to help them. They are extremely loyal in friendships; there is an old saying that goes like this: "If you have a Melancholy for a friend, you have a friend for life." Most Melancholies have a low self-image, are inclined toward depression, think "self-promotion" is tacky, are continually into "fixing themselves," are notoriously "guilty" (they have an over-active conscious), and tend to worry much too often about their health. In addition to the following characteristics listed below, the Melancholy is essentially described as being organizational and an introvert...

- Is self-conscious, easily embarrassed, timid, bashful.
- Avoids talking before a group; when obliged to they find it difficult.
- Prefers to work and play alone. Good in details; careful.
- Is deliberate; slow in making decisions; perhaps overcautious even in minor matters.
- Is lacking in self-confidence and initiative; compliant and yielding.
- Tends to detachment from environment; reserved and distant except to intimate friends.
- Tends to depression; frequently moody or gloomy; very sensitive; easily hurt.
- Does not form acquaintances readily; prefers narrow range of friends; somewhat exclusionary.
- Worries over possible misfortune; crosses bridges before coming to them.
- Is secretive; seclusive; shut in; not inclined to speak unless spoken to.
- Is slow in movement; deliberate or perhaps indecisive; moods frequent and constant.
- Often represents themselves at a disadvantage; modest and unassuming.

Temperament combinations

Following are the various temperament combinations and what they look like when they are combined together. Once you have identified your "primary temperament" and the temperament that is a close second, you are then ready to see how the two temperaments look when joined together. When looking at the various temperament options below, your "primary temperament" will be listed first — for example, if your primary temperament is a Sanguine and your runner-up temperament is a Choleric, they would be listed as "San/Chol" under the heading "Sanguine," not as "Chol/San" under the heading "Choleric" (your secondary temperament); your primary temperament needs to be listed first.

Sanguine
San/Chol–This is the strongest "extrovert" of all the blends because both primary types are extroverted. They are people-oriented and enthusiastic but with the resolutions of the Choleric tempering the lack of organization of the Sanguine. He is almost always a sports enthusiast and is ideal in sales. He can talk too much and can be obnoxious if threatened. The forgetfulness of the Sanguine and the caustic nature of the Choleric may make them hurtful without realizing it.

San/Mel – They are highly emotional people whose moods can fluctuate from highs to lows and back again quickly. The Sanguine's outgoing nature often allows the Melancholy's critical nature to surface too easily. It is very easy for a San/Mel to "get down" on themselves, and to realize their potential, it is best that they work with others.

San/Phleg – The overpowering outgoing nature of the Sanguine is tempered by the gracious Phlegmatic. These are extremely happy and carefree individuals who live to help people. They would not purposely hurt anyone but they must fight a lack of workplace motivation; they would rather visit than work.

Choleric
Chol/San – The second strongest extrovert is an active and purposeful individual; he is almost fearless and has high levels of energy. Whatever his profession, his brain is always active and engaged. His weaknesses combine the quick anger of the Sanguine with the resentment of the Choleric. He gets AND gives ulcers. He may leave people (including spouse and children) shell-shocked and resentful because of his angry outbursts.

Chol/Mel – The Choleric/Melancholy is very industrious and capable. He is both industrious and detailed. He combines verbal aggressiveness with sharp attention to detail. He is very competitive and forceful. He can be autocratic and opinionated with work habits that keep after details until the job is completely finished. He finds interpersonal relationships difficult due to the hard-to-please nature of the Choleric and the perfectionistic nature of the Melancholy.

Chol/Phleg – This is the most subdued of the outgoing temperaments. He is extremely capable in the long run though he may not impress you that way at first. He is organized and a good planner. He often gets more accomplished than other temperaments because he always thinks in terms of enlisting others to help him. His weaknesses include a tendency to quietly harbor bitterness rather than letting it out. Acknowledging weaknesses is difficult for him and he tends to worry about his performance in life activities.

Phlegmatic
Phleg/San – This is the easiest to get along with being congenial, happy, and people-oriented. They make excellent administrators and other jobs that involve getting along with

people. He may lack motivation and discipline and may fall short of his true capabilities. He may "putter around" for years without making progress.

Phleg/Chol – This is the most active of the introverts but he'll never be a ball of fire. He can be an excellent counselor because he is an active listener. He is practical and helpful and patient. He may lack motivation and may become stubborn if threatened. He may also have a tendency toward being sedentary and passive. He needs to be around other people as he is externally motivated.

Phleg/Mel – This is gracious and quiet, does the proper thing and is dependable. He wobbles between patience and criticism and may tend toward negativism. They can be afraid of over-extending themselves so may avoid involvement in a group.

Melancholy
Mel/San – They are detailed and organized; the Melancholy is tempered by the outgoing and warm Sanguine. He makes an excellent teacher as his organized side is well versed in the facts and his Sanguine side makes him enjoyable to listen to. If he goes into sales it will be sales that calls for exacting detail and the presentation of many facts. He is an emotional person – from being moved to tears to being critical and hard on others. Both temperaments can be fearful which may make this an insecure person with a poor self image.

Mel/Chol – This is both a perfectionist and a driver which may lead him into law or medicine. They mix decisiveness and determination. Because of the critical nature of the Melancholy they may be very difficult to please. If they become negative about someone or something, it will have a tendency to stay with them for a long time. Their combination can lead them to "nit-pick" others and be revengeful to those they have a grudge against.

Mel/Phleg – These are often teachers and scholars. They are not as prone to hostility as other. Melancholy blends and combine analysis with organization. They make excellent accountants and bookkeepers. Unfortunately he can become easily discouraged and may be susceptible to fear and anxiety. They may become uncooperative because of stubborn, rigid tendencies.

AJ Walton

Author, Instructor, Mentor

The founder and President of Global Tribe Inc, a not-for-profit based out of Nashville, America, helping those trapped in poverty for over 20 years.

Anthony was, for many years, the leader of the Future New Zealand Political Party, then after merging with Peter Dunne, the newly formed United Future Political Party held the balance of power—implementing over 14 policies, including the introduction of the Family Commission.

Anthony is a social entrepreneur, the architect of numerous projects, and a speaker for organizations, bands, and events throughout the US and many other countries. Startups include: Body & Soul gyms, The Club Executive Gym, Global Tribe Extreme Cafe, a partner in Channel 7 TV—a Wellington based community television station, and the CEO of White Cloud Innovations Ltd—a construction and property development company.

Global Tribe has also been a pioneer in youth development, in partnership with local government, designing spaces for young creatives since 1997; Zeal is now established in 5 locations throughout New Zealand, with many more on the drawing board. A property developer, speaker, designer, strategist, educator, and author, Anthony has now initiated GT Community, with a passion to design and build learning communities, bringing education back into the local area, utilizing the huge resource available—local mentors.

www.ingramcontent.com/pod-product-compliance
Lightning Source LLC
Chambersburg PA
CBHW082104220526
45472CB00009B/2039